T0314129

SINCE THE BOOM

Continuity and Change in the Western Industrialized
World after 1970

German and European Studies
General Editor: Jennifer L. Jenkins

Since the Boom

Continuity and Change in the Western Industrialized World after 1970

EDITED BY SEBASTIAN VOIGT

UNIVERSITY OF TORONTO PRESS
Toronto Buffalo London

© University of Toronto Press 2021
Toronto Buffalo London
utorontopress.com

ISBN 978-1-4875-0783-1 (cloth)
ISBN 978-1-4875-3705-0 (ePUB)
ISBN 978-1-4875-3704-3 (uPDF)

German and European Studies

Library and Archives Canada Cataloguing in Publication

Title: Since the boom: Continuity and change in the Western industrialized
    world after 1970 / edited by Sebastian Voigt.
Names: Voigt, Sebastian, editor.
Series: German and European studies.
Description: Series statement: German and European studies |
    Includes bibliographical references and index.
Identifiers: Canadiana (print) 20200258788 | Canadiana (ebook) 20200258818 |
    ISBN 9781487507831 (hardcover) | ISBN 9781487537050 (EPUB) |
    ISBN 9781487537043 (PDF)
Subjects: LCSH: Western countries – Economic conditions – 20th century. |
    LCSH: Western countries – Economic conditions – 21st century. |
    LCSH: Western countries – Social conditions – 20th century. |
    LCSH: Western countries – Social conditions – 21st century.
Classification: LCC HC59.S56 2020 | DDC 330.9182/10828–dc23

The German and European Studies series is funded by the DAAD with funds
from the German Federal Foreign Office.

DAAD   Deutscher Akademischer Austauschdienst
       German Academic Exchange Service

University of Toronto Press acknowledges the financial assistance to its
publishing program of the Canada Council for the Arts and the Ontario
Arts Council, an agency of the Government of Ontario.

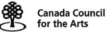
Canada Council   Conseil des Arts
for the Arts   du Canada

ONTARIO ARTS COUNCIL
CONSEIL DES ARTS DE L'ONTARIO
an Ontario government agency
un organisme du gouvernement de l'Ontario

Funded by the   Financé par le
Government   gouvernement
of Canada   du Canada

Canada

Contents

Acknowledgments   vii

Introduction   3
SEBASTIAN VOIGT

Section One: Ambiguities

1 Crisis or Opportunity? Amway and an Unfamiliar Story
of Economic Growth in the 1970s   35
JESSICA BURCH

2 Crisis? What Crisis? Mass Consumption in Great Britain
in the 1970s and Early 1980s   56
SINA FABIAN

3 Decent Work in the Home? Household Workers and the Crisis
of Social Reproduction since the 1970s   78
EILEEN BORIS

Section Two: Adaptations

4 The Clandestine Crisis: Migrant Labour in an Age
of Deindustrialization   103
MICHAEL KOZAKOWSKI

5 Challenges of Computerization and Globalization:
The Example of the Printing Unions, 1950s to 1980s   129
KARSTEN UHL

6 Soft Skills in an Age of Crises: Continuing Training as an
   Economic Coping Strategy in West German Companies   153
   FRANZISKA REHLINGHAUS

Section Three: (Dis-)Continuities

7 Deindustrialization and the Globalization Discourse
   in France since 1980   189
   ANDREAS WIRSCHING

8 Look to the Future, Embrace Your Past: Regional
   Industrialization Policies and Their Aftermath   209
   BART HOOGEBOOM AND MARIJN MOLEMA

9 The End of Long-Established Certainties: The Transformation
   of Germany Inc. since the Late 1980s   237
   HARTMUT BERGHOFF

Contributors   267

Index   269

Acknowledgments

The volume resulted from the conference "Industrial Decline and the Rise of the Service Sector? How Did Western Europe and North America Cope with the Multifaceted Structural Transformations since the 1970s?" held in Munich in 2016 and co-sponsored by the Institute for Contemporary History (IfZ), Munich–Berlin, and the German Historical Institute (GHI), Washington, DC. The conference was organized by myself and Stefan Hördler and was envisioned together with Andreas Wirsching, director of the IfZ, and Hartmut Berghoff, then director of the GHI and now director of the Institute of Economic and Social History at the University of Göttingen.

I would like to express my heartfelt gratitude to all the authors for their outstanding cooperation and great patience. Special thanks goes to Andreas Wirsching for his generous support for this volume; to Ilker Iscan, my student assistant; to Stephen Shapiro and Christine Robertson from the University of Toronto Press for their enthusiasm for the topic; to Barbara Tessman for her thorough copy-editing; and to the reviewers, whose input contributed substantially to forging the present volume into an integrated whole.

SINCE THE BOOM

Continuity and Change in the Western Industrialized
World after 1970

Introduction

SEBASTIAN VOIGT

In 2017, a study by the Organisation for Economic Co-operation and Development (OECD) on economic changes in over thirty industrialized countries between 1995 and 2015 noted the rapidly increasing segmentation of labour markets. While new jobs had been created in both the high-wage and the low-wage sectors alike, the number of typical middle-class jobs had seen a significant decrease of nearly 10 per cent during the period under review. This resulted in a cohort of well-paid and highly skilled experts coinciding with a growing number of precariously employed and poorly paid workers.[1]

Technological innovations and continuing shifts in the global economic order have further accelerated the polarization of labour markets in Western countries since the turn of the century. These tendencies have not only widened disparities in income and wealth but also have exacerbated other inequalities at various levels. These intensifying trends do not, however, constitute a recent phenomenon that has emerged only in the new century, but indeed reach back to the mid-1970s.

Over the course of the past several decades, numerous studies have identified fundamental shifts in the postwar era concerning demographics and the composition of the labour market, labour productivity and wage rates, technological changes, and the plight of the low-skilled workforce.[2] The shrinking of the middle class in Western Europe and the United States has often been attributed to the loss of jobs in manufacturing industries. In the decades following the Second World War, well-paid jobs in industries such as coal and steel, shipbuilding, and printing allowed (mostly male) workers to provide for their families and maintain a certain lifestyle. Since the 1970s, however, many of these jobs have vanished in Western industrialized countries. The simultaneous growth of the service sector has not created comparable employment opportunities on a sufficient scale. Instead, many new jobs with lower wages and insecure working conditions have appeared in their stead.

The decline of traditional industrial regions, such as the US Rust Belt, the Ruhr area of western Germany, the industrial triangle in northwestern Italy, and northern France, has had enormous social ramifications that can still be felt today.[3] The closure of the last coal mine in the Ruhr, Prosper-Haniel in Bottrop, on 21 December 2018 marked a symbolic event in this respect, concluding an important chapter in the history of industrialization in Germany.[4] This development was unsurprising, as the coal and steel industries had already been declining for decades, a process that had begun in the late 1950s and accelerated in the course of the 1970s. From this perspective alone, the 1970s seem to be of particular relevance to understanding the socio-economic changes still shaping Western societies today.

The significance of the decade has therefore been a focus among North American historians for some time. In *The Seventies: The Great Shift in American Culture, Society and Politics*, Bruce Schulman turned his focus to that decade, which had been perceived previously, much too often, as an amorphous period between the events of 1968 and the Reagan era.[5] This earlier approach does not, however, do justice to the significance of the 1970s, a time in which American society would change in lasting ways. These changes involved a shift away from the public sphere and active role of the state, which had been exemplified by the New Deal in the 1930s or the War on Poverty in the 1960s, toward a stronger private sector and a sovereign free market. At the same time, a power shift in American politics also occurred, both in terms of economics and culture. The growing importance of the South and the Sun Belt were symptomatic of this shift. For Schulman, the increasing popularity of country music, a new form of religiosity, and the New Age movement also reflected these cultural changes. At first, Watergate and the resignation of Richard Nixon in 1974 appeared to be a major victory for the Democrats and for a functioning separation of powers in the United States. Looking back, however, as Schulman points out, Watergate has chiefly been chalked up as evidence for the government's lack of trustworthiness. The scandal did not ultimately serve to stabilize democracy but, rather, sparked greater movement away from state institutions.

Jimmy Carter, elected president in 1976, serves as a symbol for the period. As the first candidate from the Deep South since the Civil War, he embodied a shift in power and the rise of the Sun Belt. Carter's reaction to the energy crisis of the late 1970s, which combined Baptist moralism with a philosophy anchored in state planning, made it clear that he had strongly distanced himself from hegemonic views of the time.

The *Zeitgeist* no longer focused on collective sacrifice but on individual self-realization.

Philip Jenkins takes another approach in his *Decade of Nightmares: The End of the Sixties and the Making of Eighties America*.[6] In it, he investigates the palpable rise in diffuse fears within US society since the mid-1970s, arguing that a conservative elite by no means intentionally instigated this paranoid tendency, but only reacted to it. The period around 1975, according to Jenkins, can be seen as a transitional moment away from a political willingness to compromise. In terms of foreign policy, American society perceived the world from an increasingly Manichaean perspective, with absolute evil posing an external threat to cohesion. This view of the world corresponded with widely circulating conspiracy theories.

Jenkins explains that several political and moral panic campaigns served to shift the United States significantly to the right during the period in question. Media reports on child abuse and pornography and their networks grew increasingly hysterical. Irrational cults gained larger followings. These developments correspond, in terms of the culture industry, with the popularity of horror films like *Halloween*. The term "mass murderer" also found its way into people's everyday vocabulary during the period. Ronald Reagan, Jenkins posits, thus did not introduce this fundamental change to US society in the 1980s; he merely accelerated and intensified a development already in progress.

In the collective volume *The Shock of the Global: The 1970s in Perspective*, the editors Niall Ferguson, Charles S. Maier, Erez Manela, and Daniel J. Sargent analyse the decade from various perspectives.[7] In the introduction, Ferguson strongly criticizes the assertion of an all-encompassing crisis during the 1970s. Outside of elite American universities, we read, such tendencies were rarely recognized. Yet, at the global level, considerable economic deregulation had taken place, while technological inventions had proven particularly crucial with regard to further development. The "post-industrial society," a concept popularized by Daniel Bell in 1973, serves several articles in that volume as a point of reference to describe the shift from production to the service sector.

In his *Age of Fracture*, Daniel Rodgers speaks more in terms of the history of ideas.[8] He writes that, in the course of the 1970s, ideas that had predominated in the United States during the decades after 1945 began to crumble. These phenomena of disintegration could be seen to stretch from the economic macro level down to the everyday lives of individual people. Rodgers posits that the flexibilization of markets and financial system undermined the economic policies of the postwar period that had been inspired by Keynesian theory, with economists and politicians now framing the market as a decisive and universally applicable source of legitimation. The previous framework of individual conceptions of identity, along with societal institutions and structures of solidarity, diminished in importance. All across the political spectrum, moreover, the focus shifted from collective structures to the preferences, wishes, and decisions of individuals. The analytical categories used to capture social reality had changed. Rodgers explains that the neoliberal expression that "there is no such thing as society" became noticeable in academic discourse as well.

Historians would soon also look into microphenomena and people's everyday lives, forgoing master narratives and theories on general developments. Emerging identity politics and French postmodernism would also support this trend. The focus on countless group identities pushed society as a collective space into the background. Rodgers thus describes the period beginning in the mid-1970s as an era of fracture.

The discussion among North American historians on the significance of the decade corresponds in many ways with the latest controversies in the field of German contemporary history, though with one important and rather unsurprising difference. The American debate deals nearly exclusively with changes within the United States. Although certain socio-economic shifts changing the basic structure of industrialized society were undoubtedly transnational if not global in character, specific national effects could be found at the centre of attention in US studies. The size of the country, along with its particular distribution of political and economic power, was certainly of importance in that regard.

The German discussion over the past several years has focused mainly on West German society, with comparisons drawn with other Western European countries. A seminal attempt to identify and relate the various changes, Lutz Raphael and Anselm Doering-Manteuffel's study *Nach dem Boom*, has been highly influential in the German debate about the decade.[9] They identify a "social transformation of revolutionary quality" based on far-reaching structural ruptures setting in during the mid-1970s.[10] Their argument rests on four central features: the decline of traditional industries, increasing market orientation, growing individualization, and a breakthrough of microelectronics. These developments in the era following the postwar boom, the authors argue, ultimately resulted in the emergence of a new kind of capitalism, that of "digital financial capitalism."[11]

The emergence of "digital financial capitalism" was the most significant consequence of the manifold changes taking place since 1970. Raphael and Doering-Manteuffel point to three central characteristics of this new model of political-economic order. The first was the spread of microchips as a new "basic material of the industrial world."[12] Their use digitized not only production but also communications, the media, and everyday life. The second was a palpable shift in the macroeconomic paradigm. The monetarism of Milton Friedman's Chicago School began to supplant the Keynesian economics of the postwar era. Whereas the demand-side Keynesian approach sought to use state intervention as a means of addressing imbalances arising from the market, expanding social security systems, and reducing economic inequalities, monetarism was geared toward the neoclassical view of a fundamentally stable economic process. This supply-side paradigm rejected any state intervention into the economy and placed trust in the self-regulatory powers of the market.

The third characteristic of digital financial capitalism was the development of a new view of humankind: the entrepreneurial self.[13] This view focuses on the creative power of the ego-driven individual. Each person is expected to be continuously active and creative and to be able to meet the requirements of modern society with complete flexibility. Individuals are thus responsible for their own success and failure, as collective solidarity fades into the background. This new view of humankind shifts the economic imperative of neoliberalism onto the individual, as life-long learning and ongoing retraining become an inescapable obligation. It realigns the relationship between individuals and society as well as between the different areas of society. To elucidate these relationships, Raphael and Doering-Manteuffel investigate the complex connections and interactions between the functionally separate areas of politics, economy, education, science, and religion.

Nach dem Boom views the early 1970s as the beginning of this period of change and the successive disintegration of the previous order. The oil crisis of 1973, with effects that included a rise in unemployment, alongside the collapse that same year of the Bretton Woods system, which had served to help stabilize international financial policy, together symbolize this development. Paradoxically, the origins of the main ideological changes can be traced back to the alternative culture movements of the late 1960s. The protagonists there held a position critical of consumption, rejecting hegemonic values and the existing social system as conformist. They instead propagated the creative breaking out of old stagnant patterns, which would unintentionally kindle a "new spirit of capitalism."[14]

The coinciding of numerous changes at the economic, political, and cultural levels served to fundamentally reconfigure Western industrial societies. The transformation processes did not, however, all run parallel or at the same speed in the individual countries of Western Europe. Their full impact would emerge only at the end of the twentieth century. Raphael and Doering-Manteuffel therefore view the phase between 1970 and 2000 as a transitional era of its own, comparable with the period in continental Europe between the French Revolution of 1789 and the democratic uprisings of 1848. Reflecting on this profound transformation of Western European societies, the authors speak of a "structural fracture" and a "social shift of revolutionary quality."[15] These propositions were the subject of intensive debate in the field of history in Germany and were met with strong opposition.[16] The criticism included, for example, that the use of the term "structural fracture" in the singular suggested a starting point from which the fracture spread. The authors therefore make this more precise in the second edition, noting that "the term structural fracture serves to combine the observation of numerous fractures in different places and at different points of time in the countries of Western Europe."[17] They explain that the term was of particular analytical use as it included numerous aspects ranging from the collapse of certain industrial segments through to the wave of privatization in European television during the 1980s.

The structural fracture thesis, furthermore, underpins the guiding hypothesis that the multiple fractures ultimately resulted in the emergence of digital financial capitalism. This "social shift of revolutionary quality" does not thus present a uniform scenario but a process that was ambiguous and specific to individual countries. Despite threads of continuity, a new order did ultimately emerge as a consequence of the dynamic changes after 1970, taking on its final contours in the early 2000s.

The economic structure of the Federal Republic of Germany, for example, underwent a considerable shift in the 1990s. The network of Rhine capitalism, with its close association of banks, insurance companies, and major industrial companies, came apart to a large degree. Throughout Western Europe, social democratic parties altered their policies, relinquishing old convictions and embracing the Third Way as proclaimed by British prime minister Tony Blair and German chancellor Gerhard Schröder. At the same time, the internet took on a globally central role, with national politics losing some of its particular relevance to transnational networks and processes of transfer.

These shifts did not have an effect only at the macro level; they also changed the everyday lives of countless people. Classical industrial segments underwent an ineluctable decline while new service sectors emerged. Many individuals would no longer be able to plan secure careers, even as employment figures for women rose continually and the education system expanded considerably.

In their summary, Raphael and Doering-Manteuffel reiterated that the infrastructure of the industrial system had been eroding since the 1970s, that Keynesianism had fallen by the wayside, and that the emerging ideological order discredited any moves to steer or plan economic processes. These trends also served to reduce the general acceptance of the state within society. The accumulation of these processes, this structural fracture, brought about the aforementioned "social shift of revolutionary quality" and culminated in digital financial capitalism. The period "after the boom" (as referenced in the title of the book *Nach dem Boom*) is hence the immediate prehistory of our present time, and the underlying processes analysed are therefore crucial to an understanding of the current socio-economic and political situation.

While *Nach dem Boom* has stimulated a contentious debate, provoked a considerable amount of criticism, and encouraged further research efforts among German historians, it has, unfortunately, yet to be translated.[18] The present volume seeks to address that oversight by assembling contributions based on empirical research that addresses the hypotheses of a "structural fracture" and a "social transformation of revolutionary quality" beginning in the 1970s. Since these developments have crossed national borders to affect all industrialized Western societies, the volume's geographical focus lies on Western Europe and the United States.

The narrative of such a structural rupture cannot be applied globally. Developments in non-Western countries generally took a different course in the 1970s. While some Asian countries such as Taiwan and South Korea underwent rapid industrialization, others such as India and China had yet to surface as emerging economies.[19] Although it would certainly be quite stimulating to the discussion, it would be beyond the scope of this volume to pursue a transnational approach comparing Western nations and those of the Global South to trace, for example, the mutual interdependencies of these counter-directional developments.

This volume's general aim, then, is to examine the validity of the "after the boom" hypothesis on the basis of empirical case studies. Notwithstanding their multifaceted topical foci and methodological heterogeneity, the chapters in this volume provide a critical discussion of whether the "long" 1970s were indeed characterized by a structural rupture. This book is a contribution toward bridging the gap between the English and the – highly productive – German debates on the 1970s.

The individual chapters deal with shifts in the labour market, the effects of socio-economic transformations on groups such as migrants and domestic workers as well as on labour unions and their various strategies to cope with the new challenges, in addition to the relationship between change and continuity when it comes to the current state of capitalism.

The contributors are guided by a variety of questions: Has capitalism been substantially transformed since the 1970s and, if so, in what ways? Can the 1970s be mainly understood as a decade of crisis? Did the oft-cited "good old times" of the postwar boom with all its well-paid industrial jobs really come to an end in the 1970s, or does this notion merely romanticize the past?

The empirical case studies present innovative results and offer a more complex picture of the 1970s that transcends the narrative of a decade solely marked by decline and the dissolution of conventional security. Their broad transnational angle, which includes examples from Germany, the United States, France, the Netherlands, and the United Kingdom, should serve to inspire further discussions and pave the way for more comparative studies.

The notion of the first decades after the Second World War as constituting "good old times" is problematic both in terms of its superficiality and its one-sidedness.[20] Populist voices in many countries have recently spoken of an allegedly idyllic industrial past and exploited this notion politically. The call of the current US president, Donald Trump, to rebuild the American steel industry has been matched by the aspirations of the German right-wing party Alternative for Germany (AfD) to re-establish traditional gender roles and work hierarchies. The current rise of right-wing politicians in Europe and the astonishing success of xenophobic populism in the United States also seem to be linked ultimately to the socio-economic transformations of the 1970s. The topic of the volume is thus not only of historical but of political interest as well.

Right-wing politicians play both on the anger of segments of the lower classes and on the fear of social decline among the middle and upper classes.[21] Populists portray immigrants and social minorities as responsible for growing economic uncertainty and the loss of a sense of security. The complexity of modern societies often leads to insecurity and anger resulting from a mixture of real changes, imagined fears, and feelings of loss of a supposed clearly structured past. Simplistic *Weltanschauungen* such as populism and crude nationalism blame these changes on easily identifiable scapegoats that personify the consequences of social transformations: specific individuals or groups are viewed both as being personally responsible for and as profiting from overall negative trends.[22]

The pervasiveness of these resentments among white male workers has been discussed extensively in recent times. In his autobiographical book *Return to Reims*, French sociologist Didier Eribon describes how the workers' milieu in northern France, where he grew up, has shifted its political affiliation over the past few decades.[23] Traditionally a stronghold of the French Communist Party, many workers now support the right-wing Rassemblement National (National Rally) of Marine Le Pen. Eribon traces the multifarious reasons for this trend, beginning in the late 1970s and early 1980s, following years of economic ruptures. He also elaborates on the ongoing crisis of the political (social democratic) left and its rejection by many of its former voters. This development has taken place not only in France but indeed in nearly all industrialized countries.[24] The moderate European left is currently in the midst of severe crisis while the populist right has been on the rise for some time. Given the recent electoral successes of the AfD, the translation of Didier's book has sparked a lively public debate in Germany as well.[25] Interestingly, it turns out that the German party's average voter is an older male with an above-average income but a generally pessimistic outlook on economic and social issues.[26] While right-wing populism is thus not embraced only by disgruntled white male workers, it does particularly thrive in regions that have been left behind in the course of socio-economic transformations.

In the United States, scholars have similarly explored the changing political terrain – changes that contributed to the success of Trump in the 2016 elections. Notably, James David Vance's book *Hillbilly Elegy: A Memoir of a Family and Culture in Crisis* about his upbringing in Middletown, Ohio, has drawn attention to the white underclass, its social situation, and its moral values and political convictions.[27] Arlie Russell Hochschild's *Strangers in Their Own Land: Anger and Mourning on the American Right* explains what motivates members of the white working class in rural Louisiana to act and vote against their presumed interests.[28] Hochschild empathically analyses their feelings of estrangement and marginalization at various levels, precipitated by the stagnation or even reduction of wages and living standards, rapid demographic change toward a more diverse society, and the perceived hegemony of a liberal culture mocking their patriotism and their Christian faith.

All these sociological studies on the changing political landscape and the rise of right-wing and populist parties regard economic factors as playing a crucial role and as resulting from developments that began in the 1970s. Taking into account the importance of socio-economic factors, it might not be mere chance that the publication of the original French version of Eribon's book in 2009 nearly coincided with the onset of the euro crisis, which was itself closely connected to the preceding global financial crisis that many economists considered to be the most serious economic crisis since 1929.[29]

In light of the grave social effects of multiple crises, ruptures in the labour market, growing poverty, and the near collapse of the economies of several (Southern) European countries, a broad debate on the economic foundations of the capitalist system set in. The voices calling for further regulations and stricter control of financial markets grew louder across a spectrum ranging from academics to political activists.

The unforeseen success of Thomas Piketty's 2013 book *Capital in the Twenty-First Century* can be understood only within this context. The study was highly praised, notably in the United States, and sold well over a million copies and was translated into numerous languages. Paul Krugman, the Nobel Prize laureate and *New York Times* columnist, for example, called the study a seminal contribution to public debates on taxation, social inequality, and the concentration of wealth.[30] It might become, he wrote, "the most important economics book of the year – and maybe of the decade."[31] The former head economist in the World Bank's research department, Branko Milanović, deemed it "one of the watershed books in economic thinking."[32]

Piketty argues that, in a capitalist society, inequality is not merely coincidental but in fact one of its central characteristics. The inherent tendency of capitalism toward greater inequality had been reversed during the period between the 1929 Wall Street crash through the mid-1970s thanks only to special circumstances. First, the precipitous economic downturn of the late 1920s, the sustained depression of the 1930s, and the effects of the Second World War had destroyed a large portion of the elite's wealth. During that period, moreover, governments intervened more often in response to the effects of economic crises, with structural policies and state interventions aimed at addressing adverse social consequences. Especially after 1945, the governments of Western Europe and the United States deliberately acted to redistribute wealth via their taxation policies. In addition, the global economic upswing after the extensive destruction of the Second World War increased the average wages of the working population, reducing the weight of inherited fortunes in the process, and rendering Western societies more equal and meritocratic. The majority of the population benefited from this development. For the first time, workers and their families could participate in the emerging consumer society. Full employment, attained in the late 1950s, further strengthened workers' social status. Strong labour union movements managed to continuously improve wages and working conditions.

According to Piketty, these trends were reversed in the mid-1970s due to changing economic policies that favoured privatization and deregulation in the era of neoliberalism. In Western industrialized nations, the political shift to the right supporting such policies began to materialize in the United Kingdom with the election of Margaret Thatcher as prime minister in 1979. It was followed by the victory of Ronald Reagan in the United States a year later and the downfall of the Social Democrat–led government in West Germany in 1982. The new conservative chancellor, Helmut Kohl, proclaimed an "intellectual-moral turnaround." Ever since, social inequality in industrialized countries has increased at many levels while inherited wealth has become more important, leading to a form of "patrimonial capitalism" today.

The studies by Didier Eribon and Thomas Piketty need to be interpreted as complementary approaches to the same phenomenon. Both intend to provide an understanding of the historical genesis of the current political and economic situation in industrialized countries. While the former sheds light on the shifting political consciousness and attitudes of the (white) workers' milieu, the latter highlights the economic transformations underlying political changes and affecting the working population. Similar to Raphael and Doering-Manteuffel, Piketty and Eribon both argue that the developments shaping the present can be traced back to processes setting in during the 1970s.

It is not only recent research that has underlined the particular importance of the decade. Contemporaries had already observed and theorized on potentially far-reaching socio-economic transformations. In 1969, the French sociologist Alain Touraine coined the term "post-industrial society,"[33] and Daniel Bell popularized the concept in his 1973 book *The Coming of Post-Industrial Society*.[34] Despite certain differences in their respective concepts, they agree in their basic assumptions – that is, the irreversible and continuing decline of the industrial sector and the rise of the tertiary service sector. Providing services and creating knowledge would quickly become more important than producing goods. This shift would have a strong effect on labour markets and would devaluate manual labour and blue-collar jobs while creating service sector jobs. Thus, highly skilled professionals were most likely to benefit from these developments.[35]

Broad debates on the qualities of the era and the ongoing structural changes in Western societies continued over the following years. Jean Fourastié, published a book in 1979, whose title evolved into a catch-phrase for the entire postwar era: *Les Trente Glorieuses, ou la révolution invisible de 1946 à 1975*.[36] He argued that the three decades following the Second World War had been characterized by a continuous economic upswing and growing productivity, with high average wages and increasing consumption. The rising prosperity had led to a generous system of social benefits in many Western European countries. This exceptional period had come to an end with the impact of the 1973 oil price crisis.

In addition to socio-economic transformation and shifts in the labour market, new cultural phenomena were debated publicly as well. In 1977, Ronald Inglehart's *The Silent Revolution* noted a profound change in values regarding religion, work ethics, family, and homosexuality, between the generations in industrialized societies.[37] He identified the emergence of an individualistic, post-materialistic attitude within the younger generation. A year earlier, on the occasion of the bicentennial of the founding of the United States, the novelist and journalist Tom Wolfe had pejoratively referred to the 1970s as the "Me Decade."[38] He bemoaned what he saw as rampant individualism and the loss of communitarian values.

At the end of the decade, historian Christopher Lasch depicted American society as a "culture of narcissism."[39] The rise of consumer culture in modern capitalism, he argued, had produced narcissistic individuals with fragile, superficial self-concepts. Lasch drew parallels between psychological changes in personality and shifts in the workplace. The decline of the agricultural and industrial sectors and the growing relevance of information and knowledge catered to a narcissistic persona, with all its social and psychological implications. That same year, the German philosopher Jürgen Habermas edited two volumes on the intellectual climate of the late 1970s.[40] Fearing a conservative backlash in the country, leading leftist intellectuals, writers, and academics illuminated different facets of the political, economic, and cultural state of West Germany. Habermas wrote of a "contemplative left" aware of the fragility of the democratic system in West Germany, thirty years after its founding. He underlined the necessity to defend the status quo against those who openly complained of "too much" democracy.

Notwithstanding their differences, these contemporary voices from different countries reflect a broad consensus in the perception of ongoing structural transformations in the fields of politics, culture, and the economy during the 1970s. Criticism was voiced on the political left, lamenting the end of Keynesianism and an upswing in neoliberal economic policies, but also by conservative thinkers who complained of an emerging superficial individualism and the rise of degenerated liberalism.

Regardless of their political stances, another opinion shared among contemporary intellectuals concerned the assumption that the implications of ongoing structural changes could be entirely understood only decades later. For example, in his book, Daniel Bell begins his chapter on the problems of organized labour by noting that "the structural changes I have been delineating pose some crucial, long-run problems for the organized trade-union movement in the United States. But long-run, in this context, means thirty years or so before these tendencies work themselves out in detail."[41] For Bell and others, the social effects of the incremental emergence of the "knowledge society" would be able to be observed to their full extent only at a minimum distance of three decades.

In a similar argument, albeit one that looks back in time and not forward, German sociologist and former director of the Max Planck Institute for the Study of Societies, Wolfgang Streeck, recently stated: "I would argue that the crisis weighing capitalism down at the beginning of the twenty-first century – a crisis of its economy as well as its politics – can be understood only as the climax of a development which began in the mid-1970s and which the crisis theories of that time were the first attempts to interpret."[42]

As the complex consequences of the various transformations of the 1970s could not be foreseen at the time, it seems now, forty years later, necessary to return to an examination of the decade. Doing so may well be the key to understanding numerous trends fundamentally shaping the present. Appreciating contemporary history as the "prehistory of the present"[43] and taking the political and economic implications of the 2008 economic crisis into consideration, it is not surprising that historians have begun to deal with the 1970s more intensively in recent years.[44]

Raphael and Doering-Manteuffel's *Nach dem Boom* paradigmatically presents recent debates in German historiography, taking up numerous contemporary observations and channelling them into a set of stimulating and thought-provoking theses. The present volume aims to examine, from different angles, core aspects of the social and economic history of the 1970s and its aftermath, while also examining the hypotheses of *Nach dem Boom*.

Whether one agrees with Raphael and Doering-Manteuffel's assessment of a structural rupture in the 1970s or not, there seems to be no doubt that the processes of digitalization and computerization accelerated in the course of the decade, affecting a great many workplaces along with the living reality of millions of workers. For example, the invention of the electronic watch led to the loss of half the jobs in the German watch industry in just the four years between 1971 and 1975. The introduction of electronic typesetting and image design occasioned the loss of more than one-fifth of all jobs in the German printing industry during the 1970s. In many industrialized nations, textile workers suffered heavily as production was outsourced to developing countries. Many trends caused by what is now known as globalization had begun to accelerate: the rise of Asian economies increased global competition, and, by the middle of the decade, unemployment had risen across all Western countries. While many politicians regarded this as a temporary phenomenon, unemployment would remain high and develop into a structural problem, bringing back social phenomena long thought to have been overcome during the postwar boom.[45] Poverty could no longer be observed only at the margins of societies but returned to their centres as well.

Within the context of this socio-economic transformation, employment patterns have become increasingly uncertain, with many typically male-dominated sectors especially thrown into crisis. The idea of a single breadwinner with a full-time job providing for an entire family has slowly disappeared, while atypical, precarious forms of employment have increased and the proportion of female workers has grown.

Currency exchange rates were, moreover, liberalized after the collapse of the Bretton Woods system in the early 1970s. In the course of the impending monetary system crisis, capital controls in West Germany were eventually suspended.[46] These trends strengthened the financial sector while lastingly changing the role of (private) banks in the economy. Several scholars have hence come to the conclusion that a new form of capitalism emerged in the process, that of financial market or finance capitalism.[47]

The lasting results of these various economic developments were, on the one hand, "the crisis of labour society," as the motto of a 1982 congress of German sociologists in Bamberg had it. On the other hand, these changes have positively affected the fortunes of women and other hitherto underrepresented groups in the labour market. This is only one example of the fundamental ambiguities or conflicting results that marked the 1970s. These internal contradictions render it difficult to find a general analytic term to characterize the decade.

Moreover, while most scholars agree that, for multiple reasons, the 1970s should be regarded as a phase of accelerated transformation, the decline in the traditional industrial sectors had begun much earlier. The problems affecting the West German coal industry, for example, first began to emerge in the late 1950s, whereas the steel crisis, provoked by global overcapacities and ruinous competition, only accelerated in the mid-1970s. Industrial areas and cities such as Youngstown, Ohio in the American Rust Belt and Bochum in the Ruhr area of West Germany were hit hard as a result.[48]

Forms of industrial decline and the rise of the service sector thus both set in before the 1970s and continued through the following decades. There are, however, good arguments for focusing on the decade as one of the centrepieces of structural economic transformation in the postwar era – even more so as its many contradictions render it especially interesting. Their implications and consequences require a large amount of empirical research at the micro-, meso-, and discursive levels. The present volume intends to contribute to a fuller picture of the decade.

Organization of This Volume

The case studies assembled here can help answer some of the questions and speak to generalized conclusions concerning the 1970s. They are also meant to highlight a number of fundamental discrepancies in individual developments and their ramifications, resulting in a more nuanced perspective.

This volume is divided into three sections, each containing three chapters. Although each contributor focuses on the situation in a specific country, their conclusions can be applied to other national contexts as well, in light of the general trends marking the period, as described above.

The chapters in the first section, "Ambiguities," deal with the upswing in direct selling in the United States, changes in individual consumption patterns in Great Britain, and transformations in domestic work. Based in thorough empirical research, these chapters demonstrate that the 1970s need to be analysed, first and foremost, as a decade replete with equivocal, even conflicting, developments.

In her chapter "Crisis or Opportunity? Amway and an Unfamiliar Story of Economic Growth in the 1970s," Jessica Burch focuses on a hitherto largely unresearched development, that of direct selling. With companies such as Amway, Avon, and Tupperware undergoing a boom in the early 1970s, direct selling grew to a five-billion-dollar industry by 1974, with nearly two million sellers involved in the business. This number increased even further with the economic downturn following the oil price crisis and rising unemployment in the second half of the decade. From early on, Amway and similar companies advertised their business model as an easy way to earn additional money and as a solution to individuals' financial troubles, thus capitalizing on the loss of well-paid industrial jobs. Amway depicted both manufacturing and white-collar jobs as precarious and unreliable while praising direct selling as a work model for the future and a form of entrepreneurship. Although their income generally remained low, direct sellers did indeed perceive their occupation as autonomous and as a way to cope with socio-economic transformations and the changing labour market. Burch writes that direct selling was not a new phenomenon but in fact harked back to the colonial era. Its boom in the 1970s nonetheless demonstrates how the decade had simultaneously led both to deindustrialization and to new forms of employment. It cannot therefore be interpreted solely as a transition from industrial capitalism to the "new economy" of the late twentieth century, as characterized by new forms of casual and contingent work. In her chapter, Burch demonstrates that the workers' perspective remained an ambiguous one. Most perceived the developments in the 1970s as both a crisis and an opportunity, with many viewing these new forms of work as providing an increase in personal autonomy over factory work, despite the comparatively modest income.

Through the integration of individual perceptions, Burch points to the contradiction between the "objective" economic crisis and "subjective" strategies for coping with changing circumstances. She furthermore explains how the economic crisis was far from affecting all industrial sectors. On the contrary, the crisis in some sectors turned out to be the very precondition for the boom in others.

Sina Fabian approaches a similar area of varying effects in the 1970s from a different perspective in her chapter "Crisis? What Crisis? Mass Consumption in Great Britain in the 1970s and Early 1980s." Based on her analysis of consumption patterns, she calls for the decade to be viewed not merely as an era of crisis and economic decline, as, from the viewpoint of individual consumption, the case is much more complicated. She argues that consumption patterns should thus play a significant role in analysing economic development in the decade.

Britain was undoubtedly hit hard by the economic downturn. In the early part of the decade, as wages continued to rise, many individuals, and members of the working class in particular, were able to spend more money on consumption, often purchasing a car or going away on holiday for the first time in their lives. As unemployment began to increase, however, a growing number of people could no longer participate at that level in consumer society, which was so widely propagated. A new wave of poverty became readily apparent in the early 1980s. Social inequalities were increasingly palpable, and the gap between different social classes continued to widen. Fabian argues that the main distinction was now between those with and those without work. Consumption patterns reflecting different forms of vacationing demonstrate this trend paradigmatically, highlighting the disparities in the impact of these socio-economic developments. Fabian demonstrates how the decline of traditional industries went hand in hand with the expansion of mass consumption and related industries, and she distinguishes between macro-trends and individual experiences.

Eileen Boris concludes the first section by elaborating on another area of disparity in "Decent Work in the Home? Household Workers and the Crisis of Social Reproduction since the 1970s." Focusing on household work in the United States since the 1970s, Boris broadens the debate on the changing nature of work. Her article concentrates on a particularly marginalized and exploited group, that of migrant female domestic workers, as the traditional model of social reproduction – that is, a male breadwinner and a female caregiver – is changing along with the shifting global economy.

For a period during the early postwar era, domestic service had been thought to be a vanishing phenomenon, given the mechanization of the household through the use of electrical appliances. The growth in middle-class women's employment in the 1970s, in fact, had a reverse effect, heralding the re-emergence of the nanny, the housekeeper, and the extra-familial caregiver for the elderly. As white middle-class women were joining the workforce, they increasingly outsourced home and care work to immigrant women. The 1970s thus witnessed the transformation of the relationship between women and the labour market in the United States at several levels. A growing number of mainly white and married women began to take up regular employment in the context of a new form of feminism and economic ruptures leading to deindustrialization. By the mid-1970s, 50 per cent of mothers with pre-school-age children were pursuing paid employment, a figure that would grow to 80 per cent by the 2000s. These developments precipitated a crisis of social reproduction that was addressed through the use of the cheap labour of immigrant women. Boris demonstrates how these women were a vulnerable, exploited group that would slowly regain agency by organizing themselves to improve their working conditions.

Immigrant, mostly Latin American, women still form the absolute majority of household workers in the United States. Boris concludes her chapter by outlining recent attempts of household workers to fight against the precarity of their status. The struggle still continues, but under new conditions and circumstances brought about within the context of neoliberal globalization. Boris's contribution to this volume thus demonstrates the ambiguity the economic changes of the 1970s entailed for women: while white women improved their status in the labour market, the price of their progress was paid by immigrant women.

The contributors to the first section demonstrate that exclusively analysing the 1970s as a decade of crisis does injustice to its contradictory aspects. Undeniably, from the perspective of (mostly white male) factory workers, economic developments in some industrial sectors were in the midst of crisis, but this label is hardly sufficient to characterize the decade as a whole. Issues such as the renaissance of direct selling, transformations in individual consumption patterns, and the changing nature of household work cannot be interpreted in a clear-cut manner. It is necessary to integrate structural disparities into the analysis in order to understand these phenomena better.

The second section of this volume, "Adaptations," looks into how different actors such as governments, labour unions, and large companies have attempted to cope with the challenges connected to socioeconomic transformations and concomitant social phenomena, and the increase in job migration in particular. Did these actors offer new answers and provide solutions, or did they revert to old concepts in dealing with the shifting political and economic environment?

In chapter 4, "The Clandestine Crisis: Migrant Labour in an Age of Deindustrialization," Michael Kozakowski focuses on the French government's immigration policy and its implications after the oil crisis of 1973. The author underscores the important role played by migrants during the postwar boom in Western countries. With a focus on France, he expands the perspective of the volume to include continental Europe.

Migrants in France took on necessary but low-paid jobs that indigenous workers were increasingly less willing to perform. The migrants hence not only contributed to economic growth in general but specifically took on the least prestigious and most difficult factory jobs, producing goods such as automobiles and refrigerators that were mainstays of mass consumption. As a social group facing discrimination, migrants tended to accept flexible and insecure working conditions. They helped expand production while keeping prices low. Due to their marginalization, however, they were also hit hardest by the socio-economic changes of the 1970s. Migrants were, for example, the first to be fired from manufacturing jobs after the oil price crisis. Subsequent changes to migratory policy made it more and more difficult for non-European immigrants to receive work permits and enter the French labour market. Unemployment among migrants was, furthermore, much higher than the national average. After having already been exploited in factories, many were pushed into even lower-paying jobs in the service sector – for instance, in restaurants or cleaning companies. As Kozakowski shows, Western societies have never fully acknowledged the significant contribution of migrant work to the postwar boom, with migrants instead coming to be perceived as a threat in the course of the economic crisis of the 1970s. These trends were not entirely new but the continuation of the flexible, precarious, short-term, and highly mobile labour force that constituted the over-looked foundation of the economic miracle, not only in France, but all throughout Western Europe. This chapter demonstrates how government policies reacting to the oil crises spurred resentment toward the most vulnerable and alienated segment of the workforce, one that, as ethnically distinct, was a particularly easy target.

As a marginalized group, migrants can help scholars examine the socio-economic changes of the 1970s. They had to deal with new immigration policies and legal frameworks when, following the oil crises, many European governments cancelled their recruitment agreements with countries of the European periphery. Migrants generally suffered the most from the economic downturn, being the first to lose their factory jobs, which, though arduous, were comparatively well paid. Many migrants who were not forced to leave Western European countries had to accept low-skilled and poorly paid jobs in the expanding service sector.

Other social groups were in a much better position to handle the shifting circumstances. Nevertheless, as Karsten Uhl shows in his chapter "Challenges of Computerization and Globalization: The Example of the Printing Unions, 1950s to 1980s," not even the German labour union representing skilled printers and typesetters, the self-styled "aristocracy of the proletariat," was immune to the consequences of a changing economic environment. Technological inventions had begun to fundamentally transform their profession in the 1960s. This process, linked to the increased use of computer technology, accelerated in the 1970s and 1980s, with desktop publishing representing a peak in the industry's computerization process, beginning in 1985.

These technological changes provoked massive labour unrest in the printing sector between 1976 and 1985. During a 1978 strike, the labour union and work councils attempted to secure the status of qualified professions in the face of technological innovation, while a 1985 strike demanded the shortening of working hours and the introduction of a thirty-five-hour week.

Those years, as Uhl argues, were further marked by a form of Europeanization, as labour politics increasingly had to cross national borders to deal with technological developments. This chapter points to the multiple challenges for labour unions at the discursive and political levels and with respect to worker self-perception in the face of shifting job realities and working conditions. Technological change proved to be a complex process, and it took a relatively long period of time for the new technologies to prevail. Uhl shows that workers and labour unions were not only reacting to technological change but were also actively involved in steering its development.

In contrast to migrant workers, skilled workers were represented by powerful organizations fighting for their interests. As Uhl demonstrates, technological progress forced German labour unions to adapt by moving beyond national borders and toward a transnational struggle.

Notwithstanding the changes affecting their industry, printers held onto their self-perception as being the "aristocracy of the proletariat" for a long period of time. This demonstrates the relevance of a high level of self-consciousness when it comes to individuals and groups dealing with socio-economic transformations, as it can help them absorb and process the shock of structural ruptures.

As the adversaries of labour unions, companies responded differently to technological progress and transformed workplaces, as Franziska Rehlinghaus illustrates in chapter 6, "Soft Skills in an Age of Crises: Continuing Training as an Economic Coping Strategy in West German Companies." Taking the Bayer chemical company in Leverkusen as an example, Rehlinghaus examines the expansion of employee-training programs in large West German companies. Although many companies expanded their on-the-job training programs in the early 1970s, Rehlinghaus does not consider this to have been a systematic strategy for coping with new socio-economic challenges. They were instead a consequence of overlapping social developments at several levels that had already begun before the crises of the 1970s, and that cannot therefore be viewed as a new trend in capitalism. These on-the-job training programs did, however, gain considerable momentum beginning in the middle of the decade as the result of rising unemployment and were mainly a product of the education reforms of the 1960s and a consequence of the first postwar recession in West Germany in 1966–7. Their popularity also reflected the growing aspirations of individuals to advance their own careers.

The training programs of the 1970s were often advertised as quasi-magical solutions for individual employees to cope with the rapidly multiplying challenges of the labour market. Meanwhile, the government pushed them as a central pillar of the education system. Since state funding was not sufficient, however, the training programs were ultimately devised and implemented by the companies themselves. Thus, it was Bayer's department for human resources that became responsible for carrying them out within the corporation. Ultimately – and perhaps unsurprisingly, given their dependence on companies rather than on the state or on unions – the programs exacerbated existing inequalities within the workforce, as not every employee could participate on the same basis. Programs originally intended to absorb the consequences of socio-economic transformations resulted instead in increasing social discrepancies within companies, likely contributing to an emerging sense of crisis among the workforce.

The contributors to the second section take a closer look at how different actors dealt with the socio-economic challenges of the 1970s. They depict the responses of a government, a labour union, and a major company to the changing circumstances. While the French government's policies essentially deprived migrant workers of their agency, unions and companies became active agents that more or less successfully shaped or at least influenced developments. Their coping strategies, however, were not genuinely new but mostly well-tested measures that were "innovative" only by virtue of being implemented within new contexts.

These chapters show how different the reactions were to the changes in the job market and the effects of technological progress. Various forms of behaviour followed established patterns, resulting from a national form of path dependency. It is thus questionable whether a "social shift of revolutionary quality" can be generally purported to have occurred in the 1970s. It would instead seem more like a gradual shift. Even when technological advances completely transformed a profession – as was the case for printers – a softer landing was possible if strong unions were present, as in West Germany. Not all of the social changes were thus revolutionary in character. This revolutionary quality stood more in a dialectical relationship with reform and gradual changes.

The chapters in the final section, "(Dis-)Continuities," discuss the significance of the concept of deindustrialization in grasping the transformations of the 1970s, from three very different perspectives. Focusing on the issue of industrial decline, they address questions such as, Is "deindustrialization" adequate as an analytical term to describe the changes? Did deindustrialization take place at all – and, if so, to what extent? How did it affect the respective societies under consideration?

Without ignoring actual shifts in economic structures, each of the contributors to this section demonstrates how "deindustrialization" as a concept is not sufficient to describe the developments of this decade. While many countries and regions still retain a strong industrial basis, others have enacted economic reforms that supported and successfully strengthened the competitiveness of their industries. Deindustrialization is therefore not only an inadequate description of the 1970s but also a problematic narrative that at least implicitly presumes that the "good old times" were indeed "better."

Andreas Wirsching's chapter on the manifold consequences of globalization in France, "Deindustrialization and the Globalization

Discourse in France since 1980," serves to further this discussion, demonstrating how the debate on deindustrialization has become ingrained in French cultural memory. This debate is now closely interrelated with how the effects of globalization are evaluated. Wirsching argues that it is possible to speak of deindustrialization only from a Western perspective, if at all. Whereas industrial decline certainly did affect areas such as northern France, the 1970s actually saw an upswing in industrial production at the global level. A deindustrialization narrative had nonetheless already been established in the 1970s. As Wirsching argues, the deindustrialization narrative needs to be evaluated critically, rather than simply promoted, with France providing an especially interesting example of its development.

Wirsching highlights the shortcomings of the current "after the boom" discussion. France has undergone profound economic, social, and cultural changes over the past several decades, and its industry has successfully repositioned itself under the new socio-economic conditions. The notion of deindustrialization, Wirsching argues, is mainly part of the country's "remembrance culture." It is generally regarded as a purely national, or even regional, issue, and is not placed in the context of a broader European or transatlantic development. In many cases, the French deindustrialization narrative instead turns into a source of regional identity connected to feelings of social exclusion. This sentiment often evokes a longing for the clearly structured postwar society that was based mainly on industrial employment. It also produces an attitude of resistance to the real and perceived demands of a postmodern, highly individualized society. Wirsching's chapter not only reveals an important desideratum for historical research but also offers an explanation for the current rise of populism.

Chapter 8, by Bart Hoogeboom and Marijn Molema, "Look to the Future, Embrace Your Past: Regional Industrialization Policies and Their Aftermath," advocates for the careful use of the term "deindustrialization." While conceding that a number of traditional industries did enter a state of crisis in the 1970s, they warn against the overgeneralization of this observation.

Complementing Wirsching's chapter, Hoogeboom and Molema provide a regional perspective with their focus on postwar economic development in the northeast Friesland region of the Netherlands. After remaining underdeveloped for a long period of time, the area was able to catch up in terms of industrialization during the postwar era as the result of efficient structural and industrial policies. Hoogeboom and Molema view the concept of deindustrialization as misleading when it comes to understanding industrial developments in northeast

Friesland. Core expectations such as the decline in industrial production and the growth in service sector jobs simply do not apply there. On the contrary, the industrial sector continues to play an important role in every municipality of the region. The coordinated structural policies of the state in the postwar decades thus seem to have been successful, refuting neoliberal assumptions about spatial-economic strategies. Hoogeboom and Molema demonstrate the merit of taking a regional perspective in differentiating socio-economic trends.

This chapter also shows how generalizations on the character of the 1970s should be avoided. From the specific regional perspective of this study, the decade does not even appear to be a particular turning point. With respect to northeast Friesland, the actual historical trajectory cannot be characterized as "deindustrialization."

The final contribution to this volume takes up this debate with regard to (West) Germany by drawing a line leading from the 1970s to the present. In his chapter "The End of Long-established Certainties: The Transformation of Germany Inc. since the Late 1980s," Hartmut Berghoff deals with the implications of the globalization processes that set in over four decades ago but began to reveal their full potential only in the early 1990s. The creation of the Economic and Monetary Union of the European Union, coinciding with the disintegration of the socialist states of Eastern Europe, marked the preliminary end of a long-term process of European integration that had accelerated significantly during the 1970s. The global economy then underwent considerable structural changes in the 1990s.

Berghoff identifies several overlapping trends that affected Germany in particular. The end of the Cold War and the integration of Eastern European economies into the capitalist global market changed the political and socio-economic landscape of Europe. The digital revolution fundamentally affected workplaces, while the global integration of markets reached ever-new heights. Neoliberal policies enjoyed a high degree of acceptance and were being implemented worldwide, with the financial sector growing in importance. Berghoff delineates the implications of these worldwide developments in his deliberations on the continuities and discontinuities in Germany in the 1990s.

Historical research on "varieties of capitalism" tends to interpret the socio-economic structure of West Germany as a corporative form often known as "Rhenish capitalism," distinguished from others by a system of social partnership between labour unions and employer associations.[49] Social concerns and strong governmental supervision have succeeded in containing market forces to a certain extent in a model that is also firmly anchored in solid vocational training.

Berghoff discusses whether this "Germany Inc." model did in fact come apart in the 1990s, as many scholars have suggested. Refuting the claim that Germany has evolved into a liberal market economy along the lines of Anglo-Saxon countries, Berghoff instead draws a more complex and nuanced picture of the current state of affairs. Examining the system of labour relations, the implications of market deregulation, and changes in the structure of companies and corporations, Berghoff concludes that Germany Inc. has not unravelled but has transformed into a hybrid state. Many pillars of the old model continue to stand: Germany has not become a post-industrial society but has retained a strong manufacturing base, notwithstanding clear changes. Germany Inc. has undergone reform and become more flexible, with ambiguous implications. While the German economy continues to thrive, social rifts have deepened, and social certainties long taken for granted have clearly eroded. Berghoff contributes to the discussion on varieties of capitalism by illustrating how a specific socio-economic nation-state structure constituted a path dependency influencing its reaction to the challenges of globalization that continue to play a major role today. Berghoff argues that while the fundamental socio-economic transformations of the 1990s originated in the 1970s, Germany's path dependency has persisted even in the face of the critical changes of the past several decades.

The chapters in part 3 demonstrate how the concept of deindustrialization, or industrial decline, cannot be applied universally in a convincing manner. In the cases presented from France, the Netherlands, and (West) Germany, continuities have clearly prevailed over socio-economic ruptures, calling into question the suitability of speaking of a period "after the boom."

These chapters make clear that one cannot speak of deindustrialization in many parts of Western Europe during the 1970s, but instead of a "catch-up" form of industrialization induced by state economic and structural policies. In light of considerable socio-economic continuities, especially as pertains to the Rhenish capitalism of Germany, it is questionable whether one can speak of digital financial capitalism as a completely new order stretching to the end of the twentieth century.

The effects of the developments discussed in the contributions to this volume continue to fundamentally shape socio-economic conditions in Europe and the United States alike. By dealing with a variety of topics from different countries, ranging from household work to direct selling and government policies toward migrants, and taking into account the various social and political actors, these chapters provide illuminating glimpses into the diverse panorama of the 1970s. It is precisely their variety that enables new insights and tests them from different angles.

Taken as whole, the chapters cast serious doubts on the validity of the concept of industrial decline in the context of the 1970s. Even as many traditional industries and industrial regions did slide into severe economic crisis during the 1970s, a generalized view of deindustrialization does not do justice to the period. The many fundamental disparities of the decade and their socio-economic, political, and cultural implications require even more thorough empirical studies. An aim of this volume is to bring diversity to the depiction of the decade, provoke critique, and stimulate further research.

NOTES

1 Cf. OECD, *OECD Employment Outlook, 2017* (Paris: OECD Publishing, 2017), last accessed 4 July 2018, http://dx.doi.org/10.1787/empl _outlook-2017-en.

2 For the United States, see Richard B. Freeman, John T. Dunlop, and R.F. Schubert, *The Evolution of the American Labor Market, 1948–80* (Chicago: University of Chicago Press, 1980); Robert I. Lerma and Stefanie R. Schmidt, *Overview of Economic, Social, and Demographic Trends Affecting the US Labor Market: Final Report* (Washington, DC: Urban Institute, 1999). For Germany, see Christian Brinkmann and Karen Schober, eds., *Erwerbsarbeit und Arbeitslosigkeit im Zeichen des Strukturwandels: Chancen und Risiken am Arbeitsplatz* (Nuremberg: IAB, 1992); Jutta Hinrichs and Elvira Giebel-Felten, *Die Entwicklung des Arbeitsmarktes 1962–2001*, Arbeitspapier Nr. 82 (Sankt Augustin: KAS, 2002), also online, last accessed 4 July 2018, http://www.kas.de/wf/doc/kas_467-544-1-30.pdf?030610110803.

3 See Jon C. Teaford, *Cities of the Heartland: The Rise and Fall of the Industrial Midwest* (Bloomington: Indiana University Press, 1993); Steven C. High, *Industrial Sunset: The Making of North America's Rust Belt, 1969–1984* (Toronto: University of Toronto Press, 2003); George Packer, *The Unwinding: Thirty Years of American Decline* (London: Faber & Faber, 2014); Stefan Goch, *Eine Region im Kampf mit dem Strukturwandel. Strukturpolitik und Bewältigung von Strukturwandel im Ruhrgebiet* (Essen: Klartext, 2002); Marco Doria, *L'imprenditoria industriale in Italia dall'Unità al "miracolo economico": Capitani d'industria, padroni, innovatori, Giappichelli* (Turin: G. Giappichelli 1998); Roberto Tolaini, Sara De Maestri, Roberto Tolaini, and Garruccio Roberta, *Storia e itinerari dell'industria ligure Copertina rigida* (Genoa: De Ferrari, 2012); Sylvie April, ed., *Les Houillères entre l'État, le marché et la société: Les territoires de la résilience, XVIIIe–XXIe siècles* (Villeneuve d'Ascq, FR: Presses Universitaires du Septentrion, 2015); Marion Fontaine, *Fin d'un monde ouvrier Liévin, 1974* (Paris: Éditions EHESS, 2014).

4 See Alexander Keßel, Matthias Biesel, and Linda Schreiber, "Prosper-Haniel: Letzte Kohle an Steinmeier übergeben, aber alle achten nur auf den Bergmann hinter ihm," *Der Westen*, 21 December 2018, last accessed 13 February 2019, https://www.derwesten.de/auf-kohle-geboren /prosper-haniel-steinkohle-abschied-zeche-bergbau-id216050303.html; Carsten Liebfrid, "Bergwerk Prosper-Haniel verabschiedet sich von Bottrop," *Westdeutsche Allgemeine Zeitung*, 2 December 2018, last accessed 13 February 2019, https://www.waz.de/staedte/bottrop/bergwerk -prosper-haniel-verabschiedet-sich-von-bottrop-id215923695.html.
5 Bruce J. Schulman, *The Seventies: The Great Shift in American Culture, Society and Politics* (Cambridge, MA: Da Capo Press, 2002).
6 Phillip Jenkins, *Decade of Nightmares: The End of the Sixties and the Making of Eighties America* (Oxford: Oxford University Press, 2006).
7 Niall Ferguson, Charles S. Maier, Erez Manela, and Daniel J. Sargent, eds., *The Shock of the Global: The 1970s in Perspective* (Cambridge, MA: Belknap Press of Harvard University Press, 2010).
8 Daniel T. Rodgers, *Age of Fracture* (Cambridge, MA: Belknap Press of Harvard University Press, 2011).
9 See Lutz Raphael and Anselm Doering-Manteuffel, *Nach dem Boom: Perspektiven auf die Zeitgeschichte seit 1970* (Göttingen: Vandenhoeck & Ruprecht, 2008).
10 Lutz Raphael and Anselm Doering-Manteuffel, *Nach dem Boom: Perspektiven auf die Zeitgeschichte seit 1970*, 2nd ed. (Göttingen: Vandenhoeck & Ruprecht, 2010), 13.
11 Ibid., 14.
12 Ibid., 9.
13 Ulrich Bröckling, *Das unternehmerische Selbst: Soziologie einer Subjektivierungsform* (Frankfurt a.M.: Suhrkamp, 2017).
14 Luc Boltanski and Ève Chiapello, *Der neue Geist des Kapitalismus* (Konstanz: UVK-Verlagsgesellschaft, 2006).
15 Doering-Manteuffel, *Nach dem Boom* (2008), 12–13.
16 Knud Andresen, Ursula Bitzegeio, and Jürgen Mittag, eds., *"Nach dem Strukturbruch?" Kontinuität und Wandel von Arbeitbeziehungen und Arbeitswelt(en) seit den 1970er-Jahren* (Bonn: Dietz, 2011).
17 Doering-Manteuffel, *Nach dem Boom* (2nd ed., 2010), 13.
18 Andresen, Bitzegeio, and Mittag, "*Nach dem Strukturbruch?*"; Morten Reitmayer and Thomas Schlemmer, eds., *Die Anfänge der Gegenwart: Umbrüche in Westeuropa nach dem Boom* (Munich: Oldenbourg, 2014).
19 See Richard Levick, "The Korean Miracle: The Challenge ahead for the Chaebols," *Forbes*, 7 October 2015, last accessed 13 February 2019, https://www.forbes.com/sites/richardlevick/2015/10/07/the-korean-miracle -the-challenge-ahead-for-the-chaebols/#3f9ca9793a82; *Michael Edson Robinson, Korea's Twentieth-Century Odyssey (Honolulu: University of Hawaii*

29

Press, 2007); Murray A. Rubinstein, ed., *Taiwan: A New History* (New York: M.E. Sharpe, 2007); Ian A. Skoggard, *The Indigenous Dynamic in Taiwan's Postwar Development: Religious and Historical Roots of Entrepreneurship (New York: M.E. Sharpe, 1996); Sven Hansen and Barbara Bauer, eds., Chinas Aufstieg: Mit Kapital, Kontrolle und Konfuzius* (Berlin: taz, 2018); Joseph Tse-Hei Lee, "The Rise of China: An Introduction," *Indian Journal of Asian Affairs* 20, nos 1/2 (2007): 1–4; John G. Ikenberry, "The Rise of China and the Future of the West: Can the Liberal System Survive?" *Foreign Affairs* 87, January–February 2008, last accessed 13 February 2019, https://www .foreignaffairs.com/articles/asia/2008-01-01/rise-china-and-future-west; Theo Sommer, *China First: Die Welt auf dem Weg ins chinesische Jahrhundert* (Munich: C.H. Beck, 2019); Harald Müller and Carsten Rauch, "Indiens Weg zur Wirtschaftsmacht," *Aus Politik und Zeitgeschichte* 22 (2008): 7–13, also online, last accessed 13 February 2019, http://www.bpb.de /apuz/31199/indiens-weg-zur-wirtschaftsmacht?p=all; Edward Luce, "In Spite of the Gods: The Rise of Modern India," *Publishers Weekly*, 11 June 2006, last accessed 13 February 2019, https://www.publishersweekly.com /978-0-385-51474-3.

20 Pia Heinemann, "Die gesunde Sehnsucht nach der guten alten Zeit," *Welt*, 14 January 2010, last accessed 13 February 2019, https://www.welt.de /lifestyle/article5655840/Die-gesunde-Sehnsucht-nach-der-guten-alten -Zeit.html; Julia Shaw, "Warum früher alles besser war," *Spiegel*, 18 November 2016, last accessed 13 February 2019, http://www.spiegel .de/wissenschaft/mensch/nostalgie-warum-frueher-alles-besser -war-a-1120337.html; Stephanie Coontz, "The Not-So-Good Old Days," *New York Times*, 15 June 2013, last accessed 13 February 2019, https:// www.nytimes.com/2013/06/16/opinion/sunday/coontz-the-not-so -good-old-days.html; Shilpa Madan, "Those Good Old Days and the Power of Nostalgia," *livemint*, 7 January 2017, last accessed 13 February 2019, https://www.livemint.com/Sundayapp/jyHvNAFpaEq9c5mo3DA1yI /Those-good-old-days-and-the-power-of-nostalgia.html.

21 Jan-Werner Müller, *What Is Populism?* (Philadelphia: University of Pennsylvania Press, 2016); Volker Weiß, *Die autoritäre Revolte: Die Neue Rechte und der Untergang des Abendlandes* (Stuttgart: Klett-Cotta, 2017).

22 See Uffa Jensen, *Zornpolitik* (Berlin: Suhrkamp, 2017).

23 Didier Eribon, *Returning to Reims* (London: Penguin Books, 2018), translated from *Retour à Reims: Une théorie du sujet* (Paris: Fayard, 2009).

24 See Frank Decker, ed., *Populismus in Europa* (Bonn: VS Verlag, 2006); Ruth Wodak, *Majid Khosravinik, and Brigitte Mral, eds., Right-Wing Populism in Europe: Politics and Discourse* (London: A&C Black, 2013).

25 Rainer Rilling, Janis Ehling, Miriam Pieschke, Christina Kaindl, and Alex Demirovic, "Klasse, Scham und die Linken: Debatte zu Eribons Rückkehr nach Reims," *Zeitschrift Luxemburg*, November 2016, last accessed

4 July 2018, https://www.zeitschrift-luxemburg.de/lux/wp-content
/uploads/2016/10/Eribon-Paper-final.pdf.; Peter Birke, "Abheben und
Verschwinden: Die Debatte zu Eribons Rückkehr nach Reims," *Sozial.
Geschichte Online*, Heft 2, 2017, last accessed 4 July 2018, http://dx.doi
.org/10.17185/duepublico/44668.

26 See Stefan Maas and Christoph Richter "Der AfD-Wähler – das unbekannte
Wesen: Eine soziologische Analyse," *Deutschlandfunk*, 21 July 2016, also
online, last accessed 4 July 2018, http://www.deutschlandfunk.de/eine
-soziologische-analyse-der-afd-waehler-das-unbekannte.724.de.html
?dram:article_id=360821.

27 James David Vance, *Hillbilly Elegy: A Memoir of a Family and Culture in
Crisis* (New York: Harper, 2016).

28 Arlie Russell Hochschild, *Strangers in Their Own Land: Anger and Mourning
on the American Right* (New York: New Press, 2016).

29 See, for example, Barry *Eichengreen and Kevin O'Rourke*, "A Tale of Two
Depressions: What Do the New Data Tell Us?" *Vox*, 8 March 2010, last
accessed 4 July 2018, https://voxeu.org/article/tale-two-depressions
-what-do-new-data-tell-us-february-2010-update; *Peter Termin, "The
Great Recession and the Great Depression,"* Daedalus *139*, no. 4: 115–24,
doi:10.1162/DAED_a_00048.

30 Paul Krugman, "Why We're in a New Gilded Age," New York Review of
Books, 8 May 2014, last accessed 4 July 2018, http://www.nybooks.com
/articles/2014/05/08/thomas-piketty-new-gilded-age/.

31 Paul Krugman, "Wealth over Work," *New York Times*, 23 March 2014, last
accessed 4 July 2018, https://www.nytimes.com/2014/03/24/opinion
/krugman-wealth-over-work.html.

32 Branko Milanovic, "The Return of 'Patrimonial Capitalism': A Review of
Thomas Piketty's *Capital in the Twenty-First Century*," *Journal of Economic
Literature* 52, no. 2 (2014): 519; http://dx.doi.org/10.1257/jel.52.2.519.

33 Alain Touraine, *La société post-industrielle* (Paris: Denoël, 1969).

34 Daniel Bell, *The Coming of Post-Industrial Society: A Venture in Social
Forecasting* (New York: Basic Books, 1973).

35 The three-sector model was developed by Allan Fisher, Colin Clark,
and Jean Fourastié. See Colin Clark, *The Conditions of Economic Progress*
(London: Macmillan, 1940); Allan Fisher, "Production, Primary, Secondary
and Tertiary," *Economic Record* 15, no. 1 (1939): 24–38; Jean Fourastié,
*Le grand espoir du XXᵉ siècle: Progrès technique, progrès économique, progrès
social* (Paris: Presses universitaires de France, 1949). For a critique of this
model, see Rüdiger Graf and Kim Christian Priemel, "Zeitgeschichte in
der Welt der Sozialwissenschaften: Legitimität und Originalität einer
Disziplin," *Vierteljahrshefte für Zeitgeschichte* 4 (2012): 479–508, also online,
last accessed 4 July 2018, DOI: https://doi.org/10.1524/vfzg.2011.0026.

36 Jean Fourastié, *Les Trente Glorieuses, ou la révolution invisible de 1946 à 1975* (Paris: Fayard, 1979).

37 Ronald Inglehart, *The Silent Revolution: Changing Values and Political Styles among Western Publics* (Princeton, NJ: Princeton University Press, 1977).

38 Tom Wolfe, "The 'Me' Decade and the Third Great Awakening," in *Mauve Gloves and Madmen, Clutter and Vine* (New York: Farrar, Straus & Giroux, 1976), 126–67.

39 Christopher Lasch, *The Culture of Narcissism: American Life in an Age of Diminishing Expectations* (New York: W.W. Norton, 1979).

40 Jürgen Habermas, ed., *Stichworte zur "Geistigen Situation der Zeit,"* Vol. 2 (Frankfurt am Main: Suhrkamp, 1979).

41 Bell, *The Coming of Post-industrial Society*, 143.

42 Wolfgang Streeck, *Buying Time: The Delayed Crisis of Democratic Capitalism* (London: Verso, 2014), 1.

43 See Hans Günter Hockerts, "Zeitgeschichte in Deutschland: Begriff, Methoden, Themenfelder," *Historisches Jahrbuch* 113 (1993): 124.

44 Thomas Raithel, Andreas Rödder, and Andreas Wirsching, eds., *Auf dem Weg in eine neue Moderne? Die Bundesrepublik Deutschland in den siebziger und achtziger Jahren* (Munich: Oldenbourg, 2009); Konrad H. Jarausch, ed., *Das Ende der Zuversicht? Die siebziger Jahre als Geschichte* (Göttingen: Vandenhoeck & Ruprecht, 2008); Jeremy Black, *Europe since the Seventies* (London: Reaktion Books, 2009); Hartmut Kaelble, *The 1970s in Europe: A Period of Disillusionment or Promise? German Historical Institute London. The Annual Lecture* (London: German Historical Institute, 2010); Ferguson et al., *The Shock of the Global*; Thomas Borstelmann, *The 1970s: A New Global History from Civil Rights to Economic Inequality* (Princeton, NJ: Princeton University Press, 2012).

45 Thomas Raithel and Thomas Schlemmer, eds., *Die Rückkehr der Arbeitslosigkeit: Die Bundesrepublik Deutschland im europäischen Kontext, 1973 bis 1989* (Munich: De Gruyter Oldenbourg, 2009).

46 Werner Abelshauser, *Deutsche Wirtschaftsgeschichte: Von 1945 bis in die Gegenwart* (Munich: C.H. Beck, 2004), 267.

47 See Paul Windolf, "What Is Financial-Market Capitalism?" edited and translated for Glasshouse Forum 2008, last accessed 4 July 2018, https://www.uni-trier.de/fileadmin/fb4/prof/SOZ/APO/FinancialMarket Capitalism.pdf; Larry Neal, *The Rise of Financial Capitalism: International Capital Markets in the Age of Reason* (Cambridge: Cambridge University Press, 1993).

48 The fates and the histories of these two cities were reflected in songs by Bruce Springsteen and Herbert Grönemeyer. "Youngstown" was written by Bruce Springsteen and released on his 1995 album *The Ghost of Tom Joad*;

"Bochum" was written by Herbert Grönemeyer and released on his 1984 album *4630 Bochum*.

49 Peter A. Hall and David Soskice, *Varieties of Capitalism: The Institutional Foundations of Comparative Advantage* (Oxford: Oxford University Press, 2001); on "Rhenish capitalism," see Hans Günter Hockerts and Günther Schulz, eds., *Der "Rheinische Kapitalismus" in der Ära Adenauer* (Paderborn: Schöningh, 2016).

SECTION ONE

Ambiguities

1 Crisis or Opportunity? Amway and an Unfamiliar Story of Economic Growth in the 1970s

JESSICA BURCH

In 1979, President Jimmy Carter declared the United States to be in a state of economic and cultural crisis. Between 1970 and 1975, national unemployment had jumped from 4.9 to 8.5 per cent. Throughout the latter half of the decade, real earnings had declined while prices rose to a historical high. Inflation had compounded the effects of unemployment as the Consumer Price Index ballooned from 116 in 1970 to 161 in 1975.[1] According to Carter, however, "the true problems of our Nation are deeper than gasoline lines or energy shortages, deeper than inflation or recession." The true challenge facing the nation, Carter explained, in what has become known as the "Malaise Speech," was a crisis of confidence. An erosion of faith in the strength of the US economy, American government, and whatever sense of social cohesion had survived the turbulent 1960s had grown into "doubt about the meaning of our own lives and the loss of unity of purpose for our Nation."[2]

Voices from across the political spectrum diagnosed the end of an economic era – one characterized by high rates of production, employment, and consumption – and raised concerns about what would come next. For those on the left, such as political theorist Michael Harrington, economist and critic of the military-industrial complex Seymour Melman, and economic historian Robert Heilbroner, the contemporary moment was one of "collective sadness" and "American capitalism in decline." Left-leaning scholars in the mid-seventies pointed to the end of the growth economy to critique, variously, the military-industrial complex, corporations' influence on the state in matters of the private economy, and the unbalanced nature of the so-called mixed economy. Although some more optimistic intellectuals, such as Harrington and Heilbroner, saw capitalism in the mid-seventies as in a state of transformation that might lead to something better, ideally something leaning toward socialism, all noted the apparent end of the "growth economy."[3]

Those on the right, too, acknowledged the pressures of economic decline and social conflict. In his 1975 State of the Union address, President Gerald Ford put it simply: "the state of the union is not good."[4]

Malaise in this decade was not exclusively American. As Sina Fabian shows in the next chapter, British politicians, too, described the period as a "winter of discontent." Historians of the United Kingdom as well as of the United States have, like public intellectuals in the 1970s, tended to view the decade through the lens of crisis and decline; a decade of lost jobs, lost labour union power, lost opportunities for alternative paths. Yet, as Fabian also argues, historians have over-read that narrative's universality and explanatory power.

This chapter turns attention to one industry – direct sales – for which the "crisis" of the 1970s also brought opportunity. Focusing on the history of the Amway Corporation as a case study, I show that the 1970s can, if viewed from a different angle, be reinterpreted as a period of growth. This is not to say that 1970s malaise was merely imagined. For many Americans, the changing structures of production and employment had very real financial consequences. Rather, I argue, as Fabian does in the case of British consumer spending, that the narrative of crisis and decline tells only part of the story.

Contrary to President Ford's diagnosis, for some sectors of the US economy, the state of the union *was* good. At the same time that high-wage blue-collar jobs were disappearing from the industrial heartland, capital was being diverted into new areas of growth. Manufacturers did scale back production in the 1970s but also relocated some of that activity to the booming American Sunbelt. Investment was being diverted, too, into new sectors of growth such as the service economy, new technology and knowledge jobs, healthcare, and industries such as tourism, professional services, and the "FIRE economy" (finance, insurance, and real estate).[5] In 1945, services accounted for only 36 per cent of the gross national product. By 1983, the service sector accounted for half of total GDP and more than half of the nation's jobs.[6] Yet new service and knowledge jobs were often either low pay or required new skills and qualifications; they therefore offered little consolation to blue-collar workers laid off from unionized jobs.

If the general shift toward the late twentieth-century service and knowledge economy spurred new areas of growth, the economic climate of the 1970s also benefited firms and industries that were historically non- or counter-cyclical. Temporary staffing and employment agencies, discount retailers, and residential leasing – as well as consumer credit, small-sum lenders, debt collectors, and alcohol producers – typically performed well during periods of economic downturn. The direct sales industry, which sold consumer goods on a person-to-person basis rather than in conventional retail spaces, also thrived over the course of the 1970s. Between 1969 and 1974, direct sales grew from a $3 billion into a $5 billion industry. By 1974, nearly two million Americans sold goods for direct sales firms, including Amway, Avon, Mary Kay, Tupperware, and Stanley Home Products.[7] Net income for the top eleven non-store sellers of consumer goods increased 81 per cent in a single year, with growth driven primarily by door-to-door and party-plan sellers of cosmetics and vitamins.[8]

In fact, Jay Van Andel and Rich DeVos, founders of the Amway Corporation, described the 1970s as the company's "best [years] ever." Founded in 1959 as a spin-off from the vitamin company Nutrilite (which Amway later acquired), Amway – short for "the American Way" – began as a direct seller of cleaning supplies; by the late 1960s it sold a wide variety of other products.[9] Between 1969 and 1978, Amway's sales force grew from 80,000 to over 300,000 sellers. Retail sales increased approximately 400 per cent over the course of the decade, growing from $125 million in 1969 to over $500 million in 1978.[10] As the executives explained in 1974, "the 'bad' years in terms of the general economy have been Amway's best growth years … because more people seek extra income opportunities and financial stability in bad times" – and as a provider of part-time, temporary sales work, Amway offered just that.[11]

In addition to evidencing the sector's success and counter-cyclical tendencies, the history of Amway provides a new vantage point from which to reassess the realities and legacies of the 1970s as a decade of crisis and decline. First, Amway's growth in the 1970s complements histories that have traditionally focused on deindustrialization as a discrete phenomenon rather than as part of the transition from a manufacturing to a service economy. Second, Amway's success in the 1970s, as well as that of the direct sales sector in general, was not in spite of the economic recession but *because* of it. Van Andel and DeVos recognized early on the power of "crisis" as a marketing strategy. While President Carter feared that spreading economic and cultural "malaise" threatened to undo social ties and national unity, businessmen Van Andel and DeVos saw in the current moment an opportunity to galvanize – and recruit – Americans uncertain about their job security and financial standing.

Van Andel and DeVos sensed something about the moment of economic transformation that, thirty years later, scholars would label "capital mobility." They understood implicitly that industrial decline and rising unemployment were not unidirectional phenomena. Rather, industrial decline opened up new opportunities for sectors, firms, and executives able to leverage the very developments that President Carter interpreted as signs of "crisis" and turn them to their advantage.

Third, the history of Amway and its distributors provides a window into the material and psychological strategies some Americans employed to survive the recession. For many Amway distributors, direct sales provided not only a means of immediate economic support but also a way to adapt to larger shifts in the structures and nature of work in late capitalism. Amway is thus part of a broader history of industrial decline and the rise of the service sector but also tells its own story.

The story of Amway in the 1970s is ultimately about how one firm and its distributors constructed a new narrative about labour and economy in the late twentieth-century United States that acknowledged the real sense of financial crisis felt by many American in this period, as well as the power of "crisis" in language and culture. At the same time, as a story of corporate growth in the 1970s, it demonstrates the limits of the 1970s declension narrative. It shows that crisis for some could be opportunity for others.

A Recession-Proof Business Strategy

Van Andel's and DeVos's marketing strategy in the 1970s drew on a common understanding within the industry – that direct sales was countercyclical. Indeed, historian Katina Manko has characterized direct sales, with its combination of inexpensive goods and person-to-person sales, as a "depression-proof business strategy."[12] During the first years of the Great Depression, the direct sales sector grew from a $100 million to over $125 million – approximately 25 per cent growth.[13] Thousands of Americans affected by the Depression in the 1930s turned to direct sales firms such as Real Silk Hosiery, Jewel Tea, Fuller Brush, and the California Perfume Company as a source of immediate income. The California Perfume Company, which was later renamed Avon, increased its sales force by 20 per cent between 1930 and 1933 and reported sales increases of 10–15 per cent every year between 1930 and 1938.

The success of direct sales during the Great Depression, and then again in the 1970s, owed much to the industry's low-cost business structure. Direct sales firms do not sell merchandise in physical stores. Rather, they rely on a model of mobile, independent salesmanship that can be traced back to the Yankee peddlers of the colonial period.

Twentieth-century direct sellers – called distributors, representatives, agents, or "independent business owners" – sell goods on a person-to-person basis, usually in a customer's home. Distributors are classified as independent contractors rather than corporate employees. Rather than receive a wage, direct sellers typically acquire goods from a manufacturer, such as Amway or Tupperware, sell that merchandise to consumers, and retain a specified share of the profits. Many direct sellers earn additional income by recruiting new distributors to sell under them as part of what the industry calls their "downline." This networked or multilevel model, which Amway popularized in the 1960s, enables distributors to earn a commission on what they sell personally *plus* a commission on all the products sold by each member of their downline.

The use of an independent sales force has made direct sales firms especially adaptive to changing economic conditions. Because direct sales firms do not sell merchandise in stores, they have fewer fixed costs, such as rent for office and retail space. Compared to conventional firms, direct sales outfits also enjoy lower personnel costs. If a conventional sales firm experiences a drop in sales, it might cut jobs to reduce payroll costs. Commission expenses, by contrast, fluctuate with production and revenue.

The independent contractor label has also enabled direct sales firms to reduce or eliminate many additional employment costs, such as benefits and payroll taxes. The direct sales industry formalized this model of labour in the 1930s in response to New Deal labour regulations such as the Fair Labor Standards Act (FLSA) and the Social Security Act (SSA), which, among other things, established a minimum wage and payroll taxes to fund social insurance programs. In this way, direct sellers have much in common with individuals, mostly women, who participated in outwork or the shadow economy as described in Eileen Boris's chapter in this volume.

Outwork, homework, care work, and direct sales are predominantly casual, part-time, seasonal, "feminized" modes of work often without a permanent contract, labour union representation, or the protection of New Deal–era regulations that police many forms of stable, wage-based white-, blue-, or even pink-collar jobs.[14] One key distinction between direct sales and other modes of casual or home-based work, however, is that, as Boris shows in this volume and elsewhere, the employment status of female homeworkers, outworkers, and care workers has been a lightning rod for larger debates about gender, labour, and state power in the labour economy.[15] As a relatively small part of the consumer and labour economies, on the other hand, direct sellers rarely garnered so much attention. Moreover, at-home and party-plan selling, particularly in a homosocial setting like a Tupperware party or a Mary Kay cosmetics consultation, fit within rather than challenged prescribed notions of women's domesticity, which made direct sales a less likely candidate for social reformers. Following the passage of the SSA and FLSA, direct sellers' independent contractor status remained unchallenged through the late 1970s.

The use of a non-wage-based independent sales force was a significant financial advantage in the 1970s. In 1977, the Internal Revenue Services estimated that the independent contractor label exempted direct sales firms in aggregate from as much as $107 million in annual employment taxes.[16] Perhaps more importantly, as Van Andel and DeVos suggested in 1974, bad economic times produced a greater need for the kind of supplemental income direct selling could provide. As in the 1930s, high rates of unemployment in the 1970s led many Americans to seek additional income, and thousands looked to direct selling. Between 1973 and 1980, Avon's sales force grew from 290,000 representatives to 425,000.[17] The Direct Selling Association, the industry's primary membership and research organization, estimated that 8 per cent of American households participated in direct selling in 1973.[18] As Van Andel and DeVos put it, "the relatively infrequent 'bad years' (recessions, slowdowns, and downturns) have turned out to be the best growth years" because more people seek supplemental or replacement income during bad times.[19]

Direct sales executives harnessed the potential for growth in the economic climate of the 1970s by promoting direct selling as a solution to labour insecurity and unemployment in that period. Executives urged distributors, too, to see the 1970s from a more optimistic perspective. Van Andel and DeVos acknowledged that "the problems [of the 1970s] are real," but for Amway distributors, they insisted, "the opportunity is [just as] real." The executives counselled distributors to "get off the worry bench and onto the field – out in the marketplace where people are waiting to buy, waiting to listen." "Like the song says," they urged, referring to the 1971 hit from Mama Cass, "Don't let the good times pass you by!"[20]

Crisis and Opportunity

As early as 1971, Amway corporate literature began pointing to the potential benefits of economic recession for the firm and its distributors. The company newsletter *The Amagram*, which circulated among Amway distributors, included regular features on the ways rising unemployment, inflation, and high energy prices made anxious Americans ripe for recruiting. To reach a growing population of Americans sensitive to financial insecurity, Amway ran a series of advertisements in 1974 and 1975 under the tagline "Do It Now." An ad in the August 1974 issue of *Time* shows a man in a bank. He nervously scratches his face as he approaches the desk of a stern-looking banker. The headline asks: "Do you run out of money before you run out of month?" The ad further enquires if, like this man who needs a loan or perhaps cannot make a mortgage payment, "the cost of living is winning the race against your income." Speaking directly to inflation and the rising cost of consumer goods, Amway suggests that "you can join the more than 200,000 enterprising independent Amway distributors ... who are proving that extra income developed through the Amway opportunity means the difference between keeping ahead and going into debt." While many Americans found themselves running out of money before the end of the month, "Amway offers you an alternative," the ad argues. It offers a chance to follow the example of other Amway distributors who, "for as little as the cost of an average pair of shoes ... not only solved their immediate budget problems, but built a secure future as well." "Do it now," the ad urges, "and you'll be amazed how much shorter each month seems!"[21]

The "Do It Now" series, which ran in publications including *Time, Businessweek,* and *Ebony,* included several similar advertisements centred on families' "budget problems." One looked in on a couple fretting over a pile of bills and suggested that "Amway helps your income keep up with your outgo."[22] Others offered images of families liberated from financial stress. Under the headline "A little moonlight can put a lot of sunshine in your life," for example, a family camps under the moon. While the ad suggests that camping under the stars can bring your family happiness, the deeper implication lay in the other meaning of "moonlight," as taking a second job. In 1970, four million Americans held more than one job, and demographic indicators projected many more multiple jobholders by 1980. Amway marketing executives were here trying to tap into this growing demographic by suggesting that moonlighting as a distributor can add "sunshine" to one's life "if you're willing to do a little extra during your leisure hours."[23]

Some advertisements played on parents' anxiety about providing for their children. One ad suggests that "if you want the best for your family but worry about the cost, Amway may be your answer." The ad features a family celebrating a son's college graduation under the headline: "The best things in life are expensive."[24] Another shows a family enjoying a day at the aquarium alongside the slogan, "A little extra money can mean a lot of extra living." "If money is all that's keeping you from a great vacation, a new car, or that special boat," the ad says, "the Amway opportunity can help you live a little." Purchasing a "special boat" would have seemed to many Americans a very far off possibility. Nevertheless, whether one wanted money for college tuition, a family vacation, or merely to pay the bills, marketing literature claimed that "Amway can show you how to stop whining and start living."[25]

The optimistic, sometimes lightly scolding, tone of Amway advertisements stood out in publications like *Time*, which dedicated most of each issue to articles on the energy crisis, inflation, unemployment, and a growing federal deficit, but Amway's advertising strategy was actually very common. Pan Am World Tours claimed that, "with so much going wrong 50 weeks of the year," its vacation packages allow "you to have 2 weeks that go right."[26] While travel agencies encouraged British citizens to embark on a road trip or vacation in Spain, as discussed in Fabian's chapter, the British Tourist Authority advised Americans that 1974 was an opportune time to travel abroad because "your dollar is worth a lot more in Britain today than it was last summer – 11% more." As an added bonus, "there is no gasoline rationing. Gas is available, and it's cheaper than anywhere on the continent."[27]

Economic recession, as Fabian also argues, did not necessarily discourage consumption. Rather, providers of consumer goods and services used advertising to justify discretionary spending – for example, a UK vacation – as a form of economy. Other sectors, like insurance companies, tried to redefine their products as necessities. The Life and Health Insurance Companies of America advised that, while "the idea of a good product at a reasonable price has taken quite a battering in the last few years," life insurance policies were more affordable, and more necessary, than ever.[28]

Companies across industries tapped into Americans' financial anxieties and desire for economy, sometimes to humorous effect. A Volkswagen advertisement highlighted the benefits of its fuel-efficient cars during the energy crisis by suggesting they help relieve "gas pains." The ad is reminiscent of Alka-Seltzer, with the Volkswagen logo sinking into a glass of water. VWs are so efficient at "getting rid of nervous upsets, maybe," like an antacid for a stomach ache, "you should take two."[29] This is all to say that Amway was one of many firms that adopted "crisis" as a central marketing motif.

Amway advertisements juxtaposed images of financial stress with the supposed peace of mind, security, and even leisure that a distributorship could provide. Yet, while some companies used the recession as a clever catchphrase – the American Wood Council argued that the best way to "weather the energy crisis" was with improved home insulation – Amway marketing materials were responding to real changes in the structures of the US labour economy.[30] A May 1974 advertisement looks in on a workplace staffroom, where a crowd of well-dressed professionals has gathered around a poster announcing a "manpower cutback." The ad indicates that labour insecurity in the 1970s was spreading beyond blue-collar employment to affect white-collar professions, the stability of which most Americans took for granted in the 1950s and 1960s. In 1971, the white-collar unemployment rate, which throughout the 1960s had hovered steadily around 2.5 per cent, jumped to 3.5 per cent. By 1975, it had climbed to 4.7 per cent. The unemployment rate among technical and managerial occupations shot up by 50 per cent in 1970.[31] "In these uncertain times," the ad reads, "many jobs are threatened by uncontrollable events," but "extra income developed through the Amway business opportunity makes an uncertain job picture less of a threat." The final paragraph urges, "Do it now, and you'll look to the future confidently through job security you build for yourself."[32]

Although unfortunate for white-collar professionals and technical workers, labour insecurity among the professional classes, Amway executives reasoned, could provide the firm and its distributors with improved access to a more experienced, better-educated pool of recruits. Amway, and direct sales in general, had long struggled with reputational problems. Going back to the nineteenth-century tradition of itinerant peddling, Americans have historically been suspicious of traveling salesmen. Selling Amway carried that stigma coupled with a popular perception that networked direct selling was a form of pyramid scheme. Americans in the professional classes had for these reasons often looked askance at direct selling and at Amway in particular. From their point of view, hawking housewares and cosmetics at sales parties could be an appropriate activity for housewives but was not a legitimate profession. Heightened levels of job insecurity, financial anxiety, and psychological disaffection, from Amway executives' perspective, could render members of the professional classes newly receptive.

Reaching members of the professional class, however, could require a different marketing message. The *Amagram* advised recruiting distributors that "there are two kinds of prospects ... one is the man who is jobless, the other is the one who is afraid he may be."[33] Whereas the jobless man turned to direct selling out of economic need, the employed professional "may be more attracted to the thought of being his own boss in a business for himself ... which is to say, where he can't be laid off."[34] Whether pitching to a jobless man or an employed professional, both approaches shared an underlying assumption that, as levels of labour precarity rose, so did the appeal of direct selling.

To reach the employed professional, Amway advertisements de-emphasized "budget problems" in favour of the themes of independence, business ownership, and security. An Amway distributorship offered a work arrangement that did not rely on a corporate employer and was therefore immune to future "manpower cutbacks." Since the early 1960s, Amway recruiting literature marketed direct selling as an alternative to the dull, docile life of a subordinate "organization man."[35] Literature in the 1970s retained the idea that corporate work was unfulfilling but added to it the notion that white-collar work was also unstable. According to a 1970 sales manual, "ordinary work has many limitations," including having to "punch [a] time clock, [and] work for someone else," with "limited potential" to realize the fruits of one's own labour or to rise to one's full capabilities. The Amway alternative set "no quotas, territories, [and] no limiting factors" to keep individuals from their full potential. "That's why," the sales manual added, "Amway is not 'employment'" but rather a business "that is always yours."[36] In comparison to the "organization man" of the 1950s and 1960s or the hired white-collar worker of the 1970s, an Amway distributor was "one of those independent businessmen" with a business "no one can take… away from you" because "you're your own boss."[37] In other words, Amway distributors were not employed; they were *self*-employed.

Amway literature implied that workers could regain control over their own life and career through self-employment, and painted that freedom and autonomy as "only a decision away." A 1974 issue of *Time* shows one of Amway's "opportunity meetings." A distinguished, middle-aged man explains to a racially diverse, mixed-gender audience that "what Amway can give to you [is] the INDEPENDENCE of another income." Whereas other advertisements foregrounded how Amway could help one afford small luxuries, pay college tuition, or merely keep out of debt in the short term, this ad focused on Amway as a longer-term "business opportunity" in which the distributor had full control. This advertisement trumpeted the language of choice: "you can decide to begin an independent business on a part-time basis. In time, it can be as small or as large as you want it."[38] Rather than punch a time clock, or take orders from a boss, distributors decided for themselves when, where, and how much to work. Without limits set by a corporate employer, workers even controlled their earning potential. In a historical moment when many Americans felt powerless in the face of swings in the labour economy, seemingly unstoppable inflation, and the whims of a corporate employer, Amway offered a work situation in which the distributor had all the power.

Amway advertisements revealed a truth about the permanency of contingent work and the ways it was supplanting presumably more stable modes of labour in the US economy. By the early 1980s, the contingent labour force – defined as workers without an explicit, long-term contract with an employer – accounted for approximately 25 per cent of the total American labour force (including many of the domestic workers discussed in Boris's chapter below). According to one estimate, more than twenty million Americans worked on a temporary or part-time basis in 1980, and nearly half of them reported they did so because they could not find suitable work.[39]

But whereas some lamented the erosion of implicit, long-term employment contracts, direct sales executives saw the growth of contingent work as an opportunity to increase the size of the direct sales force. In contradistinction to the newly apparent instability of industrial and corporate work, direct sales firms claimed to offer security through a work situation in which one's income was independent from both an employer and the welfare state. If Americans in the 1970s were growing distrustful of the US state, the labour economy, and corporate America, as President Carter suggested, then an Amway distributorship offered a source of income that seemed to bypass all three.

Coping with Crisis

One might criticize direct sales executives for capitalizing on Americans' financial and class anxieties in the 1970s. Direct selling was certainly not a viable economic option for everyone. It was difficult, time-consuming work, and distributors rarely earned enough to survive on direct selling alone. Across the post–Second World War period, the vast majority of direct sellers participated on a part-time, casual basis. According to one estimate, perhaps as few as 1 per cent of Amway distributors in the late 1970s earned $2,000 or more in any one month of the year.[40] Nevertheless, direct selling was for some Americans a crucial financial – and psychological – strategy for coping with labour and economic insecurity in the postwar period, and particularly in the 1970s.

If the history of counter-cyclical industries like direct sales enables scholars to view 1970s deindustrialization and economic decline from a new angle, the stories of individual distributors similarly reveal an understudied aspect of the period's social and cultural history. Historians know a great deal about how and why business elites relocated capital in the 1970s, how political and business decisions affected blue-collar employment and the power of labour unions, and how workers organized to try to stave off the negative consequences of capital mobility. Social and political historians have shown how economic frustrations, particularly among white men, fomented racial tensions and resentment toward women and minorities, and reshaped the political geography of the United States. We know far less, however, about the daily strategies Americans employed to make ends meet.

Joseph Hunter's story offers a glimpse into how the spread of contingent work reshaped Americans' work lives in the 1970s. Hunter participated in direct selling as he moved in and out of the temporary labour economy. Between 1973 and 1976, he held short-term jobs at a supermarket, Krispy Kreme Doughnuts, an industrial transmission company, and a tire wholesaler, among others. When asked to narrate his job history, he could not recall when or how long he worked at each because, rather than a series of distinct jobs, they ran together in his memory as one stretch of temporary work.[41] Industrial sewing machine mechanic Larry Bryant similarly used an Amway distributorship to weather a period marked by the constant threat of layoffs and factory closures. From 1975 to 1977, he worked for two different manufacturing operations at three different plants, one of which closed and laid off the entire workforce.[42]

These stories make clear that the growth of the direct sales industry did not merely coincide with industrial decline in the 1970s but was in fact closely tied to changes in the mainstream labour economy. Amway's relationship to the conventional labour economy extended beyond the rhetoric deployed in advertisements and recruiting materials. When individuals such as Hunter and Bryant turned to direct selling as an immediate solution to layoffs in the manufacturing sector, they established a concrete human link among the histories of deindustrialization, the rise of the service sector, and the spread of causal labour in the late twentieth-century United States.

Direct sellers' experiences – and the persistent growth of direct sales across the postwar period – also reveal that labour precarity in the mid-1970s was not an acute response to factors such as the "invasion of foreign business" in the late 1960s, the collapse of the Bretton Woods system of monetary regulation, or the oil crisis of 1973.[43] Frank and Rita Delisle, for example, began selling Amway in 1962 after the sudden closure of the printing firm where Frank worked. Peter and Penny Javelin became distributors in the early 1960s "after suffering economic reverses in their former business because of a strike."[44] Unprecedented levels of industrial unemployment in the mid-1970s, in other words, did not mark a "great U-turn" in the US economy; rather, such unemployment punctuated a slow erosion of labour security already underway in the 1950s and 1960s (and indeed well before).

Russell Borthem, for example, was attracted to direct selling not because of an unexpected downturn, change in employment status, or the expected aftermath of the energy crisis but by a long history of unpredictable, unstable work. When he left the military in 1967, he looked forward to a stable, lucrative career in the airline industry. He had studied mechanical engineering at South Dakota State, served eight years in the US Navy flight crew, and expected no difficulty finding work. Indeed, he easily secured a job with Braniff Airlines. After only three months, however, Braniff benched him as part of a furlough plan to reduce the airline's personnel costs. Borthem relocated to Dallas for a job as a quality control engineer for Ling Temco Vaught, an aerospace manufacturer. In 1968, he relocated again, this time to Miami, for a position as a co-pilot for National Airlines. Borthem, a qualified pilot with a decade of experience, held three different jobs in three different states in less than three years. By 1969, he was grounded yet again when the International Association of Machinists and Aerospace Workers initiated a strike against National Airlines.

The strike dragged on for four months, during which time Borthem made ends meet installing and repairing lawn sprinklers and selling Amway. His independent lawn service provided much-needed income but, as he later recalled, "it was too hard of work."[45] Through the mid-1970s, Borthem sold as much as $400 to $500 worth of Amway products per month. In 1974, he began selling Rawleigh Home Products as well. For much of the 1970s, even after returning to work at the airline, he maintained both distributorships.

On the one hand, direct selling was for Borthem a source of casual, supplemental income that eased his mind, and wallet, during periods of intermittent unemployment. On the other, he remained steadily engaged in direct selling for almost a decade while his position as a pilot grew increasingly irregular. In that light, it is difficult to interpret which of the two endeavours should be considered his primary occupation. Either way, it was not the future Borthem had imagined for himself in 1967.

The personal narratives highlighted here come from male distributors, which runs counter to popular perceptions of direct selling as a form of women's domestic commerce. Although female-oriented firms such as Tupperware and Avon have garnered the most attention from historians and in popular culture, Amway and several other firms encouraged married couples to form a distributorship as a family business. Appealing to male distributors was key to Amway's success in the 1970s because industrial and mid-level managerial jobs, positions most often held by men, were more vulnerable to layoffs. As men like Borthem and Hunter were dismissed from paid jobs, they turned to direct selling as an alternative to corporate employment – ironically, the same rationale that had for decades appealed to female direct sellers shut out from the conventional labour force.

Direct sellers are in some ways a counterpoint to the professional women discussed in Boris's chapter. Those women made important gains in the professional workplace, which raised new questions about who would maintain the home. A new generation of full-time, professional, mostly white women, Boris shows, responded to this "crisis in social reproduction" by "insourcing" tasks to domestic workers, often immigrant women and women of colour. Meanwhile, direct sellers – both men and women – responded to the collapse of the single male-breadwinner ideal not by bringing domestic workers in but, rather, by importing paid work into the home.

The importance of supplemental income, particularly during periods of high unemployment, should not be diminished. But the success of individual distributors in the 1970s can be measured in multiple ways. For some, like Borthem, it was an important financial strategy through which to cobble together a living. For others, it was a psychological strategy through which to maintain a sense of optimism and hopefulness in the face of an increasingly insecure, contingent labour economy.

According to contemporary social scientists, widespread labour insecurity in the 1970s produced among workers financial, psychological, and emotional stress.[46] Anecdotal evidence demonstrates that the appeal of direct selling was as much about combatting the emotional toll of unemployment as the financial one. For example, a former RCA engineer, who was laid off in 1972 after a factory closure, appropriated the language of self-employment when he began selling Amway. Roger Laverty never realized significant income from his distributorship; in fact, he lost more than $1,000 in 1974 and 1975. Yet, participating in Amway did give him a sense of power at a time when his job situation was out of his control. Although technically out of work, the ability to describe himself as "employed in my own business" gave him a sense of status and purpose. Identifying as self-employed was for Laverty an alternative to admitting to himself and others that he was unemployed.[47]

Direct selling appealed to the same search for meaning, belonging, and optimism that led other Americans in the 1970s to turn to sites ranging from organized religion to positive psychology and self-help literature to yoga and Transcendental Meditation. Direct selling was in many ways a mode of positive thinking, which distributors consumed at Amway rallies as well as in their daily lives. Amway rallies were elaborate and boisterous events. Thousands of distributors attended the rallies, which sometimes filled an arena. One distributor, Gerald Fackbell, attended rallies dutifully even though his Amway distributorship never earned a profit. He continued to participate for two years, attending twenty-five distributor rallies because he enjoyed hearing speakers give a "history of how well they had done in Amway, how much money they were making, how they bought new cars or new homes or quit their jobs." For Fackbell, the rallies had a "contagious atmosphere" of optimism, and he "went to as many of these meetings as [he] possibly could," even though his participation did not yield positive financial results.[48]

Direct sales firms had long stressed how important a positive outlook was in both the act of selling and in one's private life. In the 1930s, Fuller Brush Men had the cheerful motto "Fine and Dandy."[49] Mary Kay Cosmetics stressed the necessity of "the 'You can do it!' spirit." Mary Kay Ash, Brownie Wise of Tupperware, and DeVos and Van Andel translated their motivational messages into successful careers in the mainstream self-help genre. In her self-titled autobiography, Ash described work in Mary Kay as a way to make oneself into a happy person. "You see – the funny thing about putting on a happy face," she writes in reference both to wearing cosmetics and to creating a persona as an enthusiastic salesperson, "is that if you do it again and again, pretty soon that happy face is there to stay. It becomes the real you."[50] In his best-selling book *Believe!*, Rich DeVos affirms that "almost anyone can do whatever he really believes he can do." "The most powerful sentence" in the English language he adds, is "I can."[51] The emphasis on positive thinking and visualization within direct sales culture had been a powerful part of the appeal of direct selling across the postwar period, but it took on added meaning in the 1970s when reasons for optimism seemed to many in short supply.

As a form of contingent or supplemental work, the popularity of direct selling signalled the failures of the postwar growth economy, as well as the federal government's commitment, as embodied in the Employment Act of 1946, to "promote maximum employment, production, and purchasing power."[52] Turning to direct selling in the 1970s was for many distributors recognition that industrial capitalism and corporate work were no longer capable of providing basic job security.

At the same time, Amway's rhetoric reinforced very long-standing beliefs about opportunity and economic mobility in America. Direct selling, according to Amway, was a form of entrepreneurship, self-employment, or business ownership. Packaged as "do-it-yourself job security," direct selling could be not only a legitimate and respectable means of survive but also a way to prove, often to oneself, the continued strengths of American free enterprise. If Carter's Malaise Speech diagnosed American society as in a state of economic and cultural crisis, direct sales flourished in the 1970s because it seemed to many Americans a cure for both.

Conclusion

The history of direct sales in the 1970s speaks to the theme of coping with deindustrialization on multiple levels. Direct sales firms adapted to changes in the labour economy, particularly the disappearance of high-wage industrial jobs and the rise of the contingent labour economy, by explicitly capitalizing on them. For individual distributors, participating in direct selling was also a way to cope, both financially and psychologically, with apparent transformations in the nature of work in a deindustrialized or post-industrial society. For some, direct selling offered a security policy against the unpredictability of corporate employment in the 1970s. For others, it provided a way to maintain a sense of status despite regular periods of unemployment.

In other words, direct sales firms and distributors turned the traditional narrative about labour security on its head. Mainstream manufacturing labour and white-collar professional jobs were, according to Amway and its distributors, now precarious and unpredictable. By contrast, direct selling – which had all the markings of casual, contingent work – was now a safer and more reliable choice. A form of contingent work packaged as entrepreneurship, direct selling both acknowledged the changing nature of work in the late capitalist economy and constructed a new narrative about postwar labour in which contingent work was not a concession to deindustrialization, but a solution to it.

What can historians gain by refocusing on a sector that experienced the 1970s as a period of growth? On the one hand, the growth of direct selling, along with other segments of the service sector, demonstrates that the 1970s was a moment of both deindustrialization *and* reindustrialization. From that perspective, the 1970s marks less the end of a so-called golden age of American industry than a transition from one mode of capitalism to another, or the transition to what some have called the "new economy" of the late twentieth century.

On the other hand, direct selling is a very old model of labour and business rooted the early-American peddling tradition. Particularly when viewed alongside other forms of casual or contingent work – including care work, domestic work, agricultural work, and, prior to the First World War, even most industrial work – the history of direct selling highlights not the emergence but the *persistence* of casual labour. In that light, the mid-century period of high industrial productivity, which many had seen as representative of modern US capitalism, is more exceptional than typical.[53] Analysing the history of the 1970s from a different angle thus raises new questions about the sharpness of the turn from an industrial to a service economy, the aptness of the language of decline, and the very representativeness of industrial capitalism.

NOTES

1 U.S. Department of Commerce and the Bureau of the Census, Statistical Abstract of the United States 1982–1983, 103rd ed., 24. Indexed against consumer prices in 1967 (1967 + 100).

2 Jimmy Carter, "Address to the Nation on Energy and National Goals: 'The Malaise Speech,'" 15 July 1979, in Gerhard Peters and John T. Woolley, *The American Presidency Project*, accessed 20 April 2019, http://www.presidency.ucsb.edu/ws/?pid=32596.

3 Michael Harrington, "A Collective Sadness," in *50 Years of Dissent*, ed. Nicolaus Mills and Michael Walzer (New Haven, CT: Yale University Press, 1974), 111–19; Seymour Melman, *The Permanent War Economy: American Capitalism in Decline* (New York: Touchstone Books, 1974); Robert L. Heilbroner, *Business Civilization in Decline* (New York: W.W. Norton, 1976). For Harrington, Melman, and Heibroner – best-known as authors of Michael Harrington, *The Other America: Poverty in the United States* (New York: Touchstone Books, 1997); *The Permanent War Economy*; and Robert Heilbroner, *The Worldly Philosophers: The Lives, Times and Ideas of the Great Economic Thinkers* (New York: Touchstone Books 1999) – the problem was not specific to the 1970s but an inherent characteristic of capitalism. Particularly for Heilbroner and Harrington, the latter a future chairman of the Democratic Socialists of America, capitalism's tendency toward change was itself an enemy of economic stability. For more on contemporary leftist critiques, see Jefferson Cowie, *Stayin' Alive: The 1970s and the Last Days of the Working Class* (New York: New Press, 2010); Howard Brick, *Transcending Capitalism: Visions of a New Society in Modern American Thought* (Ithaca, NY: Cornell University Press, 2006).

4 Gerald Ford, 1975 State of the Union Address, 15 January 1975.

5 Bruce J. Schulman, *From Cotton Belt to Sunbelt: Federal Policy, Economic Development, and the Transformation of the South, 1938–1980* (Durham, NC: Duke University Press, 1994); Michelle Nickerson and Darren Dochuk, eds., *Sunbelt Rising: The Politics of Space, Place, and Region* (Philadelphia: University of Pennsylvania Press, 2011); Judith Stein, *Pivotal Decade: How the United States Traded Factories for Finance in the Seventies* (New Haven, CT: Yale University Press, 2010); Jefferson Cowie and Joseph Heathcott, eds., *Beyond the Ruins: The Meanings of Deindustrialization* (Ithaca, NY: Cornell University Press, 2003); Greta R. Krippner, *Capitalizing on Crisis: The Political Origins of the Rise of Finance* (Cambridge, MA: Harvard University

Press, 2011); Bethany Moreton, *To Serve God and Wal-Mart: The Making of Christian Free Enterprise* (Cambridge, MA: Harvard University Press, 2011).

6 U.S. Bureau of the Census, *Statistical Abstract* (1976).

7 Nicole W. Biggart, *Charismatic Capitalism: Direct Selling Organizations in America* (Chicago: University of Chicago Press, 1989), 51.

8 NSM Report cited in Avon Products, Inc. "On Moonlighters and Smaller Households," in *Management News Briefs* 6, no. 6 (June 1978), Avon Collection, Hagley Museum and Library (hereafter HAG).

9 Kathryn Jones, *Amway Forever: The Amazing Story of a Global Business Phenomenon* (Hoboken: Wiley & Sons, 2011); Steve Butterfield, *Amway: The Cult of Free Enterprise* (Boston: South End Press, 1985); Michael Gerard Pratt, "The Happiest, Most Dissatisfied People on Earth: Ambivalence and Commitment among Amway Distributors" (PhD diss., University of Michigan, 1994); Michael G. Pratt, "The Good, The Bad, and the Ambivalent: Managing Identification among Amway Distributors," *Administrative Science Quarterly* 45, no. 3 (2000), 456–93; Ronald J. Kuntze, "The Dark Side of Multilevel Marketing: Appeals to the Symbolically Incomplete" (PhD diss., Arizona State University, 2001); David Harris, "Of Prophecy and Profits: A Study of the Amway Worldview" (PhD diss., Harvard University, 1992).

10 Amway Corporation, "1978 Amway Annual Report," *Amagram* 20, no. 1 (1979), Amway Corporate Archives (hereafter ACA).

11 Rich DeVos and Jay Van Andel, "Don't Let the Good Times Pass You By," in Amway Corporation, *Amagram* 15, no. 4 (1974), ACA.

12 Katina L. Manko, "A Depression-Proof Business Strategy," in *Beauty and Business: Commerce, Gender, and Culture in Modern America*, ed. Philip Scranton (New York: Routledge, 2001), 142–168; Katina Lee Manko, "'Ding Dong! Avon Calling!' Gender, Business, and Door-to-Door Selling, 1890–1995" (PhD diss., University of Delaware, 2001). On the history of direct selling, see Walter A. Friedman, *Birth of a Salesman: The Transformation of Selling in America* (Cambridge, MA: Harvard University Press, 2004); Alison J. Clarke, *Tupperware: The Promise of Plastic in 1950s America* (Washington, DC: Smithsonian Books, 2001); Kathy Peiss, *Hope in a Jar: The Making of America's Beauty Culture* (Philadelphia: University of Pennsylvania Press, 2011); Biggart, *Charismatic Capitalism*.

13 John Cameron Aspley, ed., *The Sales Manager's Handbook*, 3rd ed. (Chicago: Dartnell Corporation Publishers, 1940), 30, 61, John W. Hartman Center for Sales, Advertising, and Marketing History, Duke University (hereafter JWH), LSC 11023.

14 Direct sales is descended from independent peddling and travelling salesmanship, both male occupations. Men continued to dominate

commercial travelling salesmanship. They also participated in home-based direct-to-consumer sales into the post–Second World War period – especially with Amway, which tended to attract married couples – although in lesser numbers than women. Yet the popularity of women-oriented products and firms such as Mary Kay cosmetics and Tupperware created the perception that direct sales was an exclusively female industry.

15 Eileen Boris, *Home to Work: Motherhood and the Politics of Industrial Homework in the United States* (Cambridge: Cambridge University Press, 1994); Rhacel Parreñas and Eileen Boris, eds., *Intimate Labors: Cultures, Technologies and the Politics of Care* (Stanford, CA: Stanford University Press, 2010).

16 IRS *News Release*, no. IR-1868, 6 August 1977, 4 (speech by Commissioner Kurtz before the American Bar Association), cited in North, "Employment Tax Morass," *Creighton Law Review* 11 (1978): 797.

17 *Avon Annual Report 1973* (New York: Avon Products, 1974); *Avon Annual Report 1980* (New York: Avon Products, 1981), both in Avon Collection, HAG. Sales in the United States and Canada accounted for 50 per cent of Avon's $2.5 billion in total global sales.

18 Biggart, *Charismatic Capitalism*, 51.

19 Rich DeVos and Jay Van Andel, "Don't Let the Good Times Pass You By," in Amway Corporation, *Amagram* 15, no. 4 (1974), ACA.

20 Ibid.

21 Amway Corporation, "Do You Run Out of Money before You Run Out of Month?" *Time* 104, no. 6 (5 August 1974).

22 Amway Corporation, "Amway Helps Your Income Keep Up with Your Outgo," *Time* 103, no. 6 (11 February 1974).

23 Amway Corporation, "A Little Moonlight Can Put a Lot of Sunshine in Your Life," *Time* 104, no. 1 (1 July 1974).

24 Amway Corporation, "The Most Important Things in Life Are Expensive," *Time* 103, no. 13. (1 April 1974).

25 Amway Corporation, "A Little Extra Money Can Mean a Lot of Extra Living," *Time* 103, no. 22 (3 June 1974).

26 Pan Am World Tours, "With So Much Going Wrong 50 Weeks of the Year, We'd Like You to Have 2 Weeks That Go Right," *Time* 103, no. 13 (1 April 1974).

27 British Tourist Authority, "Now Is a Good Time to Visit Britain!" *Time* 103, no. 13 (1 April 1974).

28 Life and Health Insurance Companies of America, "In Energy-Poor, Inflation-Rich 1974, One of Life's Necessities, Life Insurance, Is Lower in Price Than It Was 20 Years Ago," *Time* 104, no. 10 (9 September 1974).

29 Volkswagen of America, Inc., "If Gas Pains Persist, Try Volkswagen," *Time* 105, no. 6 (11 February 1975).

30 American Wood Council, "Why a Lot of American Home Owners Are Weathering the Energy Crisis Better Than Others," *Time* 103, no. 13 (1 April 1974).
31 U.S. Department of Labor, "A-32: Unemployment Rates by Occupations, 1958–81," Bureau of Labor Statistics Bulletin 2096, 546.
32 Amway Corporation, "In These Uncertain Times, Amway Offers You Do-It-Yourself Job Security," *Time* 103, no. 18 (6 May 1974).
33 Ibid.
34 Ibid.
35 William H. Whyte, Jr., *The Organization Man* (Garden City, NY: Doubleday Anchor Books, 1956).
36 Amway Corporation, *You and the Amway Sales Plan* (Ada, MI: Amway Corporation, 1970), 17.
37 Amway Corporation, *The American Way to Success* (Ada, MI: Amway Corporation, 1964), 2.
38 Amway Corporation, "The Path to Security Is Only a Decision Away," *Time* 104, no. 6. (5 August 1974).
39 Richard S. Belous, "The Rise of the Contingent Work Force: The Key Challenges and Opportunities," *Washington and Lee Law Review* 52, no. 3 (1995): 865, 867; Bureau of Labor Statistics, Labor Force Statistics from the Current Population Survey, Series ID: LNS 12032197, "Employment Level – Part Time for Economic Reasons, Nonagricultural Industries" and Series ID: LNS 12032199, "Employment Level – Part-time for Economic Reasons, Could Only Find Part-Time Work, Nonagricultural Industries."
40 Amway Corporation, "The Annual Marketing Strategy Review," prepared by Walt Penrose II, 13 June 1975, CS515: 3096–3162, Federal Trade Commission Archives (hereafter FTC).
41 Joseph Hunter, quoted in *Official Transcripts of Proceedings before the Federal Trade Commission, Docket No. 9023 In the Matter of Amway Corporation, Inc.* (hereafter *Official Transcripts*), 31 May 1977, 1419–21, FTC.
42 Larry Bryant, quoted in ibid., 25 May 1977, 990, FTC.
43 Bennett Harrison and Barry Bluestone, *The Great U-Turn: Corporate Restructuring and the Polarizing of America* (New York: Basic Books, 1990).
44 Jay Van Andel, "Security through Sponsoring … Sponsoring Multiplies Your Efforts: Safeguards Your Future," in Amway Corporation, *Amagram* 18, no. 1 (1977), ACA.
45 Russell Alan Borthem, quoted in *Official Transcripts*, 23 May 1977, 696, FTC.
46 *Work in America: Report of a Special Task Force to the Secretary of Health, Education, and Welfare* produced for the Subcommittee on Employment, Manpower, and Poverty of the Committee on Labor and Public Welfare of the United States Senate, 1973; Richard S. Belous, *The Contingent*

Economy: The Growth of the Temporary, Part-Time, and Subcontracted Workforce (Washington, DC: National Planning Association, 1989).

47 Roger Laverty, quoted in *Official Transcripts*, 24 May 1977, 750–8. FTC.

48 Gerald Fackbell, quoted in ibid., 1 June 1977, 1566–77. FTC.

49 Albert E. Teetsel, a Fuller Brush man from New York popularized the slogan. Alfred C. Fuller, *A Foot in the Door: The Life Appraisal of the Original Fuller Brush Man as Told to Hartzell Spense* (New York: McGraw-Hill, 1960).

50 Mary Kay Ash, *Mary Kay: The Success Story of America's Most Dynamic Businesswoman* (New York: Harper and Row, 1981), 9, 10. See also Clarke, *Tupperware*.

51 Richard M. DeVos with Charles Paul Conn, *Believe!* (New York: Berkeley Books, 1985).

52 Employment Act of 1946, Public Law 304, US 79th Congress.

53 This interpretation aligns with Jefferson Cowie's reinterpretation of the New Deal–era labour economy and political coalition, as a "long exception." Jefferson Cowie, *The Great Exception: The New Deal and the Limits of American Politics* (Princeton, NJ: Princeton University Press, 2016).

2 Crisis? What Crisis? Mass Consumption in Great Britain in the 1970s and Early 1980s

SINA FABIAN

British Labour prime minister James Callaghan arrived back in London on 10 January 1979 from a four-nation summit in Guadeloupe with the heads of government from France, West Germany, and the United States. He was greeted by journalists upon his arrival and decided to hold an improvised press conference at the airport. While he had been away, a series of strikes during what came to be known as the "Winter of Discontent" had reached a climax. A nationwide strike by lorry drivers was paralysing the country. Callaghan's absence during these crucial days had already been criticized in the media before his return. The fact that the summit had not taken place in freezing Britain but in the Caribbean did not help reduce the criticism. Callaghan, slightly tanned, good-humouredly faced the journalists. He brushed aside the question of whether it had been the right decision to attend the summit by sarcastically replying, "I'm sure everybody would have liked to have been with me, but I don't think anybody except a few journalists are very jealous of it ... And do you know, I actually swam!" In reply to a question regarding his approach to the "mounting chaos in the country," he replied: "I promise you that if you look at it from outside ... I don't think that other people in the world would share the view that there is mounting chaos."[1]

Callaghan appeared in his statements to be snobbish, condescending, and out of touch with the British people and the problems facing the country. The tabloid newspaper the *Sun* captured this feeling in its famous headline the following day. The article's opening read: "Sun-tanned Premier Jim Callaghan breezed back into Britain yesterday and asked: Crisis? What Crisis?"[2] Although Callaghan never actually said those words, the headline has been imprinted in Britain's collective memory as an example of a politician's complete misjudgment of the situation.

Yet I argue in this chapter that, if one looks at the 1970s and early 1980s from a consumer point of view, Callaghan was actually not that mistaken. For the majority of Britons, these years constituted a period of growing consumption possibilities, despite a series of economic upheavals. Looking at patterns of consumption calls into question the notion of the 1970s as a "decade of crisis" and as a major caesura that allegedly marked the end of the postwar era's economic boom.

This is not to say, however, that there were no economic challenges in the 1970s. They were manifold, and Britain was hit harder by them, and coped worse, than most other industrialized countries. The biggest problems were high inflation rates of up to 25 per cent, rising unemployment, economic recession, and severe industrial unrest.

Among contemporary commenters, a near apocalyptic mood persisted, as Tory politician Quintin Hogg, Baron Hailsham of St Marylebone, expressed in 1978: "We are living in the City of Destruction, a dying country in a dying civilization ... If we go on as we are, I can see nothing but disaster ahead, though I am quite unable to predict when, or exactly how, it will overtake us."[3] The feeling of crisis reached its peak during the Winter of Discontent of 1978–9, when strikes in the public sector brought the country to a standstill. Among those walking off the job were hospital workers, gravediggers, and waste collectors. Although these were only minor strikes and did not seriously affect the daily lives of many people, media reports and disturbing images such as piles of rubbish in London's central Leicester Square immensely aggravated the sense of crisis. In particular, one single "Day of Action" on 22 January 1979, on which an estimated 1.5 million public sector workers went on strike, came to be remembered as *the* "Winter of Discontent."[4]

The succeeding Conservative government under Margaret Thatcher deliberately reinforced this narrative and worked on establishing the myth of ungovernable Britain under Labour governments in the 1970s.[5] This myth was so thoroughly inscribed on Britain's collective memory that even Tony Blair, as leader of the Labour Party, promised during an election campaign in 1997 that "we won't go back to the 1970s."[6] The interpretation of the 1970s as a decade of crises also influenced contemporary historians and their readings of those years.[7]

With increased research interest in recent years, the 1970s do not appear all doom and gloom anymore but are frequently depicted as a progressive era with respect to women's and gay rights, for example, and the emergence of other social movements such as the environmental movement.[8] The decade is increasingly described as a dynamic period that should be analysed in its own right: it was more than just a downward path leading directly to Thatcherism.

This research points out that individualism, for example, was not a result of Thatcher's neoliberal reforms but was already prevalent before her election victory. An increase in consumption possibilities and practices enabled Britons to express this individualism.[9] In addition, Jörg Arnold has recently argued against traditional interpretations and has pointed out that the 1970s constituted a boom period for certain industrial workers (coal miners, for example), which – albeit short lived – brought rising incomes and self-assurance.[10]

It is more appropriate, then, to describe the 1970s as a decade of ambiguities, which economic catchwords such as "crisis", "decline," or "after the boom" do not sufficiently capture. Such master narratives are too narrowly focused on economic developments and accept without question the notions of contemporary observers. In Britain, the "decline" narrative has already been thoroughly deconstructed.[11] The "after the boom" narrative in Germany also needs to be further scrutinized, as it partly neglects continuities that existed throughout the turbulent decade. The catch phrase "after the boom" implies that all developments that began in the 1970s were worse than during the alleged "golden" postwar years. This was certainly not true for social reforms and movements, but even economic developments were more ambiguous than "after the boom" implies.[12]

The chapter takes up the reassessments of the 1970s and early 1980s and adds an often overlooked perspective to them – namely, personal consumption. The development of consumption patterns shows continuities rather than major "structural breaks" in the 1970s.[13] Overall, personal consumption increased during this decade. This might seem particularly paradoxical in light of acknowledged economic crises, recession, inflation, and growing unemployment. However, as is illustrated in the other chapters in this section, the 1970s were marked by seemingly contradictory economic developments. As Eileen Boris demonstrates in the next chapter, for example, women were increasingly entering the workforce, and some of those who were pursuing careers "turned their homes into workplaces for other women, whom they hired as domestic workers"; and, as Jessica Burch shows in the preceding chapter, direct selling boomed in this period.

In this chapter, I take a closer look at the ambiguous and at times contradictory developments that marked the 1970s in Great Britain. An examination of the patterns of consumption in that decade combines economic and social perspectives. Economic challenges as well as possibilities and their influences on people's everyday lives were intertwined and should therefore not be analysed separately. The chapter also stresses that not everyone could participate equally in the mass consumer society and improve their situation. The growing number of unemployed people, for instance, were largely left out.

The first part of this chapter looks at general income and consumption patterns and their changes in the 1970s and early 1980s. It also analyses the impact of the oil price crises and the following recession on consumption practices. Two main questions will be addressed in this part: Why did consumer spending increase in these years? And how was this spending influenced by the economic crises? Two consumer goods will be at the centre of this analysis: car ownership and holidays.[14] Both are expensive goods that do not belong in the category of basic goods such as food and clothing. In times of economic crises, spending on both could, in theory, be reduced and/or their consumption delayed. Both were also affected by rising fuel prices during the oil crises. Thus, both are useful for analysing the consequences of economic upheavals on consumer behaviour.

The Party Is Not Over Yet – Consumption in the 1970s

Income and Expenditure

The secretary of state for the environment and prominent Labour politician Anthony Crosland summarized Britain's economic situation in May 1975 as follows: "The crisis that faces us is infinitely more serious than any of the crises we have faced over the past 20 years ... Perhaps people have used the word 'economic crisis' too often in the past. They have shouted 'wolf, wolf' when the animal was more akin to a rather disagreeable Yorkshire terrier ... [But] for the time being at least, the party is over."[15] The years 1975 and 1976 marked the economic crisis's climax. Inflation had risen to 25 per cent. The government was forced to apply for a loan from the International Monetary Fund (IMF), and that organization demanded severe cuts in public spending.[16] But, despite these economic upheavals, disposable household income was in 1979 significantly higher than at the beginning of the decade.[17] How was this possible?

The main reason was rising disposable incomes. This rise was attributable to social reforms and the expansion of the welfare state focusing especially on less well-off sections of society and to higher wages, which were largely achieved by strikes and industrial actions.

Incomes rose especially in the early 1970s before the first oil price crisis. The "Barber-Boom," initiated by Chancellor of the Exchequer Anthony Barber's "give-away" budget of 21 March 1972, was one of the main reasons for the increase.[18] Hoping to stimulate economic growth, he announced massive tax cuts and an increase in social security benefits. Pensions, for example, which had already been increased by 20 per cent the previous autumn, would be raised again by 12.5 per cent. Personal tax allowances were also significantly raised. At the same time, purchase tax was reduced. In addition, companies profited from the budget's generous tax allowances and other incentives. These measures contributed to an average annual income growth of 6 per cent in 1972–3 and led to a boom in consumer spending in 1972–3. Car sales, for example, significantly increased in 1972, and the demand for large, powerful cars was especially high.[19]

In addition to government measures, wages, on average, increased significantly in the early 1970s in order to keep up with rising inflation. These increases were not always the result of peaceful negotiations. Large pay raises were often achieved only after long and severe strikes. The national miners' strikes in 1972 and 1973/4 ended with large wage increases. The 1972 strike forced Conservative prime minister Edward Heath to turn away from his pay restraint policy.[20] As a result of that strike, the miners achieved an average raise of 27 per cent plus additional benefits. Yet the miners were out again the following year, in an even more contentious strike. They used the oil price crisis to enhance pressure on the government. This tactic was successful. The government introduced a three-day-workweek from January to March 1974 due to fears of an energy shortage. Heath called for an early election and, in the midst of the strike, campaigned under the slogan "who governs Britain?" The Tories, however, lost their majority, and Heath resigned as prime minister. The Labour-led minority government under Harold Wilson immediately settled the dispute and granted the miners a further 32 per cent pay raise in March 1974.[21] Miners were now the top income group among industrial workers, whereas they had been near the bottom in the 1960s.[22]

Despite soaring inflation, wages did, on average, keep up with rising prices. While household incomes had stagnated or even been reduced slightly during the climax of the economic crisis in 1974–6, 1977–8 again brought significant income growth above the level of 1973. Social reforms – among them was the introduction of benefits for each child, support for lone-parent families, and a dynamic and income-based pension scheme instead of a basic pension rate – contributed to this growth.[23] These reforms, and others – including the Equal Pay Act of 1970, which granted women the same terms of pay as men – contributed to a convergence of low- and high-income groups and therefore to a reduction of social inequality in the 1970s.[24] Wages rose on average faster than salaries. Disposable household incomes were, on average,

25 per cent higher at the end of the decade than at the beginning.[25] For many industrial workers, including miners, the 1970s was not a decade of decline and doom but of income growth.[26] There was, however, one exception to these developments: the growing number of unemployed people. They were largely left out from income growth. As pensioners and lone-parent families moved up from the lowest income group, this group increasingly consisted of families with an unemployed "head of household."[27]

What did those who did experience a rise in disposable income do with their income surplus? The short answer is that they spent quite a lot on consumer goods. In particular, less-well-off sections of society were able to buy many of the durable goods that they previously had not been able to afford. The number of telephones, cars, and washing machines tripled in households of the lowest income group. Increasingly, a greater proportion of household income was spent on non-essential goods and services such as transportation and leisure activities, while the proportion spent on food and clothing declined.[28] Over the course of the 1970, the number of cars in Britain rose by 4.5 million, an increase of 30 per cent. At the same time, the number of holidays abroad more than doubled, from fewer than 6 million to 12 million,[29] and the percentage of the population that had taken at least one foreign holiday nearly doubled, from 33 per cent to 59 per cent. Many of these were skilled manual workers. Indeed, the proportion of skilled manual workers holidaying abroad rose by 40 per cent between 1970 and 1974, and, by the end of the decade, one-fifth of all foreign holidaymakers were skilled manual workers, a proportion that had doubled since the late 1960s and contributed to the half a million tourists a year who were travelling abroad for the first time.[30]

Household surpluses were also used to increase savings. Less-well-off groups, such as elderly people, were able to increase their savings rate significantly. The rates converged between different income groups. In 1973, households saved on average 10.5 per cent of their disposable household income; five years later, this had increased to 16 per cent.[31]

Consumption in a Decade of Crises

While these long-term developments in income and consumer spending were remarkably stable and there was an overall growth, despite various severe economic challenges, it is necessary to take a closer look at how consumers behaved in times of actual economic crisis. The years 1974–5 were influenced by the energy crisis, which resulted in the government declaring a state of emergency and a three-day working week.

In addition to that, the United Kingdom plunged into a recession while inflation reached 25 per cent in 1975. Household incomes stagnated and were even slightly reduced for some.

One reaction to the crisis was increased savings activity. Savings rates rose during the recession and period of high inflation.[32] Instead of buying goods, consumers decided to put more money aside, although inflation increased the risk of losing some or all of it. Consumers tried to offset the losses associated with inflation by putting more money aside. The restraints in consumption were, however, significantly less than politicians and economists had expected. Consumer spending decreased only by 3 per cent in the first quarter of 1974, despite the oil price crisis and the three-day week. Consumers spent as much in the second half of 1974 as they had done the previous year.[33]

The remarkable consumer boom of the early 1970s came to a halt in late 1973, however, as consumers postponed expensive purchases. New car registrations were reduced by a quarter in 1974. Although the overall number of holidays fell only slightly, there was a significant downward blip in foreign travel.[34] Households did not give up consumption altogether, but they economized during the climax of the crisis. Rather than buying a new car or travelling abroad, they holidayed in the United Kingdom and made do with their old car. In order to compensate for rising petrol costs, motorists cut back on maintenance costs such as inspections and repairs. And instead of spending a vacation in a hotel or guesthouse, many holidaymakers chose cheaper accommodation such as self-catering holiday flats or caravans. Consumers temporarily "downgraded" their consumption patterns.[35]

One also has to distinguish between whether consumers stated that they had or would economize and change their consumption patterns and whether they actually did so. Due to the oil price shock, fuel efficiency became a central feature when buying or driving a car. Motorists suddenly stated in surveys that petrol consumption played a decisive role when buying a new car. Before the outbreak of the first oil crisis, this factor was barely considered: the overall maintenance costs rather than just fuel efficiency were taken into account.

Awareness of fuel efficiency was one of the few long-term effects of the first oil crisis. With the rise in petrol prices, energy-saving tips appeared, and flourished. Information about how to drive economically and to save fuel was spread by the media and guidebooks.[36] By the time the second oil crisis broke out, motorists were well informed on how to save fuel. During the climax of the second oil crisis, motorists stated that petrol consumption was the most important criterion when buying a new car: it was seen as more important than safety or reliability. Yet, when asked whether they had compared the petrol consumption of different models before buying a new car, only a third admitted to having done so; moreover, only 16 per cent stated that they had deliberately chosen a model because of its fuel efficiency.[37] In the early 1980s, a survey concluded that "various surveys, including this one, have revealed that motorists may claim that petrol economy is important, but do not consider it when buying a car."[38] Similarly, motorists claimed to use their cars as little as possible and to drive economically. However, overall petrol consumption raises doubts about these statements: even at the peak of the first oil crisis, petrol consumption was reduced only slightly, by 4 per cent.[39]

Consumers adapted relatively quickly to rising prices, especially to rising petrol prices. As early as 1976, a study concluded: "It has been established that the large rises in the cash price of petrol, together with other changes in the economic climate in 1973–4, caused the post-war trends towards increased car usage and car ownership to halt and even go into reverse. But those trends have now all but recovered themselves (the car-ownership trend being slower to recover than the car-usage trend)."[40]

Despite motorists' verbal assurances that they put information about how to save fuel into practice, very few actually did. When asked directly how they had changed their driving patterns, only 10 per cent responded that they tried to drive more slowly, 7 per cent said they had changed their acceleration and braking habits, and 5 per cent stated that they sometimes walked short distances instead of using the car.[41] It is hard to say whether motorists simply stated in surveys what they deemed was socially expected or whether they were convinced that they did use their cars economically.

Despite these verbal assurances, in reality, motorists barely changed their patterns of driving or car usage. For most people, owning and using a car had become a necessity in the 1970s. Many people depended on a car in order to be able to go about their daily lives, whether getting to work, going grocery shopping, or visiting friends and families.[42] This sense of necessity explains why most motorists fairly quickly adapted to the rising costs of maintaining a car.

The economic crises of the 1970s only temporarily affected British consumers. They merely put their consumption on hiatus and consumed more hesitantly during the crises' climax. But affluence and consumption did not come to an end, despite the decline scenarios predicted by media, politicians, and social scientists. Less-well-off sections of society, which had only started to make use of their increased consumption possibilities in the early 1970s, would return to them in the late 1970s. The economic upheavals did not destroy their modest improvements in consumption.

The second oil price crisis coincided with Margaret Thatcher taking office in May 1979. Her primary ambition in the first years of her government was to reduce inflation, which had risen again to 18 per cent due to the oil crisis. In order to do so, the government raised the central bank rate to its highest-ever rate of 17 per cent. High interest rates contributed, along with the oil crisis and the increased value of the pound, to a rise in unemployment, which doubled between 1979 and 1982 to almost 13 per cent.[43] Giving priority to the reduction of inflation, the Thatcher government was willing to accept this rise in unemployment.

First-person accounts written during the early 1980s give insight into how the economic situation affected people's daily lives and their consumption patterns.[44] Apart from a socio-economic divide, there was a strong regional divide in how people were affected. In the prosperous south and southeast of England, unemployment was barely an issue. Rising prices also affected people in these regions only moderately. One middle-class person stated that fewer dinner parties were held and that it was now acceptable to bring a bottle of wine rather than expecting the host to bear the full expense of entertaining.[45] Another one said that his friends complained about rising prices but that they adapted fairly quickly to them and did not have to change their consumption patterns.[46] In these accounts, the opinion was widespread that unemployed people did not try hard enough to find a job – a view that corresponded with the image the Thatcher government popularized.

The picture looked different in other parts of Britain that depended mainly on heavy industries such as steel and shipbuilding, and, since the early 1980s, coal mining too. The north of England, Scotland, and Northern Ireland were especially affected. Traditional working-class communities were hit hard by unemployment and rising prices. These two topics dominated conversations among family as well as among neighbours and friends. Almost everyone experienced unemployment in their family sooner or later, at least for a short period of time.

For most, youth unemployment was especially worrisome. In 1984, one-third of all eighteen-to-twenty-four-year-old males had been unemployed at least once during the preceding twelve months.[47] The situation for unemployed youth worsened over the course of the decade, as the Thatcher government identified them as "prime targets" in its efforts to reduce public spending. Over the course of the 1980s, unemployment benefits were reduced, especially for young people who lived with their parents.[48]

Many people were frustrated by not being able to fully take part in mass consumer society. The mother of an unemployed young woman stated that her daughter "at times ... gets depressed and says 'I hate this world, I've got to a stage where I hate it.' She will then go out and overspend on pretty mini dresses and the next comment is 'I've spent two weeks dole money and I don't care.'"[49] Being able to fulfil even quite modest desires could require a good deal of effort by poorer households. Some households saved up several months to be able to pay for school trips or Christmas presents. The latter were often bought in cheap stores such as Woolworth. One family affected by unemployment chose sweets and basic necessities such as winter clothing and hygiene products as gifts.[50]

Less-well-off sections of society were much more affected than better-off ones by the period's economic crises. While the latter did not have to curb spending and consumption, the former, especially when out of work, had to immensely curtail their expenses. For the more affluent, expensive holidays abroad, such as those at long-distance destinations, boomed during the early 1980s, even in the midst of an economic recession, whereas cheaper domestic holidays significantly declined – a sign that others could not afford even domestic holidays. These developments are reflected in personal accounts. While wealthier households reported that they took several holidays a year and that they almost always travelled abroad, less-well-off people described that they had to stay at home or that they went camping in Britain because they could not afford to go anywhere else.[51]

Boom and Transformations – Holidays in Britain and Abroad

The British tourism industry was a booming sector in the 1970s and 1980s. This was a result of increased disposable income, and it reflected the rise of the service sector. Great Britain had been a pioneer of leisure travel since the eighteenth century. Already in the nineteenth century, many skilled workers in the Lancashire region were able to afford a holiday away from home.[52] Travel possibilities continuously increased during the first half of the twentieth century, and so did the domestic holiday infrastructure. Many holiday camps and seaside resorts – Blackpool, for example – were geared especially to working-class holidaymakers. By 1947, two-thirds of skilled workers regularly holidayed away from home.[53] Until the 1970s, travel patterns remained relatively unchanged. Around 60 per cent of the population took a vacation away from home at least once a year. The overwhelming majority stayed in Britain. Foreign destinations accounted for only 5 per cent of

Britons' holiday plans in the late 1960s. This changed rapidly within the following two decades. By the late 1980s, 40 per cent of all holidays were spent abroad.[54]

Rising incomes do not solely explain this expansion. Political, structural, and technical changes also played a role. Currency restrictions and price controls on package holidays were lifted, and larger airplanes such as the Boeing 747 could fly longer distances without stopping over and were also able to carry more people.[55]

Package tour operators and their business models were even more decisive for the foreign holiday boom. Most holidays abroad were taken as a package tour, which usually included transportation, accommodation, catering, and an English-speaking representative at the destination.[56] Tour operators were eager to tap into the new market of the affluent working class, which proved to be very lucrative. Between 1970 and 1973, the annual number of holidays taken abroad rose from 5.7 to 8 million.[57] The sudden demand in foreign holidays, however, proved to be too much for many tour operators and hoteliers. Many holidaymakers were affected by overbookings, cancelled flights, or unfinished hotels. There are no definite numbers indicating how many travellers had reason to complain; in any case, only a minority would have bothered to actually file a complaint.[58] However, criticism in the media and from consumer organizations peaked in the early 1970s. They warned holidaymakers of the small print in the operators' contracts and informed them about their legal rights.[59]

The shortcomings and reasons for complaints were largely a result of the pressure to keep up with demand but also to keep prices as low as possible. Foreign holidays were much more expensive than domestic ones. Operators therefore engaged in heavy price wars, which resulted in notoriously cheap tour offers. Most tour operators, except for highly specialized ones, offered a very similar product. Offering low prices was the only possible way to stand out. In the early 1980s, the profit margin for tour operators was only 2 per cent, roughly five pounds per individual on a tour.[60] This meant that chartered planes and hotels had to be almost fully booked for the operator to make any profit. Tour companies operated at a very high risk, which at times resulted in spectacular bankruptcies. The leading tour operator Clarksons, for example, went bust in August 1974, leaving 35,000 holidaymakers stranded abroad and over 100,000 who had already paid for their holidays.[61]

Although the press as well as consumer organizations reported widely on these shortcomings, this did not seem to deter holidaymakers, as their numbers kept increasing rapidly. Tour operators were sensitive to public criticism, which could potentially damage their image.

They tried to improve their image and reliability by informing holiday-makers early about possible changes or shortcomings. After Clarksons' spectacular failure, inclusive tour prices rose during the mid-1970s. This, however, lasted only until the outbreak of the next oil crisis and recession, when operators engaged again in heavy price wars to keep the number of travellers up.[62]

The majority of holidaymakers who spent their vacation in Western Europe booked an inclusive tour. In 1972, two-thirds went on a package tour, and the share always remained well above 50 per cent in the 1970s and 1980s. By far the most popular holiday destination for Britons was, and still is, Spain. In 1973, almost half of all holidays to Western Europe and two-thirds of the inclusive tours were spent in Spain.[63] At this time, that country was still under Franco's dictatorship, yet the geographical and climatic conditions predestined it as a holiday destination. In addition, living costs were much lower than in other Mediterranean countries such as France or Italy. The Franco regime had also massively promoted foreign tourism since the late 1950s in order to get hold of foreign currency and to end Spain's political isolation.[64]

Despite the favourable prices tour operators were able to offer, a vacation abroad still cost, on average, four times more than one in Britain. While skilled workers and their families could increasingly afford holidays abroad, semi- and unskilled workers were still mostly excluded from them.[65] What has been shown for consumption patterns in general also applied to vacations abroad: although there was a significant increase during the 1970s and 1980s, not everyone was able to participate in this boom.

The economic upheavals and oil price crises affected holidays only slightly. Foreign holidays experienced just a small downward blip in 1975. While domestic ones declined steadily after their peak in 1973, this was not necessarily due to economic crises. In 1976, for example, when domestic holidays decreased significantly, Britain experienced the hottest summer ever recorded. Therefore, many people decided not to holiday away, as they could have a nice (and sunny) time at home. The general decline in domestic vacations was offset by the rise in foreign travel.

Despite the decline in domestic travel, more than half of all holidays were still spent in Britain in 1990, with most at the traditional seaside resorts established in the nineteenth or early twentieth century.[66] The rise in foreign travel nevertheless contributed to and aggravated immensely a critical discussion of the current state and future of the British tourism industry.[67] The decline narrative was fuelled not only by the declining number of domestic tourists but also by the socio-economic structure of the remaining holidaymakers. Seaside resorts were at this narrative's centre. Renowned American travel writer Paul Theroux satirically described his impressions of a journey around the British coast in the early 1980s. A vacation there was, according to him, "no more fun than a day out on the prison farm."[68] Since working-class holidaymakers, the traditional backbone of the British seaside resort visitors, increasingly travelled abroad, domestic resorts had to look for new target groups. They found them in elderly and less-well-off tourists who could not afford, or were too scared, to go abroad. Many coastal resorts started to offer cheaper accommodation and entertainment, which focused mainly on elderly visitors. The people Theroux met in the resorts were, in his depiction, either old, unemployed, or violent youths.[69] Newspapers cynically dubbed certain British coastal stretches "Costa del Dole" because their cheap accommodations supposedly attracted unemployed youth.[70] Very similar narratives and criticism were directed at holiday camps, which, even more than seaside resorts, had been a stronghold of working-class holiday traditions over the course of the twentieth century.[71]

The changed socio-economic nature of the resort and camp visitors also meant that they spent less money during their vacation, which resulted in a lack of financial investment to modernize accommodation and entertainment facilities. Such investments might have attracted better-off visitors, but these holidaymakers could, by spending a little bit more, stay two weeks abroad in newly built, state-of- the-art resorts.[72]

One should not, however, repeat the contemporary narratives unquestioned. Those elitist narratives would lead us to question why anyone would want to spend their vacation in a resort such as Blackpool or in a holiday camp. Yet such a question disregards reports from domestic holidaymakers themselves: hardly any criticism could be found in their holiday narratives. The assumption that whoever could afford to go abroad did so does not hold true either. Some people with small children preferred to stay in Britain; others felt more comfortable at "home."[73] Many people holidayed abroad as well as in Britain. Travel biographies often included foreign vacations in exotic places as well as holidays in a British seaside resort or holiday camp. Domestic holidays were also increasingly spent as additional vacations during the Easter or autumn break, for example. Vacations in Britain were not valued any less or seen as only second best compared to overseas ones.

Yet, one factor was often decisive in choosing a Mediterranean over a domestic destination – the weather. It was often given as the main and sometimes only reason for holidaying abroad. All age and socio-economic groups offered it as by far the most important reason for travelling to Spain. Opinions such as the following were often explicitly articulated: "If only dear old England had more sunshine! Who would go abroad?"[74]

During the 1970s and 1980s, the British tourism industry, therefore, did not so much experience a decline as a transformation. As noted above, it profited from the rise in shorter second and third holidays, which were almost exclusively spent in Britain. It also saw the emergence of a new and promising holiday trend – namely, heritage tourism.[75] By marketing heritage tourism, the domestic tourism industry managed to exploit a sense of nostalgia for the past and found a unique selling point by drawing on local and national pride and by recreating and commercializing national, regional, and/or local history. Britain increasingly specialized in heritage tourism, which also appealed greatly to foreign tourists, and which resulted, among other things, in a massive boom in museums. Nearly half of all museums in Great Britain that existed in the early 1990s had originated between 1970 and 1989.[76] The rise of heritage tourism resulted partly in a move away from the seaside and into the countryside; at the same time, it made remote locations that had not been on the tourist map before increasingly accessible, a trend supported by increased mass motorization.

Heritage tourism developed in two directions. One drew on aristocratic heritage and resulted in a boom in tours and reappreciation of stately homes.[77] The other focused on industrial heritage. The rise in interest in and a nostalgic glorification of the industrial past happened alongside deindustrialization. One example is "Beamish, the north of England Open Air Museum" in County Durham, which opened in 1971 after a lengthy planning process.[78] The large open-air space comprised, among others, the recreation of a thriving pit mine and village and a turn-of-the-century town at the height of industrialization. The museum drew on an idealized industrial past focused solely on prosperous times. The location was carefully chosen not to interfere with the real mines and landscapes surrounding the museum so that visitors could fully immerse themselves in the past undisturbed.[79] This concept was highly successful. Despite its remote location and being accessible only by car, Beamish attracted 100,000 visitors in 1973. Six years later, the number had tripled.[80]

After the end of the Second World War, Cornwall became the prime domestic holiday destination, again thanks to mass motorization.[81] Its favourable climate conditions and beautiful beaches led to its being referred to as the Cornish Riviera. In addition to traditional seaside entertainment, Cornwall drew on its industrial past in order to attract visitors. As a private endeavour, a newly discovered former tin mine was named Poldark Mine after a popular novel series and marketed as a tourist attraction in the 1970s. The exhibition focused on fictionalized and glorified images of the mining past. At a mining museum owned by the local council, former coal miners who had lost their jobs due to pit closures re-enacted their profession for visitors.[82]

The fictionalization and idealization of the industrial past was already being criticized in the 1980s. Heritage – especially industrial heritage – tourism, on the other hand, transformed and expanded the British tourism industry. It created a new source of revenue and attraction apart from traditional and declining seaside resorts, and increasingly attracted foreign visitors.[83] Destinations such as the Midlands or the northeast of England appeared on the tourist map for the first time.

Conclusion

When the Labour Party released its election manifesto under the left-wing leadership of Jeremy Corbin in May 2017, the *Sun* published a reminder of the time "when everything went wrong," by which it meant the 1970s.[84] The article was illustrated with various iconic images of the "Winter of Discontent," such as piles of rubbish in London's Leicester Square. With the article and the images, the newspaper warned against voting for a "hard-Left" Labour government. This example shows how easily the narrative of the crisis and decline that allegedly dominated the 1970s can be evoked even forty years later.

Great Britain was in many ways hit harder than other Western countries by the economic turmoil of the 1970s. This was especially the case if compared to West Germany. Almost all economic indicators, including growth, unemployment, and inflation rate, were worse in the United Kingdom than in the Federal Republic. Britain also experienced fierce and manifold industrial action. Furthermore, it had to apply to the IMF for a large loan.

This chapter has argued, in accord with recent research, that it would be too short-sighted to reduce the 1970s to a decade of economic problems and crises. Contrary to this narrative lay the experiences of the majority of the people who were able to improve their economic situation and expand consumer spending. The 1970s thus were a decade of ambiguity rather than simply of crises.

Members of the working class especially profited from the expansion of possibilities of consumption by being able to afford, for the first time, expensive consumer goods such as buying a car and activities such as going on holidays abroad. The economic crises influenced consumer spending only slightly and only temporarily. They did not, as was expected at the time, result in a significant cut and other long-term changes in consumption patterns. The expansion of mass consumer society continued almost uninterrupted. In terms of consumption, the 1970s constituted neither a decade of crises nor a major caesura.

This chapter's focus on consumer spending and consumption patterns made social inequalities particularly visible. The daily lives of those middle-class and skilled workers who had a job differed greatly from the lives of the rising number of unemployed people. The gap was not between *the* working class and *the* middle classes anymore but, increasingly, between people who had a job and those who did not. The reforms of the Thatcher government widened this gap significantly in the 1980s.

The difference was spatially expressed by holiday patterns. Domestic holidaymakers were often depicted as poor, while people who could afford to increasingly went abroad. This chapter has shown that the distinction was not as clear-cut as contemporary narratives have suggested, although rising disposable incomes did result in an increase in foreign holidays. This trend contributed to a boom in package tours and thereby to a rise in the service sector. The domestic tourism industry adapted to the challenges in the industry by successfully establishing new forms of tourism, such as heritage tourism, which opened up new holiday destinations. While less-skilled workers spent their main holiday in Britain, they increasingly took up the opportunity for shorter trips to sites that showcased their industrial past and heritage, albeit in a commercialized and idealized way.

This chapter has argued that the challenges of and responses to phenomena such as economic crises and decline were not as monocausal as often has been alleged. As this study of automobile ownership and holidaymaking in the United Kingdom demonstrates, the British people dealt with economic challenges in multifaceted ways.

NOTES

1 Airport press conference, 1 October 1979, accessed 11 December 2017, https://www.youtube.com/watch?v=dX06xqN6710.

2 "Crisis? What Crisis?" *Sun*, 11 January 1979, 1.

3 Quoted in Dominik Geppert, *Thatchers konservative Revolution* (Munich: Oldenbourg Verlag, 2002), 203. For the contemporary discourse see also Dominik Geppert, "Der Thatcher-Konsens. Der Einsturz der britischen Nachkriegsordnung in den 1970er und 1980er Jahren," *Journal of Modern European History* 9, no. 2 (2011): 170–92.

4 Colin Hay, "Chronicles of a Death Foretold: The Winter of Discontent and Construction of the Crisis of British Keynesianism," *Parliamentary Affairs* 63, no. 3 (2010): 455.

5 Ibid.; Robert Saunders, " 'Crisis? What Crisis?' Thatcherism and the Seventies," in *Making Thatcher's Britain*, ed. Ben Jackson and Robert Saunders (Cambridge: Cambridge University Press, 2012), 25–42.

6 Lawrence Black, "An Enlightening Decade? New Histories of 1970s Britain," *International Labor and Working-Class History* 82 (2012): 177.

7 See Eric J. Hobsbawm, *The Age of Extremes: A History of the World, 1914– 1991* (New York: Vintage Books, 1996); Andrew Marr, *A History of Modern Britain* (London: Pan, 2009); Arthur Marwick, *A History of the Modern British Isles, 1914–1999: Circumstances, Events, and Outcomes* (Oxford: Blackwell, 2000).

8 Black, "Enlightening"; Andy Beckett, *When the Lights Went Out* (London: Faber and Faber, 2009).

9 Jon Lawrence and Florence Sutcliffe-Braithwaite, "Margaret Thatcher and the Decline of Class Politics," in *Making Thatcher's Britain*, ed. Jackson and Saunders, 132–47; Emily Robinson et al., "Telling Stories about Post-war Britain: Popular Individualism and the 'Crisis' of the 1970s," *Twentieth Century British History* 28, no. 2 (2017): 268–304; Sina Fabian, " 'Popular Capitalism' in Großbritannien in den 1980er Jahren," in *Archiv für Sozialgeschichte* 56 (2016): 273–95.

10 Jörg Arnold, "Vom Verlierer zum Gewinner – und zurück: Der Coal Miner als Schlüsselfigur der britischen Zeitgeschichte," *Geschichte und Gesellschaft* 42, no. 2 (2016): 266–97.

11 Jim Tomlison extensively and successfully worked on deconstructing the British decline narrative in "The Politics of Declinism," in *Reassessing 1970s Britain*, ed. Lawrence Black, Hugh Pemberton, and Pat Thane (Manchester: Manchester University Press, 2013), 41–60; "Thrice Denied: 'Declinism' as a Recurrent Theme in British History in the Long Twentieth Century," *Twentieth Century British History* 20, no. 2 (2009): 227–51; and "After Decline?" *Contemporary British History* 23, no. 3 (2009): 395–406.

12 Newer "after the boom" publications have taken a more nuanced stance and qualified the earlier far-reaching theses to some extent: Anselm Doering-Manteuffel, Lutz Raphael, and Thomas Schlemmer eds., *Vorgeschichte der Gegenwart: Dimensionen des Strukturbruchs nach dem Boom* (Göttingen: Vandenhoeck & Ruprecht, 2016).

13 Sina Fabian, *Boom in der Krise: Konsum, Tourismus, Autofahren in Westdeutschland und Großbritannien 1970–1990* (Göttingen: Wallstein Verlag, 2016); Frank Trentmann, "Unstoppable: Consumption after the Boom – Resilience, Adaptation and Renewal," in *Vorgeschichte*, ed. Doering-Manteuffel, Raphael, and Schlemmer, 293–307.

14 For the car in Britain, see Timothy R. Whisler, *The British Motor Industry, 1945–1994: A Case Study in Industrial Decline* (Oxford: Oxford University Press, 1999); Simon Gunn, "People and the Car: The Expansion of Automobility in Urban Britain, c.1955–70," *Social History* 38, no. 2 (2013): 220–37; Kathryn Morrison and John Minnis, *Carscapes: The Motor Car, Architecture and Landscape in England* (New Haven, CT: Yale University Press, 2012). For tourism, see Hartmut Berghoff et al. eds., *The Making of Modern Tourism* (New York: Palgrave, 2002), especially Hartmut Berghoff, "From Privilege to Commodity? Modern Tourism and the Rise of the Consumer Society," 159–81; John K. Walton, *The British Seaside: Holidays and Resorts in the Twentieth Century* (Manchester: Manchester University Press 2000); Victor T.C. Middleton and Leonard J. Lickorish, *British Tourism: The Remarkable Story of Growth* (Oxford: Butterworth-Heinemann, 2007).

15 Anthony Crosland, quoted in "Councils Are Told to Curb Rise in Spending," *Times* (London), 10 May 1975, 1.

16 Douglas Wass, *Decline to Fall: The Making of British Macro-Economic Policy and the 1976 IMF Crisis* (Oxford: Oxford University Press, 2008).

17 Central Statistical Office (hereafter CSO), ed., *Social Trends 1982* (London: HMSO, 1983), 80; Chris Cook and John Stevenson, *Britain since 1945* (London: Longman, 1996), 166.

18 Budget Speech, in House of Commons, Debate, 21 March 1972, series 5, vol. 833, cc 1343–90. For cabinet discussion on the budget, see PREM 15/818, in the National Archives.

19 CSO, ed., *Social Trends 1974* (London: HMSO, 1975), 112; Cook and Stevenson even suggest 8.5 per cent in 1972 and 7 per cent in 1973. See Cook and Stevenson, *Britain since 1945*, 166. For car sales, see Society of Motor Manufacturers and Traders (hereafter SMMT), *The Motor Industry of Great Britain* (London: SMMT, 1974).

20 Jim Phillips, "The 1972 Miners' Strike: Popular Agency and Industrial Politics in Britain," *Contemporary British History* 20, no. 2 (2006): 187–207.

21 Dominic Sandbrook, *State of Emergency: The Way We Were – Britain, 1970–1974* (London: Penguin, 2011), 613–45.

22 Arnold, "Verlierer," 277.

23 Howard Glennerster, *British Social Policy: 1945 to the Present* (Malden, MA: Blackwell, 2007); Cornelius Torp, *Gerechtigkeit im Wohlfahrtsstaat: Alter und Alterssicherung in Deutschland und Großbritannien von 1945 bis heute* (Göttingen: Vandenhoeck Ruprecht, 2015).

24 Anthony B. Atkinson, "Distribution of Income and Wealth," in *Twentieth-Century British Social Trends*, ed. Albert H. Halsey and Josephine Webb (New York: St. Martin's Press 2000), 353ff; Linda Dickens, "The Road Is Long: Thirty Years of Equality Legislation in Britain," *British Journal of Industrial Relations* 45, no. 3 (2007): 463–94.

25 Cook and Stevenson, *Britain Since 1945*, 166; CSO, ed., *Social Trends 1982* (London: HMSO, 1983), 80.

26 Arnold, "Verlierer."

27 Wiebke Wiede, "The Poor Unemployed: Diagnoses of Unemployment in Britain and West Germany since the 1970s," *Rescuing the Vulnerable: Poverty, Welfare and Social Ties in Modern Europe*, ed. Beate Althammer, Lutz Raphael, and Tamara Stazic-Wendt (New York: Berghahn Books, 2016), 307–31.

28 CSO, ed., *Family Expenditure Survey 1972* (London: HMSO, 1973), 100; CSO, ed., *Family Expenditure Survey 1980* (London: HMSO, 1981), 18, 28.

29 SMMT, *Motor Industry*, various years; Middleton and Lickorish, *British Tourism*, 207.

30 Associations' Consultative Council, ed., *Anatomy of UK Tourism: Domestic, Inbound, Outbound* (London: Travel Associations' Consultative Council, 1982), 24; Roger Bray and Vladimir Raitz, *Flight to the Sun: The Story of the Holiday Revolution* (London: Continuum, 2001), 96; English Tourist Board, ed., *Holiday Intentions Survey* (London: English Tourist Board, 1980); Susan Barton, *Working-Class Organisations and Popular Tourism, 1840–1970* (Manchester: Manchester University Press, 2005).

31 CSO, *Trends 1982*, 112.

32 Ibid.

33 "Decline in Consumer Spending Was Less than Expected during the First Quarter," *Times* (London), 19 April 1974, 19; "Consumer Spending Still Remains Buoyant," *Times* (London), 17 January 1975, 18.

34 SMMT, *Motor Industry*, 1977; Middleton and Lickorish, *British Tourism*, 207.

35 Euromonitor Publications Limited, ed., *Holiday Survey* (London: Euromonitor Publications, 1978), 35; M.J.H. Mogridge, "The Effect of the Oil Crisis on the Growth in the Ownership and Use of Car," *Transportation* 7 (1978): 47ff.

36 "Good Driving Can Help Save Petrol," *Times* (London), 29 November 1973, 33; "Oil – Why We Must Slow Down," *Daily Mirror*, 20 November 1973, 7.

37 Sylvia Gilpin and David Yelding, *UK Motorists and Car Fuel Economy: Results of a Survey* (London: Consumers' Association, 1984), 13f.

38 Ibid.

39 Roger Duffell, *Car Travel, 1965–1975, With Particular Reference to Pleasure Motoring and Highway Planning* (n.p., 1975), 557ff.

40 Peter Bonsall and A.F. Champernowne, "Some Findings on Elasticities of Demand for Petrol," *Traffic Engineering + Control* 17, no. 10 (1976): 416.

41 M.C. Dix et al., eds., *Car Use: A Social and Economic Study* (Aldershot, UK: Gower, 1983), 134ff.

42 See the special directive on the car, in Mass Observation Archive (hereafter MOA), SxMOA2/1/24 Autumn/Winter 1987 Directive (Car).

43 Jim Tomlinson, "Thatcher, Monetarism and the Politics of Inflation," in
    Making, ed. Jackson and Saunders, 62–77.
44 The accounts can be found in the MOA. The 1981 directives dealt
    explicitly with inflation, consumption, and unemployment: http://
    database.massobs.org.uk/projects_database/directivesList/. For a
    critical assessment of the mass observation files as sources, see Annebella
    Pollen, "Research Methodology in Mass Observation Past and Present:
    'Scientifically, About as Valuable as a Chimpanzee's Tea Party at the Zoo'?"
    History Workshop Journal 75, no. 1 (2013): 213–35.
45 SxMOA2/1/1 G226, MOA.
46 Ibid., D157.
47 Ibid., S496; C108; A19; M384; CSO, ed., *Social Trends 1987* (London: Central
    Statistical Office, 1988), 86; Selina Todd, *The People: The Rise and Fall of the
    Working Class, 1910–2010* (London: John Murray, 2014), 318–37.
48 Glennerster, *British Social Policy*, 181.
49 SxMOA2/1/1 S496, MOA.
50 Ibid.; SxMOA2/1/3 S496, inMOA.
51 See, for example: SxMOA2/1/1 A19; B41; B53; B83; C108, MOA.
52 John K. Walton, *The English Seaside Resort: A Social History, 1750–1914*
    (Leicester: Leicester University Press 1983), 30–5.
53 Walton, *The British Seaside*, 61.
54 Bray and Raitz, *Flight to the Sun*, 196.
55 Peter Lyth, "Flying Visits: The Growth of British Air Package Tours,
    1945–1975," in *Europe at the Seaside: The Economic History of Mass Tourism in
    the Mediterranean*, ed. Luciano Segreto, Carles Manera, and Manfred Pohl
    (New York: Berghahn Books, 2009); Bray and Raitz, *Flight to the Sun*.
56 See in more detail Fabian, *Boom in der Krise*.
57 Department of Trade and Industry, ed., *Business Monitor: Miscellaneous
    Series. M6. Overseas Travel and Tourism,* (London: HMSO, various years).
58 "Spain's Summer of Travel Discontent," *Financial Times*, 27 July 1971, 17.
59 "Warning on Holiday 'Small Print,'" *Financial Times*, 23 January 1970, 8;
    "Sun, Sand and Small Print: The Travel Trade's Dilemma," *Financial Times*,
    3 April 1973, 20.
60 Euromonitor Publications Limited, ed., *The World Package Holidays Market,
    1980–1995: Consumers and the Industry in the Five Major Markets* (London:
    Euromonitor Publications, 1988), 44.
61 "Holiday Giant Collapses," *Daily Telegraph*, 16 April 1974; "The Bubble
    Bursts," *Flight International*, 22 August 1974, 198.
62 Associations' Consultative Council, ed., *Anatomy of UK Tourism*, 5.
63 Department of Trade and Industry, ed., *Business Monitor*, various years.
64 Sasha D. Pack, *Tourism and Dictatorship: Europe's Peaceful Invasion of Franco's
    Spain* (New York: Palgrave Macmillan, 2006); Michael Barke, John Towner,

and Michael T. Newton eds., *Tourism in Spain: Critical Issues* (Wallington, UK: CAB International, 1996); Segreto, Manera, and Pohl., *Europe at the Seaside*.

65 British Tourist Authority, ed., *British Holiday Intentions* (London, various years).

66 Own estimates from Middleton and Lickorish, *British Tourism*, 207. See also Walton, *The British Seaside*, 69.

67 See, for example, "Beside the Seaside," *Times* (London), 29 August 1981, 9; "Having a Lonely Time, Wish You Were Here," *Daily Express*, 9 July 1982, 10.

68 Paul Theroux, *The Kingdom by the Sea: A Journey around the Coast of Great Britain* (London: Penguin Books, 1984), 326.

69 Ibid., 24ff.

70 "Having a Wonderful Time on the Dole," *Daily Express*, 2 June 1984, 10.

71 Sandra Trudgen Dawson, *Holiday Camps in Twentieth-Century Britain: Packaging Pleasure* (Manchester: Manchester University Press, 2011). See for criticism and decline, 221ff.

72 Gareth Shaw and Allan M. Williams, "Riding the Bid Dipper: The Rise and Decline of the British Seaside Resort in the Twentieth Century," in *The Rise and Fall of British Coastal Resorts*, ed. Gareth Shaw and Allan M. William (London: Pinter, 1997), 1–21; Walton, *The British Seaside*, 66.

73 SxMOA2/1/23 N399; A 1412; B42; N1484, MOA.

74 SxMOA2/1/23 H260, in MOA; D. Hodson et al., eds., *Package Holidays in Spain* (Manchester: Manchester University Press 1985), 102.

75 See, for responses to crisis in seaside resorts, Gareth Shaw and Allan M. Williams, "The Private Sector: Tourism Entrepreneurship – A Constraint or Resource?" in *The Rise and Fall of British Coastal Resorts*, ed. Shaw and Williams, 117–36.

76 John Urry and Jonas Larsen, *The Tourist Gaze 3.0* (London: Sage, 2011), 135ff.

77 Roy Strong, Marcus Binney, and John Harris, eds., *The Destruction of the Country House, 1875–1975* (London: Thames and Hudson, 1974); Peter Mandler, *The Fall and Rise of the Stately Home* (New Haven, CT: Yale University Press, 1997).

78 Peter Johnson and Barry Thomas, "The Development of Beamish: An Assessment," *Museum Management and Curatorship* 9 (1990): 5–24.

79 Natasha Vall, "Coal Is Our Strife: Representing Mining Heritage in North East England," *Contemporary British History* 31 (2017), https://doi.org/10.1080/13619462.2017.1408541.

80 Johnson and Thomas, "Development," 8.

81 See also SO ed., *Social Trends 1993* (London: HMSO, 1994), 139; Walton, *The British Seaside*, 64ff.

82 Neil Kennedy and Nigel Kingcome, "Disneyfication of Cornwall: Developing a Poldark Heritage Complex," in *International Journal of Heritage Studies* 4, no. 1 (1998): 45–59.

83 For contemporary criticism, see Robert Hewison, *The Heritage Industry: Britain in a Climate of Decline* (London: Methuen, 1987); Tim Hall, " 'The Second Industrial Revolution': Cultural Reconstructions of Industrial Regions," in *Landscape Research* 20, no. 3 (1995): 112–23. For a more nuanced view, see John K. Walton, "British Tourism between Industrialization and Globalization: An Overview," in *The Making of Modern Tourism*, ed. Berghoff et al., 124–6.

84 "When Everything Went Wrong," *Sun*, 11 May 2017, accessed 12 December 2017, https://www.thesun.co.uk/living/3535415/from-rubbish-piled -high-to-hospital-closures-and-endless-strike-chaos-this-is-what-britain -looked-like-the-last-time-labours-hard-left-were-in-charge-jeremy/.

3 Decent Work in the Home? Household Workers and the Crisis of Social Reproduction since the 1970s

EILEEN BORIS

The 1970s mark the transformation of women's relation to the labour market in the United States. In the context of both the new feminism and economic restructuring amid deindustrialization, offshoring, and financialization, rising numbers of women, including white women previously not in the labour force, went out of the home to fulfill their own desire to work. In addition, many married women needed another income to support their families. By 1976, nearly half of mothers with children under eighteen were in the labour force, a percentage that rose to nearly 80 per cent in 2000, only to slightly dip with the 2008 recession.[1] The growing movement of mothers with young children into employment led to a perceived crisis in social reproduction exacerbated by the lack of public provision of child and elder care in the limited (and means-tested) US welfare state. While women cut the number of hours spent doing housework nearly in half and men doubled theirs in heterosexual households, families still experienced a gap between women and men in time spent on such tasks.[2] In response, better-off women who were pursuing careers turned their homes into workplaces for other women, whom they hired as domestic workers, in an effort to balance "work" and "family."

Paying for household work involves "outwork" insofar as a woman or a household relegates tasks performed for family maintenance to another, commodifying that labour. Sometimes this displacement involved location: fast food and store-bought meals could replace home cooking, while dry cleaners, tailors, and laundries could undertake maintenance of clothing. But from the standpoint of the home as a place of employment, it is more accurate to speak of the use of domestic workers as "insourcing" because the employer brings the cleaner or carer into the home. What is being consumed is not products entering the home, but the labour of a housekeeper, paid to substitute for wives, mothers, and other family members. Paid domestic work is commodified labour, but its outputs are a mixture of intangibles and material products that forge or produce the home and its people. The results of this labour power dissipate through the very quotidian nature of cooking and cleaning or become congealed in the bodies that incorporate such offerings. Theorists refer to such work, paid and unpaid, as "reproductive labour" or "social reproduction," the making of people through daily maintenance and generational transference of norms, behaviours, and ways of being.[3] Rejecting the ideology of "like one of the family," most cleaners and carers understand that they are workers, even as they engage in what I have called "intimate labour," and even if they develop attachments to homes and families that complicate the cash nexus and exchange relation.[4]

In the early years following the Second World War, social scientists had thought domestic service would wither away as appliances, laundries, and prepared foods became increasingly common.[5] Certainly mechanization and cleaning products impacted the labour process, even if new norms for cleanliness increased household work.[6] But employment growth in the 1970s proved commentators wrong, with the return of the nanny, cleaner, and elder-care worker as private solutions to social problems. As African Americans fled domestic work whenever they could, by decade's end a new generation of immigrant women from the Americas, especially English speakers from the Caribbean, and from Asia, filled such jobs. Compelled by structural adjustment and civil unrest to leave their own homes, immigrant household workers laboured in the homes of other women.[7] As Michael Kozakowski shows for France in his chapter in this volume, a racialized migrant workforce took on some of the lowest-paying jobs in the growing service economy. In the United States, they slipped into a prior racial regime that had allocated household labour to African Americans.

The care gap and growing inequality between women, as well as the time crunch and income squeeze of many households, intensified the problem over the past half century. By 2012, in-home workers expanded to roughly two million, nearly all women and disproportionately immigrant; one out of nine women born elsewhere with a high school degree or less engaged in some kind of home care or domestic labour.[8] In the twenty-first century, many homeworkers remain in the shadow economy, difficult to count because they work without papers, labour intermittently or part-time, are paid in cash, come under the classification of "independent contractors," or work for private household-cleaning and care-worker agencies and are categorized as service workers. While the US census has captured some of this increase, surveys by domestic worker organizations suggest the actual numbers to be even higher.[9] The International Labour Organization (ILO) estimated in 2016 that, worldwide, domestic workers numbered 67 million and were 2 per cent of all workers and 4 per cent of all women in the labour market. Women composed 80 per cent of these workers, while some 17 per cent were migrants.[10]

This chapter highlights the interconnected histories of domestic workers and the women who employed them in the 1970s. More than a general crisis of the economy – which Sina Fabian discusses with respect to Britain in the preceding chapter – another type of crisis hit the United States during those pivotal years: that of social reproduction. This type of labour was essential to prepare families to address the larger economic crisis of the time: a shifting job structure and stagflation. The two-paycheque household was becoming necessary for its members to maintain a middle-class life style. Meanwhile, deindustrialization created a Rust Belt in the Midwest, replacing men's well-paying and unionized manufacturing jobs with a female-employing, lower-waged, and non-union service sector. The growth of the economy was in services, high and low, with the Sunbelt booming, as Jessica Burch shows in chapter 1.[11] How families and households would be maintained when women joined the paid labour force turned a labour question into a cultural one. As a *Washington Post* columnist opined, "Today's emancipated educated women feel that motherhood and careers can coexist and feel it is not only their right but their duty to contribute in the working world," but they were having a problem finding "adequate help" who could not only clean the floors but whom they felt comfortable leaving their children with after school. They didn't want "some indifferent woman who couldn't care less about [their children]."[12]

Women's labour force participation was only one component shaping the demand for household workers. This chapter also explores changes in immigration laws in the 1960s and subsequent struggles over what became known as the "illegal traffic in imported domestic help." Increased numbers of visa applications for what commentators called the "alien maid" responded to the growing need for household labour, though politicians hoped to improve conditions to attract more US workers by insisting on contracts containing wage and hour standards, even though domestic workers remained outside labour law.[13] Employment of immigrants occurred as African-American workers demanded rights and recognition as part of the civil rights struggle, including coverage under those very labour standards for which adherence to was a requirement of importing immigrant live-in maids. Without various forms of public services, including appropriate and affordable child care, and lacking family pensions as developed by European welfare states, the United States maintained its historic reliance on commodified racialized labour. Privatized market solutions were the answer to the question of who would care and cook and clean when mothers and wives went out to work.

Wage-Earning Mothers and the Housework Problem

The feminism of the 1970s, which both facilitated and reflected the advancement of some women into professional and full-time employment, also proved a boon for the demand for domestic workers. Throughout the decade, the labour force participation of mothers with children below school age (six years) quickly rose. These numbers included 37 per cent of wives with husbands making an upper-middle-class income. Over half of all women were in the labour force by the end of the decade; by that time, less than a quarter of households in the United States conformed to the male breadwinner, female homemaker model.[14] Women entered jobs previously dominated by men: from 1960 to 1983, the proportion of lawyers who were women expanding from 2 to 15 per cent and financial managers from 9 to 39 per cent. Women also took on jobs as butchers and bartenders, traditionally considered men's work, in greater numbers than before. By shifting out of "women's work," such wage earners gained higher incomes, but most women entered the rapidly expanding service sector doing "pink-collar" or women's lower-waged work. One estimate has women taking up three out of five new jobs during the 1970s.[15]

A range of social, demographic, and economic factors were pushing women into formal employment. They were "marrying later, having fewer children, divorcing more often, living decades beyond the lifespans of their grandmothers." Inflation encouraged the "two-paycheque family" as wages stagnated and prices increased. The retail and service sector preferred women employees, including part-time ones. Indeed, these women's jobs weathered the recession of 1974–5 better than construction and manufacturing, where men dominated. Added to these factors was the ideology of liberal feminism, which equated independence with equality in the waged workplace.[16]

Faced with double days of employment and unpaid household work, wage-earning women began a decades-long quest to solve the "work and family" balance. As historian Kirsten Swinth powerfully argues, feminists of the 1960s and 1970s sought equalitarian relationships that would transform gender subjectivities and social structures. Rather than being considered valueless, care would assume its true value, so that homemakers, poor single mothers, and household workers would gain recognition and living wages. Given feminist inability to transform the public-private divide, we can forget that there were alternatives to hiring another woman to do one's housework, sending one's children to private child care centres, or buying prepared food.[17] Republican president Richard Nixon, after all, vetoed comprehensive child care, and Congress imposed means tests and work requirements on social assistance or welfare for stay-at-home mothers. Although some employers offered child care, flex-time, or flexi-space, most businesses reorganized workplaces for just-in-time production or scheduling that made it more difficult for employees to perform reproductive labour. The culture of some offices and professions stretched out the working day rather than accommodating care work.[18]

Feminists would revalue the worth of household labour. Proclaimed New York's Democratic congresswoman Bella Abzug, one leading figure, "The women's movement is the homemaker deciding that raising children, cleaning, cooking and all the other things she does for her family is work that should be accorded respect and value."[19] A small number of Marxist feminists suggested "wages for housework," paying women for performing reproductive labour, preferably with the state the source of such monies, as the first step to revaluing such labour and ending its gendered private character.[20] Under the banner, "Every mother is a working mother," the National Organization for Women (NOW) in 1978 proposed a Homemaker's Bill of Rights. Since "it is not the homemaker who benefits most from her/his unpaid labor, but it is the community and family and through them all of society," it reasoned, "homemakers should be granted the recognition and rights of paid, skilled workers" – that is, they should receive social security on the basis of their labour and not a waged partner's. Their goods and services should be counted under the gross national product, while those on public assistance should receive adequate income to remain at home. Part-time and flexible-time employment, along with appropriate child care, should make "jobs more available to parents of young children." Other jobs should be restructured. Additional planks emphasized protection from spousal rape and domestic violence, a safe workplace and "adequate" housing, review of laws and codes "that deprive homemakers of dignity, security and recognition," and "the right to retire or change jobs."[21]

Experts looked at the monetary worth of such labour. Based on 1972 data, the Social Security Administration calculated the "average economic value of housewives and working women." It found that women aged twenty to twenty-four were worth more keeping house than employed full time. But, for every cohort forward, the worth of employment became greater than that of housework. The largest gap was among those sixty to sixty-four, where employed women earned $7,052 to the housewife's worth of $2,942, reflecting the reality that the value of bearing and rearing children, with greater need for cooking and cleaning, no longer applied to older women.[22] The National Federation of Business and Professional Women touted a higher yearly estimate of the overall worth of housework, between $8,400 and $13,364.[23] Social Security never credited housework for direct payments, and the state gave means-tested allowances only to poor single mothers under Aid to Families with Dependent Children (AFDC). Such welfare came under vicious attack in the late 1960s and 1970s, when greater numbers of Black women, having migrated to northern cities, gained access to such funding.[24]

Having male partners perform their share of domestic work was the preferred feminist solution. Yet men could not be relied upon to do so, though their participation increased over time. Pat Mainridi exposed men's reactions in the now classic "The Politics of Housework" in 1970: "The measure of your oppression is his resistance." Thus to the suggestion of sharing domestic labour, she offered one translation of his foot dragging: "Eventually doing all the housework yourself will be less painful to you than trying to get me [the husband] to do half. Or I'll suggest we get a maid. She will do my share of the work. You will do yours. It's women's work."[25] Claimed sociologist Mary Jo Bane in 1977, "Everybody's in favor of equal pay, but no body's in favor of doing the dishes."[26] Outsourcing to another woman emerged as a way to negotiate heterosexual conflict.

Employing a nanny or another household worker offered the flexibility that sending children to child care did not. During the 1970s, stories in the *New York Times* highlighted the working mothers' complaint: the shortage of good child-minders and housekeepers. Even if the *Times* reflected an elite urban group, it captured the angst of a generation of educated women who sought to use their training while having families. The situation of women in areas undergoing deindustrialization, like the middle west, upstate New York, and Pennsylvania's "Rust Belt," where men were losing well-paying unionized jobs, was much more difficult.

Household workers knew that it wasn't "rising affluence" fuelling the demand for their services but "the sharp increase in the number of working wives and working female heads of families" that led to their employment. As a *New York Magazine* commentator reported in 1971, "today's typical lady-of-the-house is probably a harassed middle-class woman who works, thinks of herself as poor because most of her salary goes for household help and taxes, and is somewhat painfully aware of the class, racial, and perhaps even feminist implications of having a maid." But, like the mistress of old, she paid the lowest wage the market could sustain, provided no benefits or sick days, had unrealistic expectations of the tasks that could be squeezed into a given time, and saw no need for an employment contract. Good work received no raise; wages at $1.35 an hour or less were typical.[27] In the early 1970s, the minimum wage stood at $1.60 an hour, rising to $2.00 an hour in 1974, the year that non-live-in private domestic workers achieved coverage under the Fair Labor Standards Act (FLSA). At the time, their median wage was under $2,000 a year, when the middle-class median income stood at $55,000.[28] Yet the cost of goods from groceries to utilities remained the same no matter one's occupation.

Low wages, stigma, and "racial tension between whites and blacks" made domestic work an undesirable occupation. According to the Bureau of Labor Statistics, the percentage of "nonwhite females" working in private households declined from 29.2 per cent to 18.6 per cent between 1965 and 1969.[29] During the previous decade, at least a million women "threw down their scrubbrushes, took off their aprons and quit," claimed Edith Barksdale-Sloan, executive director of the National Committee on Household Employment (NCHE) in 1971. Estimates suggested between 1.5 and 3 million people were on the job, almost all of them women, middle aged, and without a high school education. African Americans still dominated the sector, reinforcing the lingering tinge of slavery that hovered over the work. At least a quarter of a million domestic workers headed their own families, earning much less than the $2,400 a year guaranteed income then under Congressional consideration, which the National Welfare Rights Organization vigorously protested as "too meager" to live on. They not only lived out, as they had since the 1920s, but increasingly had to patch together a series of day jobs since work had become more irregular with shifting middle-class priorities.[30]

A study of twenty cities in 1971 reported on the difficulty of finding substitutes for a housewife's labour, especially given the outmoded expectations of some employers. Some women still wanted a maid who would get down on her hands and knees to scrub "floors with a rag and soap." Demand had expanded during the 1960s as the percentage of families earning enough to hire a housekeeper ($10,000 and above) more than doubled. However, women recoiled from the conditions of service: "low pay, poor working conditions and work benefits ... and the attitudes and actions of the average employer," especially when other opportunities were available. The civil rights revolution had opened up government and private sector employment, especially clerical work, to Black women who had previously found themselves relegated to domestic labour. "Younger girls simply don't want to be live-in maids and older women have families to take care of," one Florida employment agency manager explained, the reference to "girls" reflecting the disrespect toward Black women. Some Phoenix households bussed in high schoolers from a nearby Native American reservation on Saturdays, while others in New York, Florida, Texas, and California sought out undocumented immigrants.[31]

The labour in question wasn't only housework. Employed mothers needed care work as well. "It's almost impossible these days for a mother to feel confident about going back to work," the head of a "strictly nanny" employment agency told reporter Diana Shaman in 1977. "In a five-month period, I had six different people I tried to work with … They would start working for me, then a week later they'd call up with one excuse or another as to why they couldn't come back," a mother of two employed as a systems analyst complained. She wasn't looking for "a servant" but rather a professional. A *New York Times* article, "A Wrinkle in Housework: Wives on Job, Help Scarce – A Premium on Help around the House," reiterated her problem as one of looking for a reliable replacement for the mother who was heading out to work. Reflecting racialist assumptions, interviews with placement bureaus spoke of the scarcity of "good help." Because many Americans rejected such labour as "belittling" rather than "honest, clean work," "sponsoring" (essentially importing) nannies from Europe offered "quality personnel." But with unemployment rates hovering between 7 and 8 per cent in the mid-1970s,[32] the Department of Labor required that prospective employers prove their inability to find a suitable match after extensive advertisement and filing of the job with the state employment agency. Costs were steep, despite a recently enacted child tax credit. "If you don't make at least $300 a week, you lose money if you need full-time help," a New York City wage-earning mother claimed. Immigrant labour potentially offered a cheaper solution.[33]

As civil rights initiatives opened new employment to younger African Americans, renewed immigration meant that women from Latin America, Asia, and Eastern Europe would undertake housework.[34] The bringing in of domestic labour was not new in the 1970s, but the conditions under which workers arrived had changed. From 1885 through the 1930s, contract labour laws exempted foreign domestic workers (and nurses, an occupation often conflated with personal service) as an attempt to meet the demand of prosperous families for these workers.[35]

After the Second World War, the Department of Labor and US consuls abroad oversaw a visa program that allowed the hiring of skilled immigrant workers, especially from Europe, but household employees failed to qualify. Like housewives, they were classified as unskilled, in keeping with the general devaluation of such labour. A few came with their corporate or diplomatic employers under special visas. In contrast, with the Western Hemisphere exempt from quotas, Mexican and Caribbean women could enter the United States as domestic workers. The 1965 Immigration Act changed the system, privileging family reunification and skilled workers, even within the Americas. That year the Department of Labor placed domestic workers as "sixth-preference immigrants (skilled and unskilled workers in short supply)." As historian Martha Gardner has explained, within two years, domestic workers received 37 per cent of all visas, while over half of applicants from the Americas were for the service sector, with nearly nine of ten of these applying as domestic workers.[36]

Fear of fake maids led to new regulations. According to one Department of Labor official, "They come here as maids and then they shoot off into other jobs for more money, to the detriment of the American workers."[37] In the public mind, the employment agent or labour broker emerged as a shady operator, overcharging both migrant women and the households seeking to hire them. By 1968, experts estimated that half of some 25,000 "alien domestics" came with "fraudulent papers." Legal papers would cost the employer $70 and the worker no more than $200, but the black market in visas ran from $660 to $1,200. With brokers deducting finding fees, a woman could be left with only a quarter of her earnings.[38] Amended Department of Labor rules in 1969 would require "proof of experience and a promise of a job" to obtain a visa to come to the United States as a domestic worker. Such women were caught in a catch-22: they had to be single but had "to convince the authorities that they are not planning to enter the country primarily to look for a husband."[39] The previous year, the department had accepted only 62 per cent of applications from domestic workers, some 15,500 in total. But these numbers were deemed inadequate by women would-be employers who were desperate for live-in workers.[40]

The requirements of a privileged group of women shaped these discussions, with their needs conflated with those of all wage-earning mothers. US-born workers could fill only about a quarter of the demand for household help, desired by some 5.5 million families.[41] To an inquiry from New York Democratic congressman Richard L. Ottinger of Westchester County, Nixon's Labor Secretary George Shultz replied in October 1969, "In the absence of extenuating circumstances such as an invalid in the household, unreasonable commuting distances, a motherless household with preschool-age children, or a household where both parents work and there are preschool-age children, the duties listed above may be performed by dayworkers, live-out maids, caterers, and babysitters." Crucial was his finding that visas would be blocked if "workers are available to perform specified duties rather than on any finding that there is a shortage of workers willing to live at their prospective places of employment." But Ottinger counted that the market for live-in maids differed from that of day workers: "Many working mothers need sleep-in help and simply cannot depend on three or four different employees, as you recommend." They required weekend assistance as well.[42]

Shultz soon responded to pressure from "irate women unable to obtain satisfactory domestic help" by easing the evaluation process. If employers could demonstrate the need for live-in workers – that they were unable to restructure the work to fit into an 8 to 5 or 9 to 6 day – and no other workers were available, then the department would approve applications. Reported the *New York Times*, "the policy shift comes at a time when some employment agencies, unhappy over the losses, have been threatening to organize protest marches on the Labor Department, and some immigration lawyers have started suits challenging some of the department's actions on alien domestic applications."[43] The new Republican administration was more eager to satisfy wealthy complainers and the employment agencies than had been the previous Democratic one.

Personal Solutions, Public Struggles

New York Times columnist Linda Bird Francke tried it all. She "worked at home with child care – and without." She went out to work "part time with part-time child care and full time with full-time help." But she kept stumbling from internalized maternal expectations: "Regardless of the formula," she confessed, "it still boils down to the necessity for a bionic-mother constitution and a lifetime supply of Geritol." It didn't matter if there was a trained nanny or, as she put it, "an illegal alien, it is the mother who is still on deck."[44] Women remained caught between self-expectations and the difficulties of what political scientist Ann-Marie Slaughter decades later would call "having it all" in a political economy devoid of universal social supports.[45] But that conundrum was no excuse to disparage the very women whose labour could allow them to pursue other work. One aggrieved letter-writer to the *Times* would not let Francke get away with her race and class prejudices:

Ellen Frankfort from Manhattan called out the columnist for "ignoring the ways in which women domestic workers have traditionally been oppressed by poor working conditions as well as by sexism" and for "referring to 'illegal aliens' as some kind of vermin."[46]

Poorer women never had the luxury to cut down on employment, but they sometimes could take advantage of government programs, like Headstart for early childhood education and subsidized care after school for older children. But such wage-earning mothers still had to make do through informal arrangements when their hours of employment, including commuting time, deviated from the hours of institutional child care. Working-class women long relied on family, neighbours, and children themselves in order to juggle employment with other family labour. When they could, they often took work into the home rather than going out to work. They brought their children to their jobs. Under workfare rules, conditions that required recipients of public assistance to provide community service or labour for their benefits, some mothers began minding other poor mothers' children as their "work."[47]

The economic stagnation that brought married mothers into the labour force meant, when recession hit, cutbacks in the income of the household workers they increasingly depended upon. "Within the last year, there's been a pinch – money is tightening, and girls who used to work five days have been cut down to two or three," noted one taxi driver in 1976, who shuttled inner-city commuters from the train to affluent neighbourhoods in suburban Great Neck, New York. Domestic workers complained of jobs being reduced and "hard to find," with one woman blaming "Spanish girls" who "work for less." Apparently these recent immigrants would do jobs that older African-American women refused, like washing outside windows, would labour for longer hours, and would walk miles to suburban trains stations rather than ask for carfare.[48] At the same time, some employers in Montgomery, Alabama, reportedly reduced hours or fired their domestic workers rather than pay higher wages when the going wage inched up in 1974 to $15.20 from between $7 and $9 for an eight-hour day. "Many mothers turned to day care centers or relatives to keep their children" rather than pay more to a household worker.[49]

Domestic workers and their allies organized against such working conditions.[50] The fight to place domestic workers under labour law sought to reverse their originary exclusion. Asked whether the FLSA, passed in 1938, would "force" Southern housewives to "pay your negro girl eleven dollars a week," President Franklin Delano Roosevelt had replied that no wage and hour bill would "apply to domestic help."[51]

Roosevelt needed Southern votes to pass major New Deal legislation; to gain those votes, this legislation omitted occupations dominated by African Americans and immigrants of colour, especially household service and agriculture. While formulators of Social Security in 1935 felt that administrative problems precluded inclusion of domestics, some professional women had a vested interest in a cheap supply of servants, and housewives did not view themselves as employers. In contrast, women reformers, through the National Committee on Household Employment, attempted to upgrade the occupation through training classes and model contracts. Their voluntarist approach reinforced the feeling that household labour was different, that individual negotiation was more appropriate than social regulation.[52]

Change was slow. Amendments to social security in the 1950s – for those who worked for one employer at least twice a week and earned at least $50 in a calendar quarter and for others who earned the same amount in the quarter but with multiple employers – allowed some domestic workers to receive retirement and unemployment coverage.[53] As of 1972, only Wisconsin, New York, and Massachusetts included domestic workers under state minimum wage laws; only New York and Hawaii provided some state unemployment compensation. Household workers themselves organized to secure the New York and Massachusetts laws. In 1971, the Senate first considered homeworkers' inclusion in the FLSA, but it took until 1974 to overcome Republican opposition and an earlier presidential veto to come under the federal minimum wage.[54]

In the 1970s, a reconstituted National Committee on Household Employment led the organizing to improve domestic work. As one activist explained, "the garbage men have been upgraded to sanitation workers, with all the benefits, and that's just what we have to do."[55] In 1964, the US Women's Bureau – along with national women's organizations of Jewish, "Negro," and Protestant women– had sparked the formation of a new NCHE as a non-profit corporation "to coordinate the efforts of all groups with a mutual interest in the problems in household employment." Initially, liberal and labourite women, many of them employers of household labour, dominated the organization, which established government-funded model projects and sought to educate the larger public. It investigated conditions and publicized various community programs to expand opportunities for household workers.[56] It promoted a voluntary "Code of Standards," with provisions for minimum wages, overtime, Social Security, sick leave, vacations, paid holidays, and a "professional" working relationship.[57]

In 1972, the NCHE brought local organizations of household workers together to form the Household Technicians of America (HTA).

Changing the name of the occupation to refer to household technician was another step toward dignifying the work. By that time, the NCHE had become a Black feminist organization, demanding "pay, protection, and professionalism" and the end to economic "slavery."[58] Executive director Edith Barksdale-Sloan, who came from the US Commission on Civil Rights, cast the NCHE trajectory as a move from "employers (who wanted 'better' maids)" and a "program ... to train welfare mothers and make them economically independent" to a membership of domestics dedicated to "winning good wages and benefits, raising consciousness and educating consumers of domestic services."[59] Besides assisting local worker associations, the NCHE pushed for coverage of domestic work under the FLSA and for enforcement of labour laws, and fought against the worsening economic conditions of the 1970s. By 1974, the year that Congress included private domestic workers in the wage and hour law, local associations numbered thirty-seven, with 25,000 members.[60]

Domestic workers understood the connections between their labour and that of the women who hired them. As Josephine Hulett, an African-American worker from Ohio who became an organizer for the HTA, explained to the feminist audience of *Ms.* magazine in a 1973 interview: "There's a sense in which *all* women are household workers. And unless we stop being turned against each other, unless we organize together, we're never going to make this country see household work for what it really is – human work, not just 'woman's work.' "[61] A *New York Magazine* commentator saw the problem that organizers faced when noting that "every housewife is a potential scab, willing to moonlight at two jobs, if necessary."[62] This conjuncture of work led opponents of recognizing domestic workers under the FLSA to claim, as Richard Nixon's secretary of labor Peter Brennan testified before Congress, that "domestic service is in some aspects unique from other forms of employment. A householder who hires a maid typically has just so much budgeted for that purpose with no more available. She also has no opportunity to pass on any higher wage cost. It if comes down to it, the housewife can substitute her labor and that of other family members for the domestic. Few employers in other fields can do so."[63]

Professional and managerial women wanting equal pay and domestic workers seeking minimum wages supported each other for inclusion in the FLSA. Congress discussed the two together: the sending of the Equal Rights Amendment to the states for ratification encouraged Senator Harrison Williams (D–New Jersey), the main proponent of amending the FLSA, to call for rectifying the exclusion of domestic workers. He underscored the connection between the housewife and the servant:

> The lack of respect accorded domestics is in many ways an unfortunate reflection of the value we place on the traditional role of women in our society. The housewife's job has always been considered of secondary importance, even though it is the housewife who is entrusted with our most valuable resources and our most valuable material possession, our children and our home. In hiring a domestic, most employers expect her to accept many of the responsibilities of the homemaker, thereby creating a situation in which a dollar value is being placed on her everyday duties.[64]

Politicians of all sorts assumed that the domestic worker substituted for the labour of the married woman, whose responsibility was to manage the home. Even Michigan representative Martha Griffiths (D), a supporter of equal rights, reinforced the gender division of labour. She responded to Congressional opponents by insisting on the worth of household labour, exclaiming, "What the gentleman really is saying is what that woman does in a home is of no worth. I should like to differ with him. What she does in that home is a thing that makes life livable." New York's Bella Abzug also connected the low wages of the domestic worker to the unpaid labour of the housewife. Rejecting the assumption "that they're 'part of the family,'" she argued that "even if the 'lady of the house' works a 20-hour day for free, she should not expect her helper to do so. (This is one of the belated realizations that dawn on us women as the concept of our sisterhood grows.)"[65] In contrast, conservatives such as Arizona's Republican senator Peter Dominick envisioned recordkeeping to be such a burden that either a housewife would force her husband to undertake the task or insist on his sharing the housework, by-passing the services of a domestic worker all together and thus contributing to unemployment. But, as New York Democratic representative Shirley Chisholm, whose Barbadian immigrant mother was a domestic worker, mocked, "this may come as a shock to the Members of this House, but in most homes it is the wife who handles the family budget, and bookkeeping …To suggest that women do not know how to add and subtract is an insult."[66]

Activist domestic workers, such as HTA chair Geneva Reid, warned that without raising wages and improving conditions, the day would soon come with "the affluent and Congressmen cleaning up after themselves because the women of the household have become liberated and have joined the work force and will not have time to cook, clean, wash, iron, and take care of the children" and domestic workers would be no where to be found.[67] Her prediction proved only partially true: "the women of the household" went out to work, but, despite inclusion of most day workers into the wage and hours law, domestic workers remained underpaid, since enforcement was so difficult in the private home. One group of previously covered household labourers – home-care aides and attendants – were written out of the law in 1975, when the Department of Labor promulgated its interpretation of the new amendments: they were redefined as "elder companions," equivalent to the casual babysitter, and thus not subject to FLSA.[68]

Complaints over the inclusion of "babysitters" exposed the problem at the heart of wage and hour improvement for household workers. Take the testimony of a white manager of the Department of Labor, Training, and Employment Service from rural Georgia. He asked, "Why should a working mother be responsible for paying her maid $1.90 an hour when service workers, waitresses, cashiers, sales clerks, and yes charwomen for doctor's offices are not covered under this law?" Mothers who laboured in textile and garment factories, he claimed, had to let go their maids. Some service sector counterparts also suffered from low wages, and those in hospitality came under the lesser "tipped" wage. In his reckoning, the maids lacked the skills to replace their previous employers as factory operatives, once they were forced to stay home. Reflecting the racism of the period, this state manager told his Congressman: "The maids themselves ... are usually elderly, uneducated black females who have great difficulty in securing employment; most are also untrainable." Welfare was their only alternative, but the goal was to "break up" that system. He proposed that wages be "based on family income at least."[69]

If women could not afford a maid, however, there were other "equitable" solutions. Answered Barksdale-Sloan, women with child-care or cleaning needs could act cooperatively. They could take advantage of the already existing tax dedication for hiring a full-time babysitter. One didn't have to end the private family home, as economist John Kenneth Galbraith suggested, or use mechanized cleaning services to afford household workers. As Barksdale-Sloan argued, "the relatively marginal wage of one group of workers is not a sound or just reason to legally allow them to pay less than the minimum set by law to persons whom they employ in their homes."[70]

Not all household workers or their advocates saw a community of interests, however. As one organizer put it, "If you're tough enough to talk back to your big man on Sunday, don't tell me you're afraid of Miss

Suzy on Monday."[71] Detroit leader Mary McClendon recounted that, "when the prospective employer asks for a worker's references, 'I turn right around and ask her for her references. We want to talk to people who have worked for her. It's a two way street, you know, and it's long overdue."[72] Auburn, Alabama, activist Jessie Williams contended that anything less than treatment with dignity evoked slavery days. Workers demanded "respect." She announced, "We won't go in the back door anymore. We won't be told to eat scraps in the kitchen and stay out of the living room except when we are sweeping. We feel domestic work is just as professional as any other job." Then she warned: "If people go on making it degrading, there won't be any workers doing it much longer."[73] Barksdale-Sloan concurred. Addressing the first national convention of the NCHE in 1971, she had threatened, "Unless there are some changes made, 'Madame' is going to have to clean her own house and cook and serve her own meals, because everyone is going to quit."[74] Organizing domestic workers rejected being called by their first name. They objected to having their work dismissed as unskilled, and they demanded better pay. "The skills which a household worker employs are of no less value than any other skills, her time is of no less value and the energy she expends is of no less value than that of any other worker, be she a laborer or a professional," Barksdale-Sloan insisted. This assumption, that domestic work was like any other work or should be like all other work, lay behind calls for its inclusion in labour standards.[75]

A poor woman's movement could not sustain itself without foundation grants, but funding agencies were fickle. In 1977, NCHE became a project of the National Urban League.[76] There they became absorbed in a larger battle to improve the conditions of the service sector. Shifting occupational demographics made organizing by African-American civil rights groups more difficult. Though leery of competition from "illegal immigration," advocates did not "want to find ... black workers being pivoted against Mexican-Americans ... by *employers* who don't want to provide 'expensive' ways to get difficult jobs done." Instead they continued their call for upgrading the occupation, hoping to exclude the untrained immigrant rather than restrict all immigrants.[77] Ultimately, though, the expanding political conservatism and neoliberal economic order made any labour advances difficult.

Conclusion

By the twenty-first century, a shifting global economy had undermined the male breadwinner/female caregiver model of social reproduction.

Mothers from most classes remained in the labour force or returned as soon as they could. At the same time, they still were responsible for tending to the home and its inhabitants. A 2016 ILO-Gallup poll sampling men and women in 142 locations worldwide found that women desired employment, and men "agreed" with their labour force participation, yet women faced obstacles from an inability to undertake care while earning income. Lack of "work-family balance / access to care," what became known as the "care deficit," blocked the way to equality in the world of work. Drawing upon time-use surveys from sixty-seven nations, composing a majority of the world's population, the ILO calculated that women carried out over 75 per cent of unpaid care work, 3.2 times as much as men. Mothers of young children particularly suffered a care penalty.[78]

In this context, building a new care economy emerged as the solution to winning equality – a measure that some national organizations, like Caring across Generations in the United States, touted.[79] As the second decade of the twenty-first century was coming to a close, the ILO promoted improving the care-work economy, both to allow women to combine work and family and to upgrade the conditions of paid care work. Redistribution of care between men and women and between households and society appeared imperative to level the playing field. Care policies involved a mixture of direct provision of services; "care-relevant infrastructure"; labour regulations, like maternity protection and family leave; and social protection transfers and benefits, like tax rebates and cash for care.[80] Nonetheless, women turned to other women, often migrants, to take up the slack: either by entering their dwellings to cook, clean, and care, or by performing such labour in institutional or commercial spaces.

Household workers became a social force. Yet, as they sought inclusion in laws, becoming the new face of labour, the very labour standards regime of collective bargaining and the employment contract – guarantees of minimum wages, maximum hours, occupational safety, and benefits – has unravelled. The historical circumstances of their labour – part-time, low-paid, insecure, and subject to personalism and arbitrariness – looks less like the past and more like the future for workers denied employee status throughout the economy. Their tactics and strategies, nonetheless, offer an alternative vision of interdependency, of "caring across generations," that envisions a different basis to organize not just liv'in, but living: that is, they would place social reproduction at the centre of social life, valuing the woman who cares as well as those for whom she cares.

NOTES

1 US Women's Bureau, "Labor Force Participation Rate of Mothers by Age of Youngest Child, March 1976–2012," accessed 7 July 2018, https://www .dol.gov/wb/stats/facts_over_time.htm.

2 Kim Parker and Wendy Want, "Americans' Time at Paid Work, Housework, Child Care, 1965 to 2011," *Modern Parenthood*, 14 March 2013, Pew Research Center, accessed 7 July 2018, http://www.pewsocialtrends .org/2013/03/14/chapter-5-americans-time-at-paid-work-housework -child-care-1965-to-2011/.

3 Leopoldina Fortunati, *The Arcane of Reproduction: Housework, Prostitution, Labor and Capital* (Brooklyn: Autonomedia, 1989); Evelyn Nakano Glenn, "From Servitude to Service Work: Historical Continuities in the Racial Division of Paid Reproductive Labor," *Signs* 18 (Autumn 1992): 1–43; Silvia Federici, *Revolution at Point Zero: Housework, Reproduction, and Feminist Struggle* (Oakland, CA: PM Press, 2012).

4 Evelyn Nakano Glenn, *Forced to Care: Coercion and Caregiving in America* (Cambridge, MA: Harvard University Press, 2010).

5 Lewis Coser, "Servants: The Obsolescence of an Occupation Role," *Social Forces* 52 (1973): 31–40.

6 Susan Strasser, *Never Done: A History of American Housework* (New York: Holt, 2000); Ruth Schwartz Cowan, *More Work for Mother: The Ironies of Household Technology from the Open Hearth to the Microwave*, 2nd ed. (New York: Basic Books, 1985).

7 Rhacel Salazar Parreñas, "Migrant Filipina Domestic Workers and the International Division of Reproductive Labor," *Gender and Society* 14, no. 4 (August 2000): 560–80; see also Pierrette Hondagneu-Sotelo and Ernestine Avila, "'I'm Here, But I'm There': The Meanings of Latina Transnational Motherhood," *Gender and Society* 11, no. 5 (October 1997): 548–71.

8 Of course, where in the United States influenced who and how many. Heidi Shierholz, "Low Wages and Scant Benefits Leave Many In-Home Workers Unable to Make Ends Meet," Briefing Paper 369, Economic Policy Institute, 26 November 2013, accessed 7 July 2018, http://www.epi.org /publication/in-home-workers/.

9 Moni Basu, "The Invisible World of Domestic Work: Report Documents Abuses," CNN, 17 November 2012, accessed 7 July 2018, http://inamerica .blogs.cnn.com/2012/11/27/the-invisible-world-of-domestic-work-report -documents-abuses/.

10 International Labour Organization, "Decent Work for Domestic Workers: Achievements since the Adoption of C189," accessed 7 July 2018,

http://www.ilo.org/wcmsp5/groups/public/---ed_protect/---protrav
/---travail/documents/briefingnote/wcms_490778.pdf.

11 See also Bethany Moreton, *To Serve God and Wal-Mart* (Cambridge, MA: Harvard University Press, 2010) and Tracey Neumann, *Remaking the Rust Belt: The Postindustrial Transformation of North America* (Philadelphia: University of Pennsylvania Press, 2016).

12 Myra MacPherson, "She Hired a Housekeeper and Cried Over Boiled Steak," *Washington Post*, 11 January 1970.

13 Tom Crane, "Illegal Traffic in Imported Domestic Help under Scrutiny," *Washington Post*, 25 April 1968.

14 Diana Shaman, "A Wrinkle in Housework: Wives on Job, Help Scarce – A Premium on Help around the House," *New York Times*, 30 October 1977; Lisa Levenstein, "'Don't Agonize, Organize!' The Displaced Homemakers Campaign and the Contested Goal of Postwar Feminism," *Journal of American History* 100, no. 4 (March 2014): 1117.

15 George Guilder, "Women in the Work Force," *Atlantic,* September 1986, accessed 7 July 2018, https://www.theatlantic.com/magazine/archive/1986/09/women-in-the-work-force/304924/; Sarah Kuhn and Barry Bluestone, "Economic Restructuring and the Female Labor Market: The Impact of Industrial Change on Women," in *Women, Households, and the Economy*, ed. Lourdes Benería and Catherine Stimpson (New Brunswick, NJ: Rutgers University Press, 1987), 9.

16 Georgia Dullea, "Vast Changes in Society Traced to the Rise of Working Women," *New York Times*, 29 November 1977.

17 Kirsten Swinth, *Having It All: Feminist Struggles for Work and Family, 1963–1978* (Cambridge, MA: Harvard University Press, 2018).

18 Deborah Dinner, "The Universal Childcare Debate: Rights Mobilization, Social Policy, and the Dynamics of Feminist Activism, 1966–1974," *Law and History Review* 28, no. 3 (2010): 577–628; Arlie Russell Hochschild, *The Time Bind: When Work Becomes Home and Home Becomes Work* (New York: Metropolitan Books, 1997).

19 Quoted in Swinth, *Having It All*, 125.

20 Silvia Federici, *Wages against Housework* (Bristol: Falling Wall Press, 1975); for documents from the time, see Silvia Federici and Arlen Austin, eds., *Wages for Housework: The New York Committee 1972–1977. History, Theory, Documents* (Brooklyn: Autonomedia, 2017).

21 "NOW's Homemaker's Bill of Fights," reprinted in Amber E. Kinser, *Motherhood and Feminism* (Berkeley: Seal Press, 2010), 82–3; see also, 80–1.

22 Keith Love, "Do You Put a Price Tag on a Housewife's Work?" *New York Times*, 13 January 1976.

23 Levenstein, "'Don't Agonize,'" 1125.

24 Lisa Levenstein, *A Movement without Marches: African American Women and the Politics of Poverty in Postwar Philadelphia* (Chapel Hill: University of North Carolina Press, 2009); Marissa Chappell, *The War on Welfare: Family, Poverty, and Politics in Modern America* (Philadelphia: University of Pennsylvania Press, 2009).

25 Pat Mainardi, "The Politics of Housework," 1970, The Feminist eZine, accessed 1 July 2018, http://www.feministezine.com/feminist/modern/The-Politics-of-Housework.html.

26 Robert Reinhold, "The Trend toward Sexual Equality: Depth of Transformation Uncertain," *New York Times*, 30 November 1977.

27 Susan Edmiston, "While We're at It, What about Maids' Lib?" *New York Magazine*, 28 June 1971, 24, 26.

28 "Domestics Uniting for More Pay – And Respect," *New York Times*, 18 July 1971.

29 Peter Millones, "Government Easing Entry of Foreign Domestics," *New York Times*, 2 December 1969.

30 Papers of the National Committee on Household Employment, National Archives for Black Women's History, Washington, DC (hereafter NCHE papers): S5, B1, Newsletters file, Mrs. Edith B. Sloan, "Keynote Address," *NCHE News* 2, no. 7 (July 1971); S1, B6, Fact Sheet, 1976 file, NCHE, "Facts about Private Household Employment"; S5, B1, Brochures file, NCHE, *A Profile of Household Workers in the U.S.A.*, c. 1965. See also Premilla Nadasen, *Welfare Warriors: The Welfare Rights Movement in the United States* (New York: Routledge, 2005), 157–86.

31 "More Can Afford Domestic Help ... Fewer Can Afford to Do It," *New York Times*, 23 March 1971.

32 "US Unemployment Rate by Year," accessed 7 July 2018, http://www.multpl.com/unemployment/table.

33 Shaman, "A Wrinkle in Housework."

34 Grace Chang, *Disposable Domestics: Immigrant Women Workers in the Global Economy* (Boston: South End Press, 2000); Pierrette Hondagneu-Sotelo, *Doméstica: Immigrant Workers Cleaning and Caring in the Shadows of Affluence* (Berkeley: University of California Press, 2001).

35 Martha Gardner, *The Qualities of a Citizen: Women, Immigration, and Citizenship, 1870–1965* (Princeton, NJ: Princeton University Press, 2005), 103–6.

36 Ibid., 212–14, 216.

37 Paul Delaney, "Live-In Maids Face Tighter Visa Rules on Entering United States," *New York Times*, 3 November 1969.

38 Crane, "Illegal Traffic."

39 Delaney, "Live-In Maids."

40 Millones, "Government Easing Entry"; for portraits of potential employers complaining about the shortage, see MacPherson, "She Hired a Housekeeper"; MacPherson, "Quotas Restrict Immigrant 'Help,'" *Washington Post*, 12 January 1970.

41 Crane, "Illegal Traffic."

42 Richard L. Ottinger, remarks, "Labor Department Approval of Alien Domestics," 12 December 1969, "Extensions of Remarks," *Congressional Record*, 91st Congress, First Session, House Proceedings, vol. 115, pt. 29 (1969): 38984–5.

43 Millones, "Government Easing Entry"; "Labor Department Approval."

44 Linda Bird Francke, "Hers," *New York Times*, 3 November 1977.

45 Anne Marie Slaughter, *Unfinished Business: Women, Men, Work, Family* (New York: Random House, 2012).

46 Ellen Frankfort, "Letters: Service and Disservice," *New York Times*, 10 November 1977.

47 Sonya Michel, *Children's Interests / Mother's Rights: The Shaping of America's Child Care Policy* (New Haven, CT: Yale University Press, 1999); Ellen Reese, *Backlash against Welfare Mothers: Past and Present* (Berkeley: University of California Press, 2005).

48 "Different Commuters," *New York Times*, 15 February 1976.

49 Betty Vereen, "Maids Suffering from Cutback Seek State Welfare Payments," *Alabama Journal* (Montgomery), 21 May 1974.

50 Premilla Nadasen, *Household Workers Unite! The Untold Story of African American Women Who Built a Movement* (Boston: Beacon Press, 2015).

51 Vivien Hart, *Bound by Our Constitution: Women, Workers, and the Minimum Wage* (Princeton, NJ: Princeton University Press, 1994), 166.

52 On the reluctance of the Committee on Economic Security to include domestics, speculating on how their support for professional women impacted on this position, see Mary Poole, *Segregated Origins of Social Security: African Americans and the Welfare State* (Chapel Hill: University of North Carolina Press, 2006), 35–8, 90–6; Phyllis Palmer, *Domesticity and Dirt: Housewives and Domestic Servants in the United States, 1920–1945* (Philadelphia: Temple University Press, 1989), 118–35.

53 "Extension of Old-Age and Survivors Insurance to Additional Groups of Current Workers," Report of the Consultant Group, in US Congress, House of Representatives, Committee on Ways and Means, *Hearings before the Committee on Ways and Means on H.R. 7199, Social Security Amendments of 1954*, 83rd Congress, 2nd sess. (Washington, DC: GPO, 1954), 865.

54 "More Can Afford Domestic Help"; "Employment: Farewell to Dinah," *Newsweek*, 2 August 1971.

55 "Domestics Uniting for More Pay."

56 Speech of Elizabeth Koontz before Project SURGE, NCHE papers, S1, B12, NYCCHR 1971 file; Esther Peterson to Muriel Lockhart, 6 October 1966, NCHE papers, S1, B15, State Activities, California 1967 May–June file. See also Dorothy Sue Cobble, *The Other Women's Movement: Workplace Justice and Social Rights in Modern America* (Princeton, NJ: Princeton University Press, 2004), 198–200; Phyllis Palmer, "Housework and Domestic Labor: Racial and Technological Change," in *My Troubles Are Going to Have Trouble with Me: Everyday Trials and Triumphs of Women Workers*, ed. Karen Brodkin Sacks and Dorothy Remy (New Brunswick, NJ: Rutgers University Press, 1984), 86–7.

57 NCHE, *A Code of Standards*, NCHE papers, S1 B5, Brochures file.

58 "Pay! Protection, Professionalism: The 3 P's of Household Work," NCHE papers, S1, B8, Houseworkers Organizations, 1971–1972 file.

59 HTA decided to have Chicano and Native American members on its board of directors and discussed "strategies on how to contact White, Indian and Chicano household workers." NCHE papers: Edith Barksdale-Sloan, comments, "Planning Meeting, Coalition of Feminist Funding," NOW LDEF, 28 and 29 June 1974, 4, S1 B5, Correspondence July 1974 file; Sloan to NOW president Wilma Scott Heide, 1 March 1973, S1 B4, Correspondence 1973 January–April file; Minutes, Board of Directors Meeting, Household Technicians of America, 12 April 1972, 1, S1 B8, HTA 1971–1974 file; Resume Edith Barksdale-Sloan, S1 B15, 1974 Vita file. On NWRO, see Nadasen, *Welfare Warriors*, and Felicia Kornbluh, *The Battle for Welfare Rights: Politics and Poverty in Modern America* (Philadelphia: University of Pennsylvania Press, 2007).

60 Sloan, "Planning Meeting, Coalition of Feminist Funding"; "Domestics at Session Ask Gains," *New York Times*, 10 October 1972, 47.

61 Cited in Nadasen, *Household Workers Unite!*, 139.

62 Edmiston, "While We're at It," 30.

63 *Legislative History of the Fair Labor Standards Amendments of 1974*, 94th Congress, 2nd sess., Prepared by the Subcommittee on Labor of the Committee on Labor and Public Welfare, United States Senate, August 1976, vol. 2 (Washington, DC: GPO, 1976), 1814.

64 Senator Williams, *Legislative History of the Fair Labor Standards Amendments of 1974* (1818).

65 Martha Griffiths, *Congressional Record* (House), 6 June 1973, FLSA Amendments of 1973 (Washington, DC: GPO, 1973), 282; Bella Abzug, Hearings before the General Subcommittee on Labor of the Committee on Education and Labor, House of Representatives, *Fair Labor Standards Amendments of 1973*, 93rd Congress, 1st sess. (Washington, DC: GPO, 1973), 86–7.

66 Dominick, in *Legislative History of the Fair Labor Standards Amendments of 1974*, 1717; Chisholm, *Congressional Record* (House), 5 June 1973, 279.

67 Reid testimony, Hearings before the General Subcommittee on Labor of the Committee on Education and Labor, House of Representatives, *Fair Labor Standards Amendments of 1973*, 93rd Congress, 1st sess. (Washington, DC: GPO, 1973), 205–6.

68 I have extensively discussed this in Eileen Boris and Jennifer Klein, *Caring for America: Home Health Workers in the Shadow of the Welfare State* (New York: Oxford University Press, 2012).

69 Letter from Sidney D. Dell to Hon. Dawson Mathis, 7 June 1974, on H.R. 15200, in "Extension of Remarks," *Congressional Record* (House), 12 June 1974, E3812–13.

70 Edith Barksdale-Sloan to Sidney D. Dell, 19 June 1974, NCHE papers, S1, B11, Minimum Wage 1974 March–June file; Edmiston, "While We're at It," 30.

71 "Domestics Uniting for More Pay."

72 Jeannette Smyth, "Union Maid: A Two-Way Street," *Washington Post*, 17 July 1971.

73 Philip Shabecoff, "Domestics, a Minimum Wage Is a Raise," *New York Times*, 6 June 1973.

74 "Domestics Uniting for More Pay."

75 Barksdale-Sloan to Dell, 19 June 1974.

76 Ernest Holsendolph, "Social Action Hit by Financial Foes," *New York Times*, 8 November 1974, 20; Press release, "Practical Workers' Congress: Strategies for Greater Opportunity and Respect," 20 October 1977, 2, NCHE papers, S1, B3, 5th NCHW Conference 1977 file; Strategies *NCHE News* 11 (July 1979), 1, NCHE papers, S5, B1, Newsletters, 1969–1979 file.

77 "NCHE Reviews Carter Proposals on Illegal Immigration," *NCHE News* 8 (Fall 1977), 3–4.

78 International Labour Organization, The Women at Work Initiative, accessed 7 July 2018, http://www.ilo.org/global/about-the-ilo/history /centenary/WCMS_480301/lang--en/index.htm; see also "Millions of Women Worldwide Would Like to Join the Workforce," 8 March 2017, accessed 5 July 2018, https://news.gallup.com/poll/205439/millions -women-worldwide-join-workforce.aspx.

79 See the Caring across Generations website, at https://caringacross.org/, accessed 25 June 2018.

80 International Labour Organization, *Care Work and Care Jobs for the Future of Work* (Geneva: ILO, 2018).

SECTION TWO

Adaptations

4 The Clandestine Crisis: Migrant Labour in an Age of Deindustrialization

MICHAEL KOZAKOWSKI

Migrants in France and elsewhere in northwestern Europe made invaluable contributions to the post–Second World War "economic miracle" (in French, *Trente Glorieuses* – thirty glorious years). Approximately two-fifths of the growth in France's labour force between 1946 and 1975 was due to migration.[1] By increasing the size of the workforce, providing flexibility in working conditions, demonstrating willingness to move to where the work was, and accepting often modest pay, migrants expanded production while keeping prices low.[2] Even more important than their gross contribution to the economy were specific contributions migrants made in this industrial "golden age," when the fruits of industry and innovation became accessible to the masses. The largest sectors of male migrant employment in France – manufacturing, construction, and public works – were precisely those that brought modern goods like automobiles, refrigerators, and apartments with central heat to the masses, changing modern lifestyles. By 1973, as one union official acknowledged, migrants built 5 out of 10 cars, 9 out of 10 kilometres of highway, 5 out of 10 apartments, and 1 out of 7 machines.[3] Another contemporary in 1974 estimated that 80 per cent of construction workers in the greater Paris region were migrants.[4] Migrants figuratively and literally transformed the landscape of French life. They also played a pivotal role in the economies of their "home countries," like Spain, Italy, Algeria, Turkey, and Morocco. The "safety valve" theory may overstate the effect of emigration on unemployment. However, emigrants had a demonstrable effect on underemployment and were openly and rightly acknowledged as supporting struggling regions and helping balance the trade deficit through remittances and social security payments made on their behalf.[5] Finally, they were also imagined as transferring vocational and professional skills, acquired in France, that were needed for development "back home."[6]

Yet if migrants fostered industrial growth during the postwar boom, they would also bear the burden of the protracted economic downturn and transformation away from an industrial-based economy in the 1970s. It was precisely the industries that employed the most male migrants, such as construction and manufacturing, that were hit the hardest by rising inflation and interest rates, increasing automation, and (for manufacturing) greater foreign competition, hurting both employment and wages. As this chapter shows in the case of France, within these industries, migrants were often the first to be laid off or become seemingly trapped in low-wage posts. Concomitant with these processes, migrants faced a legal crisis as policymakers in multiple countries took advantage of the first oil crisis of 1973–4 to declare moratoriums on labour migration. These were in fact only part of a broader effort to restrict opportunities for migrants' legal employment. However, the result was that migrants, who already faced challenges in enjoying the fruits of their labour – frequently working long hours for modest pay and literally living on the margins of the industrial cities they helped build – had to contend with what I argue was a "dual crisis," in which legal and economic challenges were intertwined.[7]

Many histories of French migration take the 1970s as a beginning or end of an era.[8] Several commendable works tackle the causes of the change in migratory policy or the growing politicization of migration in the 1970s.[9] However, few examine in depth the effects of the 1970s on migrant labour in France.[10] While migrants were far more than just workers, as Max Frisch famously pointed out, most migrants in France in the early 1970s worked, regardless of their motivations for migrating.[11] Thus, particularly in an era of increasing insecurity and renewed links between work and residency status, understanding what jobs were available to migrants and how migrants navigated the job market is of crucial importance. Moreover, a study of migrant labour reveals the broader crisis – or more accurately, increasingly visible crisis – in wage labour and "Fordist" norms across all economic sectors and groups of workers during the transformations of the "1970s."

This chapter argues that the "1970s" – a period bookmarked in France by the protests of 1968 and oil crisis in 1973, on the front end, and Mitterrand's switch of economic policies in 1983 and beginnings of economic recovery around 1985, on the back – ought to be understood as a "dual crisis" for migrants. As I will demonstrate in the first section, legal and economic challenges operated dynamically and compounded the effects of one another for migrants. While the policy part of this story is increasingly known, I have compiled and analysed a macroeconomic database to understand the effects of this dual crisis on migrant jobs. In the subsequent two sections, I use this database to analyse how migrants responded to economic challenges, both through older strategies of "return migration" – innovatively (if ineffectively) incentivized by new policy responses – as well as through newer strategies to find jobs in one of the few areas of economic growth: the service sector. I show that political and economic developments facilitated return migration as a successful strategy primarily for "European" migrants and not always in accord with the wishes of government officials. At the same time, a confluence of factors – including the specifics of France's political economy – made for a particularly difficult transition to the service sector. The final section argues that the ongoing challenges of migrants to secure stable, well-remunerated, and recognized work – more apparent than new during the 1970s – should temper analyses of a radical break in the 1970s, as well as celebrations of the supposed glories of the "boom years."

The Dual Crisis

The postwar economic boom in France came to a screeching halt in 1974, as the effects of the first oil crisis, which began the preceding autumn, began to ripple throughout the economy. The combination of rising inflation, rising unemployment, and slowing output began to compound the stresses already present, and in retrospect visible, in the late 1960s. To understand the effects of the crisis on the migrant labour market during the "1970s," it is necessary to turn to the few – and, to my knowledge, hitherto underused – sources of labour statistics in France: the annual tabulations of overall migrant employment and the more detailed, but less frequent, census data. By building a dataset from the 1968, 1975, and 1982 census results, based on a sampling of one-twentieth of the population, it is possible to compare levels of foreign employment over time by sector, industry, nationality, and gender.[12] The underlying data have some important limitations. For example, they are reliant on respondent self-reporting, likely undercounting the informal labour market and migrants in irregular migratory situations. They do not distinguish between naturalized migrants and those born as French citizens, and do not distinguish between those migrants who found new jobs and those who were new entrants in the labour market. Nevertheless, the resulting dataset is based on large numbers, provides a reasonably representative national sample, employs relatively constant methodology, and allows for observation of detailed trends over time. As such, it is far more extensive and comprehensive than the quantitative micro-studies available and complements qualitative accounts, helping both to contextualize these smaller studies and enable original analysis. Unless otherwise noted, the statistics in this chapter come from this dataset.

One of the first and most important results of the crisis – seemingly simple in its effect but brutal in its consequences – was a precipitous drop in the number of formal jobs held by foreigners. Overall, in 1982, there were 160,000 fewer formal jobs held by foreign nationals than in the previous census in 1975 – an 11 per cent drop – despite a net gain of over half-a-million formal jobs in the French economy during this time. Much of the drop occurred precipitously, between October 1973 and October 1976.[13] In the secondary sector in particular, which had been the greatest source of formal foreign employment at the start of the economic crisis, a quarter of all formal jobs held by foreigners were lost.

Migrants in industry and the secondary sector not only suffered as part of broader processes of "deindustrialization," they disproportionately bore the brunt of these processes in comparison to their French colleagues. The net drop in foreign employment in the secondary sector was equivalent to one in three job losses in this sector between 1975 and 1982, even though foreigners had occupied only one in eight jobs. In the automotive industry, the drop in foreign employment was equivalent to two-thirds of overall automotive job losses. The construction sector, the largest sector of migrant employment, shed 135,000 jobs – of which over 100,000 were jobs held by foreigners. In fact, in nine out of the top ten branches in which foreigners were employed in the secondary sector in France, the proportion of job losses by foreigners exceeded what would be expected, based on the percentage of jobs they previously held in that branch.

A direct result of this drastic loss of jobs was a sharp increase in migrant unemployment. The number of unemployed foreigners tripled in the seven years between 1975 and 1982, with the foreign unemployment rate hitting 14 per cent in the latter year, in contrast to 8.4 per cent among the French. Yet these figures masked high variation. The unemployed were more likely to be Algerian (22 per cent of Algerians were unemployed), the young, those who had never held a job before, or women, who accounted for one in three unemployed foreigners, although they held only one in five jobs. (The unemployment rate for foreign women soared to 20 per cent, compared to 12 per cent for foreign men.) In contrast, the Portuguese unemployment rate was slightly lower than the French rate.[14] All this is to say that unemployment struck hardest those migrants groups that were already most socially marginalized.

These challenges were compounded by the new legal environment, in which political and economic challenges interacted dynamically to the detriment of migrants. For example, on 3 July 1974, the recently appointed French secretary of state for immigrant workers, André Postel-Vinay, used the oil crisis to persuade his counterparts in the Council of Ministers to impose a moratorium on migration. The moratorium included a halt in the recruitment of migrant workers, a pause in the introduction of their family members (overturned in 1975 by the Constitutional Council), and severe restrictions on the regularization of migrants already in the country. Following the government's official line, the media framed the decision as dictated by the economic situation and risk of unemployment, protecting the French labour market while providing a "pause" that would enable officials to address supposed problems in migrant integration and housing, especially shantytowns (*bidonvilles*).[15] In contrast, the emerging scholarly consensus is that economic reasons were only one of several factors in a process of bureaucratic restrictions already underway since 1968. These efforts to "tame" migration – particularly directed at inadequate migrant housing, irregular means of entry, unskilled labour, and non-European workers – reflected the scepticism of immigration "experts" in the bureaucracy about North African migrants, concerns about unemployment among unskilled workers in an increasingly skill-based economy, and the desire to assert their bureaucratic competence.[16]

While the moratorium was only partially a result of the economic situation, it nonetheless had severe consequences for migrants' employment opportunities. Ostensibly a temporary measure, the decisions taken in July 1974 set the tone for French migration policy for the rest of the decade. For example, the National Immigration Office (ONI) had legally recognized an average of 140,000 new foreign workers (not on seasonal or temporary permits) each year in the period 1969–73. In 1974, this number fell to approximately half, before falling to an average of 22,000 per annum for the rest of the decade.[17] While neither European Economic Community (EEC) nationals nor Algerians were counted in these totals, migration of the former had already slowed substantially by the 1970s, as the Federal Republic of Germany became the primary European destination for Italian migration, while Algerian migrants faced a domestic moratorium on migration, imposed by President Boumédiène in 1973. In other words, migration to France did not stop, but was less frequent and less frequently legal. What migration was legally recognized tended to fall into the categories of seasonal workers, family members, and asylum seekers. However, these newly prominent legal categories often came with restrictions on legal employment (or, in the case of seasonal workers, long-term employment). Other migrants, already legally in the country, found it difficult to renew residence and/or work permits, particularly if unemployed – a situation increasingly common in the midst of economic crisis.[18]

Thus, the moratoriums should be seen less as a stop in migration and more as a shift in its characteristics and, particularly, an increase of barriers to *legal employment*. While work and residence permits were increasingly hard to come by, travel and entry into France by would-be migrants (either as tourists or by virtue of post-colonial settlements) was harder to stop. In other words, de facto migration continued, and migrants present in the country remained. (They may, in fact, have been more reluctant to leave, for fear of being frozen out of the country if they left.) Yet few new migrants could have their work legally recognized. This stood in sharp relief to the 1960s and, to a lesser extent, the 1950s. While the ONI had elaborate procedures for screening and placing migrants, most Spaniards and later Portuguese in the 1960s entered the country as "tourists," found a position, and then regularized their status. This method of migration was so common that, by 1968, 82 per cent of non-Algerian foreign workers who gained first-time work permits did so through the process of regularization.[19] (For their part, Algerians were legally exempt from most controls on movement and employment except during the Algerian War of Independence, by virtue either of their status as French citizens before 1962, or of the Evian Accords at the time of independence.)[20] Thus, irregular migration was not new; it had long been an integral, even encouraged, part of postwar French migration.[21] What was new was the inability for most migrants to regularize their status, thus freezing many migrants in a state of legal limbo and exclusion from formal labour markets.

As both new and existing migrants often found themselves increasingly frozen out of opportunities for legal employment and increasingly at risk of deportation or other sanctions, their "clandestinity" severely restricted the types of jobs they held, their ability to switch jobs, and their ability to improve wages or conditions on the job. Furthermore, because social security provisions, such as child allowances, were such a large component of the average worker's total compensation,[22] not to mention her or his sustenance in time of disability or unemployment, the increase in long-term irregular employment meant that the compensation and fates of many migrants diverged sharply from those of other workers. Thus, the moratorium, adopted in the name of addressing economic security and improving migrants' living conditions, in fact made the lives of many migrants more precarious.[23]

Old Strategies and New Policies of Return

In response to this dual economic and legal crisis, many migrants looked to time-honoured strategies: so-called onward and return migration. Migrant unemployment in France was increasing rapidly, providing ammunition for those who wanted a more aggressive policy of slowing (legal) migration and encouraging (or forcing) returns, the failures of which produced an even greater sense of "crisis." For migrants themselves, the linkage between employment status and the renewal of one's documentation meant that the increasingly unfavourable legal environment was intertwined with an increasingly harsh economic environment. Because many other governments, like that of the Federal Republic of Germany, imposed moratoriums of their own on migration, opportunities for onward migration to other countries were limited. Because the global nature of the downturn meant that job prospects were similarly gloomy across the Mediterranean basin, whence most migrants came, the majority chose to remain in France. However, thousands of migrants took their chances by returning to their country of origin, though often resettling in different cities or regions than one's origin, thus blurring the lines between "onward" and "return" migration.

The willingness of migrants to take their chances by "returning home" varied greatly by gender, age, and nationality. The number of foreign men in their twenties and early thirties legally registered in France dropped remarkably, as young men left the country and were not replaced by new arrivals. Some left as previously planned, while others left due to the new legal and economic challenges. It is possible that part of this drop was due to the increasing difficulty of legally registering in France. However, the increase in number of women registered in these age groups, as well as of men of most other ages, suggests that young working men – those least likely to have families or whose families were in their countries of origin – disproportionately favoured return migration as a strategy for dealing with the crisis, accelerating what was already a high turnover rate in this demographic.

Despite economic challenges across the region, other migrants may have been more likely to pursue strategies of return when the relative advantage or disadvantage of staying or leaving was narrow. For example, the number of Spanish nationals living in France fell by nearly half between 1968 and 1982, as departures accelerated and new arrivals fell sharply. Spanish workers lost the highest percentage of net, formal jobs in the secondary sector, as well as across all sectors. However, such job losses reflected not just a deterioration of legal and economic conditions in France, but new economic and political opportunities in Spain. Spanish industry, including in its Catalan and Basque strongholds, went through a profound crisis in the late 1970s and 80s. However, the boom of the 1960s and the death of Franco in 1975, followed by a rapid democratic transition, created a sense of optimism and progress that offset what appeared, at first, to be temporary economic headwinds. Furthermore, the shift to a consumer society and an expansion of easy credit (the rapid expansion of which was particularly remarkable in Spain) reduced the incentive to migrate in order to save.[24]

Italian migrants also "returned" in large numbers during the crisis, with high job losses and large numbers of departures, though new arrivals had already slowed to a trickle before the economic crisis. The combination of long-term economic convergence between Italy, Spain, and France, as well as a loss of employment opportunities in France due to the crisis, considerably dampened the advantages of Italians and Spaniards of staying in France.[25] In contrast, the Portuguese community in France, which had experienced a later boom in the second-half of the 1960s and first-half of the 1970s, and was experiencing a democratic renaissance of its own, remained effectively constant in size. The number of formal jobs held by Portuguese in France remained relatively constant during the economic crisis, as many migrants continued pursuing strategies of circular migration, observed in high levels of turnover in terms of jobs and migratory movements.

In contrast, return migration was a riskier strategy for the North African community in France and was less frequently undertaken. This was likely due to a combination of factors, including fewer alternative economic opportunities in the Maghreb, as a population boom and rising numbers of participants in the workforce offset many of the advantages of economic growth, as well as fear that, were migrants to leave France, they might not be able to come back. Algerian migrants suffered the highest absolute number of net job losses, which would likely have been even higher were it not for the continuing growth of the Algerian population in France. The net result of this was not, as French officials hoped, a significant increase in departures, but rather a significant increase in unemployment, as previously noted. The Moroccan and Tunisian migrant communities, though their origins can be traced to the period around the First World War, were relatively small in comparison to their Algerian counterparts until the late 1960s, before increasing five- and three-fold, respectively, between 1968 and 1982. Because of the relatively small number of existing, formal jobs in the secondary sector they held at the start of the crisis (in comparison to the other major migratory groups), and because of the high numbers of new migrants, the result tended to be both access to new jobs as they opened and, particularly, booming unemployment and underemployment. To provide one illustration, the Moroccan population in France increased by over 180,000 between 1975 and 1982[26] but gained only 780 net, formal jobs in that period.

Given the reluctance of many migrants to leave France, and the rising unemployment of those who remained, successive French governments increased the pressure on migrants to return to their countries of origin through various policies. While "return" had been less of an explicit norm than in the Federal Republic of Germany, where migrants were referred to as "guest workers" (Gastarbeiter), it was widely hoped in France that only those migrants who were culturally or genetically most assimilable would become French citizens (possible after three years of legal residence). Others, it was hoped, would come to France to fill temporary needs in the labour market and would depart when they had fulfilled their own financial goals or were no longer "needed" in France.[27] In the end, however, the French government had limited ability to expel residents. Despite an increase in media coverage and migrant protests around the topic, most migrants who lived and/ or worked irregularly in France were not deported. As in the 1930s, the Interior Ministry found it far easier to deny someone a residence or work permit than to ensure that they left the country and did not return.[28]

In 1977, as it was clear that unemployment in both the migrant and overall populations was increasing, the Barre government began to introduce cash incentives for migrants to leave. When cash payouts were first introduced, the measures were strictly voluntary and open to foreigners registered as job-seekers or receiving unemployment benefits. In exchange for surrendering their residency permits and renouncing their rights to future social assistance (e.g., welfare and retirement pensions), migrants would receive a one-time payoff. When the desired exodus failed to materialize, despite a loosening of restrictions, the government enacted the so-called Stoléru Law in 1978 to make departures mandatory and set a target of half a million forced "repatriations" in five years. EEC nationals, Spaniards, and Portuguese were to be spared, leaving Algerians and, to a lesser extent, Moroccans and Tunisians the primary targets of these measure. Ultimately, the numbers of migrants who were repatriated – voluntarily or otherwise – fell far short of government targets, most came from the Iberian Peninsula, and many, according to the critics, simply received compensation for a return they would otherwise have made by choice or as a result of the lack of employment opportunities.[29] Likewise, the Bonnet Law of 1980, which significantly increased the risk of deportation, was abrogated the following year after Mitterrand came to power, thus having limited effect. In short, policy innovation did not result in lasting or desired change, and the failures of successive voluntary and mandatory repatriation schemes revealed the limits of the French government's ability to significantly change the numbers of foreigners in the overall labour market (as opposed to the number of formally employed foreigners).

More innovative – and arguably even less successful – were bilateral efforts to find jobs for returning migrants. Return migration – voluntary or otherwise – threatened to exacerbate problems in the labour markets of their countries of origin. As one member of the Spanish Institute of Emigration (IEE) complained, returns of migrants were normal, but when promoted by foreign governments during a recession, they represented a transfer of unemployment from one country to another.[30] For migrants who chose or were forced to "return," finding gainful employment could prove challenging, in no small part because the economic downturn and long-term shifts in sectors of economic activity were global phenomena. Furthermore, despite expectations that returning migrants would bring back valuable skills and professional experience, job openings rarely matched migrants' qualifications.[31]

Therefore, the French Ministry of Labour, working with the semipublic Association for Adult Vocational Training (AFPA), foreign governments, and a host of associations and businesses, developed and expanded a fairly new type of vocational training program, known as "training to return" (*formation-retour*). Whereas vocational training had traditionally been a tool used by the Ministry of Labour to promote migrant integration *into* the French labour market, training to return was aimed at assisting migrants to find jobs in their countries of origin as they *left* the French labour market. It had been one area of Franco-Algerian cooperation since 1962 but tended to be operated on a small-scale, often under the umbrella of other development aid projects. In 1974, the concept of training to return was institutionalized as French governmental policy in the 25 Point Program and was considered a potential policy for aiding the French labour market, as well as the Algerian. That same year, even as recriminations flew in other matters concerning Algerian migration, the AFPA and the Algerian National Office of the Labour Force (ONAMO) increased bilateral cooperation programs in the area of training to return. For its part, the EEC attempted to facilitate such "reinsertion" in the workforce through European Social Fund allocations and the efforts of the European Centre for the Development of

Vocational Training (CEDEFOP), founded in 1975. Again, however, the results of such training to return and reinsertion programs, both at the European and bilateral levels, were meagre, due in part to the price tag of such efforts, and in part to underlying structural challenges in the labour markets.[32] Despite these challenges, in France – as in the Federal Republic of Germany, as shown in Franziska Rehlinghaus's chapter in this volume – retraining and further training would continue to attract interest and funding as an attempt to help workers navigate a changing labour market.

The Fraught Transition to a Service-Based Economy

Because most migrants stayed in France, even as the secondary sector shed jobs and unemployment soared, many pursued new opportunities in the service sector. While employment in the primary sector continued its long-term decline and increasing reliance on temporary and informal labour, and the secondary sector rapidly shed formal jobs, the tertiary sector was one of the few bright spots in the French economy after the oil crisis. Depending on how one counts, it was around the time the crisis began that, for the first time, the majority of jobs in France were found in the tertiary sector. Whereas between 1975 and 1982, over a million jobs were lost in the primary and secondary sectors combined, more than 1.6 million jobs were added in the tertiary sector.

Yet migrants gained just a fraction (6 per cent) of the new net jobs in this sector, disproportionately low compared to the percentage of foreigners in the foreign labour market, and far below the level of net job losses foreigners experienced in the primary and secondary sectors. When one combines these numbers with information in narrative accounts or qualitative analyses of the era, it is clear that, as a whole, migrants experienced difficulties participating in the transition to a service-based economy. That said, this overall picture masks considerable variation. In the period 1975–82, there were four branches of the service sector with meaningful gains in net jobs for foreign migrants: sales, transportation, hospitality, and other market services. On the other hand, there were three branches with virtually no net job gains (or even net job losses) for foreigners: telecommunications and post, finance and related business, and non-market services (meaning services generally not sold to individuals and firms, and often paid for by the government, such as teaching or firefighting).

Several factors prevented foreign migrants from participating more in the increasingly service-dominated labour market. Many new jobs in the service sector went to French women, who, after a postwar decline in (formal) workforce participation rates, were entering the formal workforce at a much faster rate (and staying longer in it), particularly since the 1970s. For example, nearly 80 per cent of the growth (1.4 million individuals) in the French workforce in 1975–82 was due to the increased numbers of French women working or looking for jobs, even as the number of active foreigners decreased slightly.[33] Unemployed migrants were effectively competing against French women, many of whom enjoyed educational or linguistic advantages compared to migrants, but like them, suffered disadvantage and discrimination. Now, France was not alone in witnessing a rapid increase in women's participation in the formal labour market during the long 1970s. A similarly dramatic increase, for example, was observed in the United States, albeit from higher existing levels. In the United States, those years marked a period of substantial job growth in which the number of women who were employed rose steadily and the overall employment level rose substantially, if less steadily, notwithstanding several recessions.[34] In France, in contrast, the net gain of 1.4 million women who were looking for or found jobs in the years 1975–82 was almost three times higher than the overall growth in jobs. That is to say, the French economy created an insufficient number of service-sector jobs for French or foreigners, women or men.

In searching for service-sector jobs, migrants faced several disadvantages compared to French workers, often due to a combination of language barriers and/or discrimination. Nationality and national-based hiring preferences likely also played a role. During this time of economic stress, many jobs were provided by the government at different levels, yet these were mostly closed to foreigners. Areas dominated by the public sector – post, transportation, and non-market services – added more than half a million net jobs between 1975 and 1982, yet only 21,000 net job gains went to foreigners. Almost all of these gains were in transportation, where migrants slowly gained access to jobs as bus drivers, mechanics, and other public transportation jobs, even as they lost in prestige. Growth in high-prestige and high-paying jobs in finance, insurance, and real estate were likewise largely closed to foreigners. Similar stories could be told of the liberal professions or upper management jobs. Linguistic and educational gaps account for only part of these stories, as there was also the problem of having one's degrees or credentials recognized. EEC recognition of qualifications in services and the professions was still at a very preliminary stage, as was the harmonization of educational degrees. Of course, it was not that no foreigners had high-level service-sector jobs calling for advanced education. However, even if one counts not just the liberal professions, but all types of mid- and upper-level management jobs and professions, both public and private, only 2 per cent of the 4.5 million positions in these professions in France in 1982 were held by foreigners. Moreover, they tended to be held by EEC nationals or citizens of the most-developed countries, rather than by nationals from the major countries of labour migration.

Insofar as migrants had very limited access to public jobs and high-end private jobs, opportunities for re-employment (or new employment) in the service sector tended to be in less prestigious jobs, such as sales, hospitality (increasing reliant on flexible, and often clandestine, migrant labour), and other services, particularly domestic services like cleaning and concierges. As in the United States, migrant women often assumed household and domestic work as French women joined the workforce in increasing numbers, but the lower rate of dual-income households meant that there were fewer opportunities for household and domestic work in France than in the United States (see the chapter by Eileen Boris in this volume).

The concentration of service job opportunities for migrants at the low end of the sector was reflected in wages. A 1970 survey by the Ministère de l'Equipement found that, while white-collar, often service-sector, foreign employees (*employés*) earned more on average than blue-collar foreign workers (*ouvriers*), these *employés* still earned less than the average French member of the workforce, regardless of position. Furthermore, unlike foreign *ouvriers*, whose wages tended to follow a normal distribution whose amount increased with skill, the wages of *employés* followed a bimodal distribution. Simply put, as a foreign *employé*, one tended to earn well or earn poorly, and most foreign *employés* earned poorly compared to the national average.[35] Furthermore, there is some evidence that predominantly high-end service-sector jobs were less likely to be associated with unemployment than low-end service-sector jobs.[36]

Given these obstacles to employment, many migrants during the crisis turned to self-employment. There was a long, if small, tradition of migrant self-employment in France, most famously epitomized by North African cafés and small grocers. Self-employment helped migrants cope with discrimination, language barriers, non-recognition of qualifications, and other obstacles to employment. They also enabled the pooling of capital and labour by individuals tied together by family, kinship, village of origin, and other bonds. However, self-employment could be hindered by bureaucratic obstacles, such as the requirement to obtain a *carte de commerçant*. During the 1930s, French governments had introduced a series of decrees and laws that strictly regulated migrant self-employment as liberal professionals, independent artisans, and merchants. Such measures did not just purport to give authorities (in the 1930s, departmental prefects) the ability to regulate the commercial, liberal, and artisanal labour market through defined juridical status; they were imagined as explicitly protectionist measures to reduce competition during the Great Depression. Furthermore, these fields (and the foreigners who plied their crafts in them) were often seen as "unproductive" and even "parasitic" – drawing, at times, on long-standing, anti-Semitic tropes.[37]

While departmental prefects had lost much of their prerogative to national immigration officials after the Second World War, the potent regulatory mechanisms for limiting foreign self-employment, and well-organized employer and professional associations with an interest in limiting competition, remained a defining feature of France in the "1970s," limiting the possibilities of migrants to become self-employed. One study of Tunisian migrants found that a *carte de commerçant* was frequently refused, particularly for those seeking to open businesses in the food or construction fields. At the same time, the factors associated with success in obtaining a *carte de commerçant*, such as large amounts of capital and a French diploma, were often difficult for established migrants dealing with the effects of the crisis. At least for Tunisian migrants, self-employment provided for job security but little income security.[38] The lack of large-scale success for migrant entrepreneurs is borne out by the fact that, in 1982, less than 3 per cent of owners of firms in France with at least ten workers were foreigners; and a majority of these foreign owners were of European origin. Nearly all such foreign owners were men, though it is possible that some enterprises were in the hands of French spouses.

While migrant women often had little success in owning small- to medium-sized enterprises, they were – at least on paper – able to benefit in other ways from the increasing number of jobs in the tertiary sector. Migrant women and men had long toiled side-by-side in the fields, and migrant women had long been an integral part of the workforce of several industries, such as the textile mills of the north. Yet, like their French counterparts, the majority of foreign women who were legally recognized as working, worked in the service sector. About 70 per cent of foreign women who worked in 1982 did so in the service sector, where they comprised about 40 per cent of foreign workers. As in the past, many of these jobs were in low-paying and sometimes abusive positions as household assistants, concierges, cleaners, and shop assistants. Despite personal ambitions of saving, self-improvement, and occupational mobility, at least for Spanish female migrants, there tended to be significant limits to mobility, which was generally limited to changing jobs within a given sector (e.g., from work in domestic households to cleaning entire houses or offices, or transitions from domestic employment to adjacent sectors like child care).[39] Furthermore, one in five foreign women who were registered as seeking jobs in 1982 were unable to obtain one; many more had doubtless dropped out of the labour market or were too discouraged to try. These trends should make us treat the trope of submissive foreign woman, trapped in foreign systems of patriarchy, with some scepticism, and instead question the ways in which French society systematically discounted the potential of women who wanted to work and were not given the opportunity.

"Migrant Work" and the Limits of "Fordism"

The experiences of women migrants draw attention to the parallels between, and, in some cases, convergence of, "women's work" and what could be termed "migrant work." The increasingly extensive scholarship on the gendering of certain jobs as "women's work" points to the ways in which certain attributes of or skills associated with the job are said to be well adapted to the job holder's "nature." Such work tends to be imagined as low-skilled, generally has lower wages and fewer legal protections, and often creates reinforcing cycles in which men, or other more privileged participants in the workforce, leave the sector for more prestigious and better paid jobs. A similar process can be observed with respect to jobs held by migrants – especially female migrants – around the 1970s. The devaluation of some migrants' skills and wages created a vicious cycle by which certain positions in a firm, or even certain types of jobs, could become known as "migrant work." Entire sectors of the economy, like domestic service, construction, agricultural labour, mining, and often factory floor jobs, increasingly lost their French workers and became underpaid and undervalued "migrant work" by the mid-1970s, just as other professions became undervalued as "women's work." Thus when the Marcellin-Fontanet circulars of 1972 squeezed migrants' access to the legal job market and tried to give preference to registered job-seekers, it was not uncommon for unemployed French workers to refuse to take these "migrant jobs."[40]

There were many reasons for the association of "migrant work" with low-skilled and low-wage jobs. Migrants were at a particular disadvantage when it came to having their skills recognized, and thus earning equal pay. With collective bargaining agreements tying skills to wages, employers had a clear financial incentive to undervalue workers' skills so as to pay them less. For example, a foreigner who performed the duties of a skilled (OP1) position might be assigned a semi-skilled (OS2) pay grade, instead.[41] Language and training also contributed to the confusion about skills. For example, a skilled worker was an *operaio specializzato* in Italian, which sounded dangerously like a "specialized" or semi-skilled worker in French. Migrants' difficulties speaking French also created a situation of vulnerability that certain employers could exploit. Furthermore, the variety of training and educational systems across countries led to ignorance of what exactly each entailed and a discounting of unfamiliar candidates and qualifications. This is a problem that has plagued the free movement of workers in the EEC and later European Union (EU) for more than half a century. In recent years, it has led to the well-known Bologna Process to standardize bachelor's, master's, and doctoral degrees across Europe. But the issues were similar in blue-collar work.[42] During the late 1940s and early 1950s, for example, Italian migrants, the Italian Foreign Ministry, and chambers of commerce complained that French employers did not recognize Italian qualifications, and they called for bilateral working groups or the International Labour Office to jointly define workers' skills by occupation. French employers preferred to administer their own written and/or practical tests. However, culture, education, and customs could prevent migrants from obtaining top marks on "objective" tests, even in translation.[43]

The discounting of migrants' skills and the fact that many truly did not have previous experience as skilled workers led to disproportionate numbers of migrants in unskilled and semi-skilled positions. Not only did this hurt migrants and their families directly, but this classification as lower-skilled workers (for whatever the reason) also explains at least some of the wage gap observed between migrant and French workers, who generally had more favourable classifications. Furthermore, even before the crisis, "good factory jobs," even if they provided good wages and job stability, tended to limit migrants' chances for internal upward mobility, particularly in contrast to their French counterparts.[44]

The challenges of migrant social mobility led to a series of famous strikes. In France in the 1970s and 1980s, migrant workers struck at the car factories of Citroën, Renault-Billancourt, and elsewhere, complaining that they were passed over for promotion and were destined to remain "semi-skilled worker[s] for life" (*O.S. pour vie*). These strikes began before the oil crisis itself – for example, at Renault-Mans in 1971, at the Peñarroya processing plant in Lyon in February 1972, and at Renault-Billancourt in spring 1973, though there is some debate about whether they should be seen primarily as "immigrant" or "worker" strikes. However, the underlying dynamics were exacerbated after the oil crisis and a decade of stagnating opportunities, leading to a spectacular series of strikes in the early 1980s, unambiguously in the name of migrant workers, at Peugeot-Sochaux, Renault-Billancourt, Renault-Sandouville, Citroën-Aulnay, Talbot-Poissy, and Renault-Flins.[45] Their complaint, "O.S. pour vie," became the title of sociological analyses by the late Abdelmalek Sayad, and the trope of the unskilled or semi-skilled migrant also became something of a stock character in literary and artistic depictions of migrants, for example, the plays of Kateb Yacine.[46]

This growing perception of a certain type of "migrant work," whether domestic service, construction, or entry-level factory jobs, went hand-in-hand with an othering of migrants and increasing pessimism about migrant assimilability. Postwar surveys of the French public demonstrated persistent scepticism about the unskilled migrant worker's ability to adapt to French life. For example, when the 1973–4 INED survey asked how occupation affected a migrant's chances of adapting to French life, regardless of nationality, the response by a 4-to-1 ratio was that skilled workers' prospects were favourable. In contrast, two-thirds of respondents thought that unskilled labourers were at a disadvantage in adapting.[47] As French workers, and to some extent Spanish and Italian migrants, moved up the labour hierarchy, abandoning unskilled jobs, the stigmatization of unskilled labour only increased. Unskilled and irregular positions became increasingly occupied by North and sub-Saharan Africans,[48] making these jobs more closely associated with "migrant" work. Both employers and the public long assumed that North and sub-Saharan Africans were supposedly the worst workers and least able to assimilate, whereas "Europeans" – a category that included French and select migrant groups (such as the Spanish, Italians, and later Portuguese) were increasingly viewed as skilled and assimilable.[49]

The result of these dynamics was not, as other scholars have observed in 1920s France or for the end of the twentieth century in other countries, a bimodal labour market, with migrants as a sort of "underclass,"[50] but rather a more complex, fluid, and intersectionally constructed labour hierarchy, with "non-masculine," "unskilled," and "non-European" "migrant" workers (not all of whom are foreign born or formally meet these other definitions) occupying the lowest rungs. Yet while the definition of these lowest rungs on a hierarchy of labour, as well as the economic sectors, shifted as a result of the 1970s crisis, there were striking similarities – on both sides of the crisis and across the twentieth century – in the flexibility, insecurity, and limited rights and protections of these workers. Consequently, scholars should not just quantify the degree of changes wrought by the crisis but should question the extent to which "Fordist" norms of lifelong employment, career progression, and social rights were limited to privileged groups of workers even before the crisis.

Conclusion

The economic effects of the "1970s" on the migrant labour market, pushing French and "European" migrants up or out of the industrial economy and solidifying (and making more visible) the position of women, African, and (increasingly) Asian migrants within the least prestigious ranks of both the industrial and service sectors, reinforced the very sense of crisis for those wishing to "tame" a tide of migration imagined as unskilled and unassimilable. These twin assumptions about skill and assimilability drove many of the changes in migratory policy in the late 1960s and 1970s that created a dual crisis for migrants and ultimately restricted non-European and non-skilled migrants' access to work and residency permits. In so doing, they made the racialized hierarchies of labour increasingly visible, even as they obscured the contributions migrants made during the *Trente Glorieuses*– and, in fact, continue to make – to French prosperity.

They also made increasingly transparent the crisis in the conditions of wage labour, seen across a wide range of industrial and service jobs. Even before the 1970s, migrants and others who were socially marginalized faced significant challenges in experiencing substantial occupational mobility or ultimately securing high-wage jobs. During the dual economic and legal crisis in the wake of the first oil crisis, formal employment of migrants plummeted in construction and manufacturing, while unemployment bloomed. Migrants who kept their manufacturing jobs often felt themselves trapped in low-wage positions with few opportunities for advancement, while the service sector provided few opportunities for re-employment or new employment, outside of the least prestigious and poorly paid positions.

In this increasingly hierarchical labour market, dominated by wage growth at the top end of the service sector, the jobs disproportionately held by women, foreigners, and foreign women, in particular, were those where labour is often discounted in terms of low wages and the perception of low skill.[51] In many ways, this occupational division, often based on the perception of skills, proved as detrimental to migrants as division by sector or industry. Whether in the secondary or tertiary sector, "migrant jobs" sometimes experienced expansion, such as in transportation, waged cleaning and domestic service jobs, and the hotel, cafe, and restaurant sector, but they were unlikely to pay long-term dividends in terms of generous pay. In contrast, jobs requiring recognition of advanced educational credentials and public-sector jobs were largely growth sectors closed to migrants during the 1970s. An analysis of this decade reveals not just the importance of the government in adding jobs (and often desirable jobs) in this time of economic transition, but also the limits of migrants' ability to assume jobs in the service sector when governmental and semi-governmental authorities were major employers, disproportionately hired nationals, and were responsive to (well-organized) constituencies of shopkeepers, artisans, liberal professionals, and other self-employed persons.

Since the 1970s, many migrants have been better positioned to participate in a range of (private-sector) service jobs. In this, they have been aided by the rise of multinational corporations that manage global workforces, EEC and EU regulation that in recent decades have begun to seriously tackle the question of recognizing foreign qualifications in regulated professions, EU regulations that bar discrimination on the basis of nationality, and a shift in attitudes in French society during the extended postwar period, leading to a greater acceptance of foreigners working in the liberal professions.[52]

If migrants help us better understand the service-sector-dominated economy that was increasingly apparent since the 1970s, they also dampen undue celebration of the postwar industrial economy. As impressive as average wage growth in real terms was during the postwar era, there were frequent complaints that workers' – or at least migrant workers' skills – were routinely discounted, with the result being that they qualified for lower wages in collective bargaining agreements. Furthermore, the postwar French economy relied heavily on a flexible – and, from a cynical perspective, expendable – labour force, most visibly in fields like construction. The massive job losses experienced by migrants across the secondary sector, and the short average duration of migrant careers in factories such as Renault-Billancourt,[53] suggest that, even outside of construction, the postwar boom relied on lower wages, higher worker mobility, and greater flexibility than Fordist norms would have us believe. Here the example of agriculture is instructive. It was not just the case that the number of French making their living in agriculture continued to steadily decline in the decades after the Second World War, or that there was a steady increase in capitalization and industrialization of agricultural production; many crops relied heavily on an increasingly foreign seasonal labour force.[54] This portrait of a flexible, short-term, international, highly mobile labour market (in the sense of geography and jobs, but not necessarily social advancement), often only partially covered by social rights and protections, is more reminiscent of depictions of contemporary, supposedly "post-Fordist" labour markets. Migrants point to the persistence of such labour market traits, and their growth and increasing visibility, rather than to the emergence of such phenomena due to the shift from an industrial to a service-based economy.

NOTES

1 Calculated from Institut national de la statistique et des études économiques (hereafter INSEE), "Tableaux rétrospectifs à partir des recensements antérieurs à 1999," accessed 17 February 2014, http://www .insee.fr/fr/themes/detail.asp?ref_id=ir-rp99pipe&page=irweb/rp99pipe /dd/rp99pipe_retrospectif.htm.

2 Centre des archives contemporaines (hereafter CAC), 19950493, art. 6 DPM, Sous-direction des mouvements de population, "Etude R.C.B. sur l'immigration: I. Analyse des résultats de l'étude des variantes quantitatives de l'immigration réalisée par la Direction de la Prévision à l'aide du modèle FIFI" (September 1971); Derek Aldcroft, *The European Economy, 1914–1990*, 3rd ed. (London: Routledge, 1993), 143; Edward Fulton Denison, *Why Growth Rates Differ: Postwar Experiences in Nine Western Countries* (Washington, DC: Brookings Institute, 1967), 300–18; Jean-Louis Reiffers, *Le rôle de l'immigration des travailleurs dans la croissance de la République Fédérale Allemande de 1958 à 1968* (Geneva: International Labour Organization, March 1970).

3 "Intervention de M. Edmond Maire secrétaire général de la CFDT," *L'Algérien en Europe, organe de l'émigration algérienne* 176 (1–15 October 1973): 16; Barry Eichengreen, *The European Economy since 1945: Coordinated Capitalism and Beyond* (Princeton, NJ: Princeton University Press, 2008), 198.

4 "L'immigration," JT 20H, Office national de radiodiffusion télévision française, 8 October 1974, video, 4:52, accessed 21 April 2019, http://www .ina.fr/video/CAF96034465/l-immigration-video.html.

5 Carmen Ródenas Calatayud, *Emigración y economía en España, 1960–1990* (Madrid: Biblioteca Civitas, 1994); María Fernández Vicente, "Emigrer sous Franco: Politiques publiques et stratégies individuelles dans l'émigration espagnole vers l'Argentine et vers la France, 1945–1965" (PhD diss., École des hautes etudes en sciences sociales, 2006), 84; Ana Fernández Asperilla, "La emigración como exportación de mano de obra: El fenómeno migratorio a Europa durante el franquismo," *Historia Social* 30 (1998): 65; Archives nationales, F/1a/5126, Service des affaires Musulmanes to M. Crémieux-Brilhac (Directeur de la Documentation, Secrétariat général

du gouvernement), "Situation actuelle et perspectives d-avenir de la
population musulmane algérienne en France métropolitaine" (19 March 1962).

6   Madeleine Trébous, *Migration and Development: The Case of Algeria* (Paris:
Organisation for Economic Co-operation and Development, 1970), 7, 137;
Mohamed Khandriche, *Développement et reinsertion: L'exemple de l'émigration
algérienne* (Paris: Editions Publisud, 1982).

7   Schierup et al. use the phrase "dual crisis" to refer to what they perceive
as the dilemma facing contemporary European societies, which is
simultaneously an identity crisis manifest in racism and xenophobia
directed at migrants, and a demographic/social crisis, as the employment
of migrants is nonetheless necessary to finance an underfunded welfare
system catering to an aging (national) population, Carl-Ulrik Schierup, Peo
Hansen, and Stephen Castles, *Migration, Citizenship, and the European Welfare
State: A European Dilemma* (Oxford: Oxford University Press, 2006), 3.

8   Among others, see Gérard Noiriel, *Le creuset français: Histoire de
l'immigration, XIXe–XXe siècles* (Paris: Seuil, 1988); Gérard Noiriel,
Population, immigration et identité nationale en France: XIXe–XXe siècle (Paris:
Hachette, 1992); Abdelmalek Sayad, "The Three Ages of Emigration,"
in *The Suffering of the Immigrant*, trans. David Macey (Cambridge: Polity,
2004); Alexis Spire, *Étrangers à la carte: L'administration de l'immigration en
France, 1945–1975* (Paris: Grasset & Fasquelle, 2005); Patrick Weil, *La France
et ses étrangers: L'aventure d'une politique de l'immigration, 1938–1991* (Paris:
Gallimard, 2005).

9   Sylvain Laurens, " '1974' et la fermeture des frontières: Analyse critique
d'une décision érigée en turning-point," *Politix* 21, no. 82 (2008): 69–94;
Daniel Gordon, *Immigrants and Intellectuals: May '68 and the Rise of Anti-
Racism in France* (Pontypool, UK: Merlin, 2012); Abdellali Hajjat, "The
Arab Workers' Movement (1970–1976): Sociology of a New Political
Generation," in *May 68: Rethinking France's Last Revolution*, ed. Julian
Jackson, Anna-Louise Milne, and James Williams (London: Palgrave
Macmillan, 2011), 109–21; Weil, *La France et ses étrangers*, 95; Patrick Weil,
"Racisme et discrimination dans la politique française de l'immigration,
1938–1945/1974–1995," *Vingtième siècle* 47 (July/September 1995): 74;
Michelle Zancarini-Fournel, "La question immigrée après 68," *Plein droit*
53–4 (March 2002), accessed 7 November 2012, http://www.gisti.org/doc
/plein-droit/53-54/question.html.

10 For notable works on the relationship between work and migration,
see Abdelmalek Sayad, "The Immigrant: 'OS for Life,' " in *The Suffering
of the Immigrant*, trans. David Macey (Cambridge: Polity, 2004), 162–76;
Bernard Granotier, *Les travailleurs immigrés en France*, 2nd ed. (Paris:
François Maspero, 1976); and, primarily for other eras, Mary Dewhurst
Lewis, *The Boundaries of the Republic: Migrant Rights and the Limits of*

Universalism in France, 1918–1940 (Stanford, CA: Stanford University Press, 2007), 84; Spire, *Étrangers*, 109, 140–1; Elisa Camiscioli, *Reproducing the French Race: Immigration, Intimacy, and Embodiment in the Early Twentieth Century* (Durham, NC: Duke University Press, 2009), 51; Amelia Lyons, *The Civilizing Mission in the Metropole: Algerian Families and the French Welfare State during Decolonization* (Stanford, CA: Stanford University, 2013), 84; Maryse Tripier, *L'immigration dans la classe ouvrière en France* (Paris: Harmattan, 1990); Marianne Amar and Pierre Milza, *L'immigration en France au XXe siècle* (Paris: Armand Colin, 1990); and Federico Romero, "L'emigrazione operaia in Europa, 1948–1973," in *Storia dell'emigrazione italiana-Partenze*, ed. Piero Bevilacqua, Adreina De Clementi, and Emilio Franzina (Rome: Donzelli, 2001), 397–414.

11 Max Frisch, foreword to *Siamo italiani: Gespräche mit Italienischen Arbeitern in der Schweiz*, ed. Alexander Seiler (Zürich: EVZ, 1965), 7.

12 INSEE, *Recensement général de la population de 1982: Résultats du sondage au 1/20, de 1982, Les étrangers* (Paris: INSEE, 1985), 46.

13 Carl-Ulrik Schierup, "The Immigrants and the Crisis," *Acta Sociologica* 28, no. 1 (1985): 27.

14 INSEE, *Recensement général de la population de 1982: Résultats du sondage au 1/20, de 1982. Les étrangers* (Paris: INSEE, 1985), 46.

15 "Immigration: Une nouvelle politique," JT 20H, Office national de radiodiffusion télévision française, 4 July 1974, video, 2:17, accessed 21 April 2019, www.ina.fr/video/CAF91045099/immigration-une -nouvelle-politique-video.html.

16 Marcel Berlinghoff, *Das Ende der "Gastarbeit": Europäische Anwerbestopps 1970–1974* (Paderborn: Ferdinand Schöningh, 2013), 335–45; Laurens, "1974," 69–94; Sylvain Laurens, *Une politisation feutrée: Les hauts fonctionnaires et l'immigration en France, 1962–1981* (Paris: Belin, 2009), 38, 146, 218; Neil MacMaster, "The 'Seuil de Tolérance': The Uses of a 'Scientific' Racist Concept," in *Race, Discourse, and Power in France*, ed. Maxim Silverman (Aldershot, UK: Gower Publishing, 1991), 17; Maxim Silverman, *Deconstructing the Nation: Immigration, Racism, and Citizenship in Modern France* (London: Routledge, 1992), 95–105; Weil, *La France et ses étrangers*, 104–16.

17 INSEE, *Annuaire statistique de la France* (series, various years).

18 Vincent Viet, *La France immigrée: Construction d'une politique, 1914–1997* (Paris: Fayard, 1998), 383–6, 408; Laura Oso Casas, *Españolas en París: Estrategias de ahorro y consumo en las migraciones internacionales* (Barcelona: Bellaterra, 2004), 254; Weil, *La France et ses étrangers*, 102; Berlinghoff, *Das Ende der "Gastarbeit,"* 345–53.

19 Calculated from the ONI statistics on new permanent foreign workers found in CAC 19950493, art. 6. Vidal of the DPM: Sous-Direction des

Mouvements de Population, "Note sur l'évolution des régularisations: Modalités d'immigration des travailleurs permanents étrangers" 24 June 1974; Viet, *La France immigré*, 383.

20 Assemblée Nationale, séance du 29 Novembre 1966, *JORF-D* (30 November 1966), 5034–7; Todd Shepard, *The Invention of Decolonization: The Algerian War and the Remaking of France* (Ithaca, NY: Cornell University Press, 2006); CAC 19950493 art. 6 Ministère du Travail, de l'emploi et de la population, signed Charles Barbeau (directeur de la Population et des migrations), "Note pour Monsieur le Ministre," 25 June 1973.

21 Spire, *Étrangers*, 107; Michael Kozakowski, "From the Mediterranean to Europe: Migrants, the World of Work, and the Transformation of the French Mediterranean, 1945–1974" (PhD diss., University of Chicago, 2014), 107, 170–1, 249–56.

22 Susan Pedersen, *Family, Dependence, and the Origins of the Welfare State: Britain and France, 1914–1945* (New York: Cambridge University Press, 1993), 390–2; Jacques Hochard, *Aspects économiques des prestations familiales* (Paris: Union nationale d'allocations familiales, 1961), 22, 175; Lyons, *The Civilizing Mission*, 94.

23 Gordon, *Immigrants and Intellectuals*, 171. For a comparative perspective, see Mae Ngai, "The Civil Rights Origins of Illegal Immigration," *International Labor and Working-Class History* 78 (Fall 2010): 93–9.

24 Oso Casas, *Españolas*, 196.

25 Ibid., 197.

26 INSEE, *Tableaux rétrospectifs*.

27 Spire, *Étrangers à la carte*, 83 and 113; Kozakowski, "From the Mediterranean to Europe," 102; Silverman, *Deconstructing the Nation*.

28 Viet, *La France immigré*, 378.

29 Vincent Viet, *Histoire des Français venus d'ailleurs* (Paris: Perrin, 2004), 250–3; Weil, *La France*, 144.

30 MTIN-SEIE archive, IEE, Gabinete de Estudios y Publicaciones, "Intervención de la delegación española en la reunión de altos funcionarios de Estocolmo, 6–8 de noviembre 1978."

31 "Les offres d'emploi en Algérie," *L'Algérien en Europe* (May 1968): 8; Trébous, *Migration and Development*, 130–1, 191–4; Timm Voß, *Die algerisch-französische Arbeitsmigration: Ein Beispiel einer organisierten Rückwanderung* (Königstein: Hanstein, 1981), 109.

32 Michel Wagner, "Vers une politique de coopération entre les peuples: La formation-retour, quelques expériences récentes," *Migrants-Formation*, special issue, n.d. [1966?]: 17–18 and "Les travailleurs immigrés et la formation professionnelle," *Migrants-Formation* (October 1976): 98–101; Voß, *Die algerisch-französische Arbeitsmigration*, 123; Khandriche, *Développement et reinsertion*; Antonio Varsori, "Vocational Education

and Training in European Social Policy from Its Origins to the Creation of CEDEFOP," in *Towards a History of Vocational Education and Training (VET) in Europe in a Comparative Perspective*, vol. 2, ed. Antonio Varsori (Luxembourg: Office for Official Publications of the European Communities, 2004), 82–3.

33 INSEE, "Tableaux rétrospectifs."

34 "Civilian Labor Force Participation Rate: Women," "Employment Level: Women," and "Civilian Employment Level," Federal Reserve Bank of St. Louis Economic Research, accessed 21 April 2019, https://fred.stlouisfed.org/categories/32444.

35 Roland Granier and J.P. Marciano, "La rémunération des travailleurs immigrés en France," *Revue internationale du travail* 111 (1975): 167.

36 Anne-Sophie Bruno, *Les chemins de la mobilité: Migrants de Tunisie et marché du travail parisien depuis 1956* (Paris,:Éditions de l'EHESS, 2010), 248.

37 Claire Zalc, "De la liberté du commerce pour tous à la carte de commerçant étranger, 19ème siècle–1938," *Clio* (October 2003), accessed 21 April 2019, http://barthes.enssib.fr/clio/revues/AHI/articles/preprints/ent/zalc.html.

38 Bruno, *Les chemins*, 198, 251–3. For a comparative perspective finding similar outcomes, see Schierup, Hansen, and Castles, *Migration*, 212.

39 Oso Casas, *Españolas*, 197.

40 Catherine Gokalp, "Chronique de l'immigration," *Population* 28, nos. 4–5 (1973): 931–3; Laura Lee Downs, *Manufacturing Inequalities: Gender Division in the French and British Metalworking Industries, 1914–1939* (Ithaca, NY: Cornell University Press, 1995), 79–80; Joan Wallach Scott, *Gender and the Politics of History*, 2nd ed. (New York: Columbia University Press, 1999), 53, 97, 167; Nancy Green, *Ready to Wear and Ready to Work: A Century of Industry and Immigrants in Paris and New York* (Durham, NC: Duke University Press, 1997), 161–87; Dorothy Sue Cobble, ed., *The Sex of Class: Women Transforming American Labor* (Ithaca, NY: ILR Press, 2007), 15, 35; Eileen Boris and Jennifer Klein, *Caring for America: Home Health Workers in the Shadow of the Welfare State* (Oxford: Oxford University Press, 2012), 218; Thanh-Dam Truong, *Migration, Gender, and Social Justice: Perspectives on Human Security* (Heidelberg: Springer, 2014); Camiscioli, *Reproducing the French Race*, 48.

41 Andrée Michel, *Les travailleurs algériens en France* (Paris: Centre national de la recherche scientifique, 1956), 84–6; Trébous, *Migration and Development*, 135; Laure Pitti, "La main-d'œuvre algérienne dans l'industrie automobile (1945–1962), ou les oubliés de l'histoire," *Immigration et marché du travail* 1263 (September–October 2006): 52. "La vie quotidienne des immigrés à Marseille," *A la bonne heure*, TF1, 21 Nov. 1978, 15:36, accessed 12 August 2018, http://www.ina.fr/video/CAA7801518701/la-vie-quotidienne-des-immigres-a-marseille-video.html.

42 Christina Boswell and Andrew Geddes, *Migration and Mobility in the European Union* (Basingstoke, UK: Palgrave Macmillan, 2011); Peo Hansen and Sandy Brian Hager, *The Politics of European Citizenship: Deepening Contradictions in Social Rights and Migration Policy* (New York: Berghahn, 2012).

43 CAC 19790259 art 1. See in particular the comptes-rendus of the 17 and 25 November 1950 meetings of the Commission-mixte franco-italienne; Laure Pitti, "De la différenciation coloniale à la discrimination systémique?" *La revue de l'IRES* 46 (2004): 69–107; L. Berlioz, "Étude de la réussite en F.P.A. normale des Stagiaires Nord-Africains," *Bulletin du Centre d'Études et Recherches Psychotechniques* 3, no. 2 (1954): 43.

44 Granier and Marciano, "La rémunération des travailleurs," 167; Pitti, "De la différenciation coloniale," 74, 81.

45 Laure Pitti, "Les luttes centrales des O.S. immigrés," *Plein droit* 63 (April 2004): 46; Berlinghoff, *Das Ende der "Gastarbeit"*, 319–20; Laure Pitti, "Grèves ouvrières versus luttes de l'immigration: Une controverse entre historiens," *Ethnologie française* 31, no. 3 (2001): 465–76; Vincent Gay, "De la dignité à l'invisibilité: Les OS immigrés dans les grèves de Citroën et Talbot, 1982–1984" (masters thesis, École des Hautes Etudes en Sciences Sociales, 2011), 127; Gérard Noiriel, *Immigration, antisémitisme et racisme en France, XIXe–XXe siècle: Discours publics, humiliations privées* (Paris: Fayard, 2007), 611.

46 Sayad, "The Immigrant," 162–76; Kateb Yacine, "Mohamed, prends ta valise," *Boucherie de l'espérance: Œuvres théâtrales* (Paris: Seuil, 1999); Gabrielle Varro and Anne-Sophie Perriaux, "Les sens d'une catégorisation: 'Les O.S. immigrés,'" *Langage et société* 58 (1991): 11, 27.

47 Alain Girard, Yves Charbit, and Marie-Laurence Lamy, "Attitudes des français à l'égard de l'immigration étrangère: Nouvelle enquête d'opinion," *Population* 29, no. 6 (1974): 1015–69.

48 Kozakowski, "From the Mediterranean to Europe," 34.

49 Melissa K. Byrnes, "French Like Us? Municipal Policies and North African Migrants in the Parisian Banlieues, 1945–1975" (PhD diss., Georgetown University, 2008); Naomi Davidson, *Only Muslim: Embodying Islam in Twentieth-Century France* (Ithaca, NY: Cornell University Press, 2012); Neil MacMaster, *Colonial Migrants and Racism* (New York: St. Martin's Press, 1997), 209; Clifford Rosenberg, *Policing Paris: The Origins of Modern Immigration Control between the Wars* (Ithaca, NY: Cornell University Press, 2006), 109; Ralph Schor, *L'opinion française et les étrangers en France, 1919–1939* (Paris: Publication de la Sorbonne, 1985); Joan Wallach Scott, *The Politics of the Veil* (Princeton, NJ: Princeton University, 2007).

50 Gary S. Cross, *Immigrant Workers in Industrial France: The Making of a New Laboring Class* (Philadelphia: Temple University Press, 1983); Gary P. Freeman, *Immigrant Labor and Racial Conflict in Industrial Societies: The French*

and *British Experience, 1945–1975* (Princeton, NJ: Princeton University Press, 1979); Schierup, Hansen, and Castles, *Migration*.

51 Schierup, "The Immigrants and the Crisis," 29.

52 Andrew Geddes and Peter Scholten, *The Politics of Immigration and Migration in Europe*, 2nd ed. (New York: Sage, 2016), 69; A. Girard and J. Stoetzel, *Français et immigrés*, Institut National d'Études Démographiques, Travaux et documents, no. 19 (Paris: Presses Universitaires de France, 1953), 144; Girard, Charbit, and Lamy, "Attitudes," 1015–69.

53 Pitti, "De la différenciation coloniale," 74, 81.

54 Venus Bivar, *Organic Resistance: The Struggle over Industrial Farming in Postwar France* (Chapel Hill: University of North Carolina, 2018); Laure Teulières, *Immigrés d'Italie et paysans de France, 1920–1944* (Toulouse: Presses Universitaires du Mirail, 2002); INSEE, *Annuaire statistique de la France, 1981* (résultats de 1980), 62.

5 Challenges of Computerization and Globalization: The Example of the Printing Unions, 1950s to 1980s

KARSTEN UHL

"I have never seen an industry that is going to be more completely changed in the next decade as a result of automation – nor one which today realizes it less."[1] With these categorical words, American automation expert and business consultant John Diebold described the printing industry in April 1963. In Diebold's eyes, the industry was a perfect example of both managers and workers turning a blind eye to inevitable technological change. However, as a technocrat engaged in the development, Diebold himself understood the issues. He gave this speech in front of a group of people who were among those most affected by the predicted changes: those attending the convention of the American Society of Newspaper Editors. Soon this quotation became well known among print and press experts, but Diebold also turned to another aspect of the transformation often overlooked by contemporaries: the "tremendous human problems." He pointed out that the "need for social innovation" would be "fully as great as the need for technological innovation."[2]

Those who were engaged with issues related to "human problems" received the message of a vastly changing industry, even in Europe, which was still lagging somewhat behind American technological development: just one and a half years after Diebold's speech, the German unionist Richard Burkhardt quoted him during a lecture on "graphical technology's development in the age of automation" at the Vienna congress of the International Graphical Federation (IGF), a grouping of printing unions from all over the Western world.[3] They were all aware of the fact that transformation had already started. In December 1962, the first newspaper corporation introduced computers to the composing room, which seemed to mark the forthcoming end of the printing craft.[4] Large corporations – Mergenthaler, RCA, and IBM – were offering computers capable of producing justified and hyphenated tape, and, on 1 December 1962, the *Los Angeles Times* installed the RCA 301 for typesetting.[5] Just a few weeks after Diebold's speech, in July 1963, the most prominent American labour leader in the printing industry, Bertram Powers of the New York Typographical Union No. 6, visited these computers in action. Powers described them as the beginning of an era of total automation in printing and therefore as requiring new union strategies: "Those members who doubt the effects of total automation, or rely on economic theories of the past to stabilize our industry, had better re-examine their thinking."[6]

In this chapter, I will survey the technological, social, and cultural transformations in the printing industry in this era of "total automation," from the 1960s to the 1980s. It is crucial to focus on this context in order to investigate the trade union crisis of this period. In general, visions of automated factories without workers were common in West Germany during the 1970s. However, in most industries, the real conditions lagged far behind these expectations.[7] German unions, especially the metal workers' union, became aware of the automation challenge as early as in the 1960s. Yet, they were optimistic about union power being able to shape the technological impact in favour of the workers.[8] During the economic crisis of the 1970s, this optimism faded, and "there was a clear change in the union's attitude toward technology and the first signs of a shift in strategy." Nevertheless, the West German metal workers' union never did "abandon its fundamental acceptance of technological change."[9]

For printers, the transformation caused by new technology was fast and comprehensive. Therefore, the printing unions experienced particularly harshly the outcome of the union crisis: for decades they had been in a relatively comfortable situation in industrial relations because the printers and typesetters formed a strong force of skilled workers who conceived of themselves the "aristocracy of labour."[10]

In this chapter, my main focus will be on the extensive development and application of computer technology during the 1970s and 1980s; the establishment of desktop publishing in 1985 then marks the beginning of the final stage of computerization in the printing industry.[11] I will cover technological developments and debates relating to automation in international scope but, for practical reasons, will concentrate on union politics in West Germany. However, union politics often crossed the national borders, as did corporate interests. To some extent, the union movement Europeanized itself, and the IGF became an ever-important player. In the West German printing industry, labour conflicts culminated in the nationwide strikes of 1976, 1978, and 1984. The 1978 collective action in particular was mainly about technological change: trade unions and work councils sought to defend the status of qualified workers even though the challenge of automation was a watershed for working conditions in printing. This defence was crucial because the labour movement's power rested on a strong force of qualified workers.[12]

In the following pages, I will examine the role technological change played in the trade union crisis. Automation – which, in the printing industry, took the form of computerization – challenged the unions in three ways. First, on the discursive level, labour's traditional belief in technological progress in general became fragile, as union members discussed whether automation's social impact could still be shaped by union power. Second, on the level of political action, the unions' most important power resource became vulnerable: companies found ways to cope with strikes because computerization permitted production outside the factory and even without skilled workers. On the one hand, unions had to sort out new paths to international cooperation; on the other hand, alternative approaches to union technology policy, like engagement in technological development, emerged. Third, on the level of workers' self-perception, the image of printers and compositors belonging to an aristocracy of labour became obsolete in the context of computerization. Their formerly distinct self-perception as skilled blue-collar workers, of utmost importance for union stability, split into a multitude of qualification profiles and self-perceptions combined with the rise of white-collar jobs in the printing industry. This chapter will show in which respects these three levels were interconnected, and whether changes at one level affected the others.

Technological Progress and the Belief in Union Power

Even during a period of intense automation, printing union strategies showed a strong sense of continuity with the traditional union belief in technological progress. Only a minority of union members voted for categorical rejection of technological change. Most union functionaries argued for cooperation, proposing concepts for the concrete configuration of technological change, considering this the best option to defend qualified workers. These concepts were based, in turn, on the respective expectations related to further technological development, on the one hand, and for approaching the idea of technological progress in general, on the other. Hence, I will first examine anticipations about technology, and union concepts for securing qualifications under conditions of automation. Union functionaries started discussing technological change both on a national and an international level soon after Diebold's dark prophecy in 1963. From the 1960s, the printing unions were aware of coming technological changes, particularly computerization.

Even at the very convention where Diebold gave his speech, the labour issue was prominent. US secretary of labor William Willard Wirtz gave a lecture immediately preceding Diebold's. Three aspects of his speech stayed at the heart of union politics for the next two decades: embracing automation, merging unions, and protecting the worker rather than the concrete job. In these respects, the position of the state – in this case, the Democratic US administration – was very close to that of the trade unions. With regard to the first goal, for Wirtz, automation was necessary, as "the only alternative to automation" had been "stagnation." In addition, he noted that, to ease the introduction of new technology, it would be most important to merge the various printing unions. In particular, the unions in North America and Great Britain faced this problem, while the West German printing union (Industriegewerkschaft Druck und Papier) had consolidated different occupations inherent to the sector. Lastly, Wirtz emphasized the best labour policy to be "the protection of the man rather than of the job."[13] With this formula, he provided a defensive strategy against the implications of automation. He did not even consider opposing the new technology as an option, and he recognized that profound changes in job profiles seemed to be inevitable. For Wirtz, practical politics had to concentrate on helping workers not to have to exit the trade, even if they had new professional tasks and possibly lost skilled jobs.

In the following year, the debate crossed the Atlantic. The first International Computer Typesetting Conference took place at London University in July 1964, bringing together 275 delegates from fourteen Western countries. These experts discussed "computer typesetting" in a broad sense, defined by the president of the London Institute of Printing, Gordon S. Allen, as "the use of some form of general-purpose or specialized computer operation as part of the typesetting process."[14] Follow-up conferences were held in the United Kingdom in 1966 and 1972;[15] these included some participants from Japan and the socialist state of East Germany, but none from the Global South. The first conference in 1964 had demonstrated the unions' early interest in the new technology: the largest of the UK printing unions, the National Graphical Association (NGA), was represented by general president Fred Simmons and twelve other participants. Simmons emphasized that unionists were anything but Luddites: his union had "never opposed or retarded technical progress." On the contrary, the NGA was supporting technological innovation and even made plans for offering its members "a short full-time course of training on computer typesetting."[16] This did not mean that the NGA ignored social problems caused by automation. One union official, John Willats (whom we will meet again fifteen years later), even considered the "human problems" to be "the cardinal point at this conference." Not yet having had any first-hand experience with the new technology in the United Kingdom, Willats asked American conference attendants about their experience with computer typesetting. Their responses assured him that economic growth would be the best antidote for redundancies caused by technological change. They noted that the new technology would enhance productivity, but at the same time there would be so much more work to do in a booming sector that no jobs would be lost.[17] It was symptomatic of the state of the discussion that even the most profound experts – with the exception of Diebold – underrated automation's pace and impact. The underlying assumption was that automation would merge the skills of man and machine. Indeed, the conference started with a keynote speech by C.J. Duncan of Newcastle University stating that there "will always be hyphenation decisions in really tip-top work which will require human beings ... There is always going to be room for human beings."[18] This belief in human skill being irreplaceable was combined with a concept of automation as never being total. As one panellist pointed out, the "under-current fear that man will be unnecessary" was "absolutely unfounded" because more than "eighty per cent automation" could never be reached, and he compared the current situation to the invention of the first Monotype and Linotype typesetting machines in the late nineteenth century.[19]

The unionists of the International Graphical Federation held similar views, concerning both the permanency of skilled work and the idea of technological and social transformation similar to that following the initial introduction of mechanized composition. At an IGF convention in 1958, Richard Burkhardt, head of the German printing union's economy and technology department, had declared the speed of technological development overrated: automation would surely take more time. In particular, typesetting would depend on human work for the time being.[20] Thus, he was convinced that automation would be introduced gradually, that unions had enough time to adapt to the coming situation, and that union power would definitely allow the social shaping of technology. In the long run, technological and social progress would go hand in hand.[21] Just six years later, he had had to revise his position. The new reality of computer typesetting dominated Burkhardt's paper on the development of graphical technology in the age of automation given at the 1964 IGF convention, even if at that moment very few of the new machines were being used in Europe and none in Germany. Nonetheless, the trend seemed to be unstoppable. According to Burkhardt, computer-aided typesetting represented a kind of "perfect automation."[22] Computer typesetting had become an option even for small enterprises. Moreover, newspapers in the United States, Japan, the United Kingdom, and Sweden were already using long-distance transmission.[23] However, the union's optimism did not vanish, and its technology strategy did not change significantly. Burkhardt's successor as head of the German printing union's technology and economy department, Erwin Ferlemann, stayed optimistic, even as, in 1965, computer typesetting made its premiere in Germany.[24] At the 1970 IGF convention in Copenhagen, Ferlemann gave a lecture on technological progress and graphical unions' future tasks. By that time, computer typesetting was still relatively unusual in German print shops, although more than forty shops were using it.[25] In any case, Ferlemann was firmly convinced that skilled work would remain essential for the transforming printing industry, because even computers needed skilled operators.[26]

The unions' political strategies for facing the challenge of computer typesetting drew on their historical experience. Because the German printing union looked back on a success story of coping with earlier technological innovations, it still believed in union power being strong enough to defend skilled workers' interests against challenging new technologies. The union used the introduction of mechanical composition as the most prominent example: in 1900, the union had succeeded in inscribing staffing guidelines for the new mechanized printing presses in their contract with entrepreneurs. Decades later, unions continued to model their policies on this episode.[27] A strong belief in union power combined with the belief that technology was neutral in principle: indeed, during a dispute over extensive use of computer typesetting in 1978, the German printing union's board member Detlef Hensche continued to insist that "the new technology – by itself – is neutral."[28] In other words, the union thought it was possible for it to cope with technological innovations: it had no fear of new technologies becoming entrepreneurs' newest weapons against labour interests. Instead, unionists were quite optimistic that their organization had the power to shape the social effects of technological change.

Thus, even in 1978, during the German labour conflict concerning the introduction of computer composition, the narrative remained the same: the printing union headquarters distributed a model speech to local union functionaries that strongly resembled Ferlemann's words at the IGF convention in 1970, emphasizing that qualified labour would not disappear with the introduction of the new technology. Apparently, the first broad experiences with computer typesetting in the 1970s did not challenge the union's concept of automation or the strategies to cope with it. Almost a decade later, its representatives were still maintaining that, "by experience, we know that even the computer needs an operator."[29] However, this time the unionists were not as successful as their predecessors had been during the introduction of mechanical composition at the end of the nineteenth century. The labour agreement in 1978 had staffing guidelines – mostly, about qualified typesetters starting work at the new computers – but the guidelines were limited to a period of eight years.[30]

In the 1980s, discussions within the printing industry focused on whether union support for computerization was still an adequate response in a transforming industry. Yet the Confederation of German Trade Unions was not willing to change its strategy: the union leaders were convinced that the rejection of technological innovation was no option at all. In their opinion, union technology policy was all about the social shaping of technological impact.[31] Only after the deep consequences of computerization had become clear did union strategies began to change. It was not until 1982 that the International Federation of Journalists (IFJ) and the IGF finally intensified cooperation, combining the interests of blue-collar and white-collar workers. The delegates to a joint working group meeting pleaded for concerted action of all media unions with respect to technology and vocational training. It would take guts to reject new technology in certain areas, but not doing so would mean there would not be any chance to counteract entrepreneurs' strategies.[32] In retrospect, though, it seems that the decisive point of computerization had already been reached.

The End to Local Strikes?

The technological changes and the economic transformations of the 1970s challenged both union power and union strategies as multinational corporations grew in importance in the printing industry. In this context, an unlikely meeting between German unionist Ferlemann, who had become the printing union's deputy chairman, and his British fellow unionist Willats took place in front of a Turkish-owned plant near the Frankfurt airport in April 1979. By that time, the "human problems" that NGA board secretary Willats had spoken of at the Computer Typesetting Conference fifteen years earlier had become tangible. Innovations at the London *Times* provide a clear example of the developments and conflicts in the printing industry. In 1978–9, the British newspaper faced a tough confrontation between the owner – the multinational Thomson Corporation – and the paper's workers, who were represented by eight different unions. The unions rejected the planned invention of computer composition, or, more precisely, they insisted on "double-key stroking" – that is, where typesetters rekeyed copy that had already been keyed by its writers. Thus, the dispute was mainly about staffing issues – the unions did not oppose the new technology as such. The NGA did not accept management's request that journalists and advertising personnel key their own copy, because the union sought to protect the jobs of its members, the typesetters. As the dispute escalated in December 1978, the corporation stopped the production of the *Times*. The paper was not published again until 13 November 1979.[33]

During this long period of eleven months, the very technology that caused the strike made it possible to transfer the production of the newspaper – both composition and print – to another country. So, in April 1979, the *Times* management secretly made plans to publish an entirely new weekly paper, also called the *Times*, to be published outside Britain for the European and North American markets. These markets were particularly important because foreign advertising made up more than a third of the paper's advertising sales. Moreover, prior to the strike, the *Times* had sold about 35,000 copies abroad each day.[34]

This project became possible because, unlike the print workers' unions, the *Times*'s chapter of the National Union of Journalists (NUJ) decided by a narrow majority to authorize the resumption of its members' work in April.[35] Journalists wrote the articles in London; only five members of the editorial staff were secretly flown to Germany to oversee editing and production. A week before the new paper's publication date of 30 April, an impromptu office was arranged at a Frankfurt hotel, and London sent copy to Germany by courier.[36] The editors then transferred the texts to the nearby city of Darmstadt, where the small shop of Otto Gutfreund and Son did the typesetting. Gutfreund had only twenty employees, but their use of computer-aided typesetting enabled them to do the job. Importantly, only two of the typesetting shop's employees were unionized, and therefore the German printing union was not permitted by law to call a strike in response to the shop's doing this work.[37]

Before the scheduled publication date, which was mere days before the 3 May British general election, the international trade union movement intervened. The *Times* management had made the decision on 19 April to produce the new weekly edition and had informed the unions without giving further details of where and how. Soon rumours started circulating about the place of production.[38] Most unionists assumed that the paper would be printed at a Dutch facility because, due to a Cold War conflict between social democratic and communist unions, the Netherlands was the only Western European state without IGF representation.[39] On 21 April, the *Times* competitor the *Guardian* featured an article on the foreign weekly plan and even suggested that Frankfurt was most likely the place for printing.[40] Soon, the NGA informed its fellow European unionists about the *Times* strike escalation and the edition being produced abroad, and the IGF informed its members that they were obliged to support the British union. In this, the Germans were repaying a debt of gratitude after several European unions had shown international solidarity during the German printing dispute in 1978 and hindered the transfer of newspaper production in their countries.[41]

Yet, by 25 April, when the German printing union was informed of the virtual transfer of composition to Darmstadt, the typesetting was apparently already complete – or so the union believed, because Gutfreund told it so. The union accepted Gutfreund's story and so focused on possible printing locations where it could intervene. *Sunday Times* journalist Eric Jacobs later plausibly claimed that only half of the typesetting work had been done at that moment: for example, the sports results were still to be included. The last pages were set only late in the afternoon of the 29th.[42]

British and German media uncritically disseminated another narrative connected to the Gutfreund typesetting: the story of revolutionary technological innovation. Later, on 1 June 1979, the *Times*'s editor-in-chief William Rees-Mogg published an article in the *Daily Telegraph* that was widely reported in the German press.[43] He praised the Germans' efficiency, a quality he claims was missing in Britain. According to the *Times*' editor, the female German workers had been three times as fast as English typesetters – a pace he attributed to the supposedly superior technology used at the German typesetting shop. Rees-Mogg drew a picture of the extraordinary performance of a small German typesetting shop equipped with the latest computer technology. But the technology at Darmstadt was less revolutionary than he claimed. In fact, Gutfreund and Son applied a hybrid technology combining the old and the new, which was not so unusual at this still early period of computer typesetting. For example, the *New York Daily News* introduced computerization in a gradual manner, first producing tape to drive old-fashioned hot metal typesetting machines. Only in a second stage did photocomposition replace the old machines in the early 1970s.[44] The German publishing house Gruner + Jahr took the same approach in 1978–9,[45] thereby avoiding both a labour dispute and the possible disruption of a "big bang" approach in transitioning to new technology too abruptly.[46]

At Gutfreund, the gradual transition to computer typesetting happened a bit differently and without hot metal. Regarding the organization and division of labour, most of the work was done in a quasi-pre-industrial fashion resembling a cottage industry or, more precisely, an early type of telework (which should later play an important role in printing during the 1980s).[47] Eight women did most of the typesetting while working at home using a 1950s technology – perforators – to produce punched tape. Then, at Gutfreund, the tapes were electronically transformed to a modern type of tape, which drove the photosetters.[48] Of course, editors and managers preferred the streamlined story of technological innovation immediately revolutionizing the industry. It seemed to prove that reorganization of work was necessary and non-negotiable. They omitted the political dimension of the decision to use a new technology. Rather, they provided a misleading version of the actual process and then presented it as if there were no alternative.

Largely due to the misinformation from Gutfreund, the German printing union spared the typesetting shop but was paying close attention to hindering the last step of newspaper production: printing. The *Times* commissioned the nearby TER-Druck at Neu-Isenburg just outside Frankfurt to print the paper. The German union was notified but again could not arrange an official strike, due to the fact that TER-Druck (the publisher of the fascist Turkish paper *Tercüman*) employed mostly Turkish workers, who were not organized in the German printing union.[49] On the afternoon of 27 April, the British unionist Willats and his German colleague Ferlemann spoke at a rally in front of the printing house, calling for "international solidarity."[50] Through "solidarity action," the union blocked the plant and hindered workers and trucks from entering. After the third day of the blockade, the company cancelled production.[51]

In the end, this cancellation seemed to be the outcome of transnational union action, which involved a lot of actors: the British NGA, the transnational IGF, the German printing union, and last but not least the Association of Turkish Workers in Germany. The bilingual members of the Turkish association made it possible to contact the workers at TER-Druck, most of whom spoke only Turkish.[52] The inclusion of Turkish workers in this cooperation had roots in the early 1970s, when these workers had played a leading role in several strikes in West German industry, which had made the German unions at least gradually acknowledge them as follow workers who shared their political goals.[53]

A similar phenomenon was evident in other European countries: as Michael Kozakowski points out in his contribution to this volume, immigrant workers participated in French strikes in the early 1970s too.

Most participants of the TER-Druck solidarity action were members of local union branches, but Willats and Ferlemann also took part at the blockade. "International solidarity" became a key term during this campaign, and it foiled the *Times'* quest for alternative production sites. At the end of May 1979, management developed plans for printing the foreign edition in Portugal, but the Portuguese unions hindered this action.[54] As similar plans arose in their countries, the Greek and Swiss printing unions also resisted immediately.[55]

The failed German *Times* adventure was not the first time the production of a newspaper had been transferred to another country due to national strikes. As early as in 1959, during a labour conflict, British papers transferred production to Belgium and Germany, but the German printing union hindered the printing.[56] And, during the German printers' strikes in 1976 and 1978, the British unions, among other European unions, prevented the production of German papers in Britain.[57]

However, computer composition increasingly made the outsourcing of production at short notice possible. In 1952, the *Wall Street Journal* had already developed the Electro-Typesetter to automatically operate hot metal typesetting machines. Thereafter, the *Journal* could be produced simultaneously in its different composing rooms all over the United States by transmission of electrical impulses.[58] Eight years later, the *New York Times* became the first large daily to introduce Teletypesetters (tape-perforating machines). Globalization proved to be a most important force of automation: new technology made it possible to commit the articles to tape and wire them without delay to Amsterdam, where the international edition of the *New York Times* was printed.[59] Some years later, in the mid-1970s, the *Wall Street Journal* again marked the beginning of a new era expanding the possibilities opened by computer typesetting by starting to use communication satellites. Due to the high costs of satellites, for some years it was still more usual to transmit facsimile pages via land wire and radio link; for instance, the *Herald Tribune* used this technology for sending pages from Paris to London.[60]

The *Times* Frankfurt episode of 1979 demonstrates that local action was no longer an adequate reaction in a sector transformed by computerization and globalization. Instead, international trade union networks that had existed for decades gained importance. The trade union crisis caused by new technology and powerful multinationals impelled the Europeanization of the union movement. In direct reaction to the *Times* dispute, the IGF, in May 1979, decided to establish an international solidarity fund to support future actions.[61] Moreover, the unions realized the need for coordination: already in autumn 1977, the German printing union had been pleading for collaboration with European fellow unions to unify the tariff policy regarding the new technologies.[62] Nonetheless, international solidarity had its limits. In 1984, an IGF working group summed up how difficult it was to mobilize unionists to support their comrades abroad.[63] Even in 1978, the German printing union's president, Leonhard Mahlein, wondered how long it would be possible to hinder international corporate cooperation by means of union solidarity action.[64]

The *Times* strike marked a watershed, but what was the outcome? A few days after the blockade of the *Times* production at TER-Druck ended, Margaret Thatcher won the election and became the British prime minister. Breaking union power was at the top of her agenda. Still, the *Times* dispute ended in November 1979 with the unions finally succeeding in having their demands met. As Les Dixon, the president of the NGA, put it, "We won the battle for the new technology."[65] They might have won the battle, but it was a pyrrhic victory: in the long run, they surely lost the war. The *Times'* owner sold the paper to Rupert Murdoch, who closed down the iconic office in London's Fleet Street and opened a new plant at the London harbour. It was widely computerized, and there was no place for the skills of printers and typesetters.[66] The German unionists' hopes failed, too. Soon after the *Times* settlement, one of the leaders of the TER-Druck blockade, the regional union functionary Manfred Balder, expressed the hope that it opened the chance for the German printing union to extend the staffing guidelines that were part of the agreement in 1978 but would end after eight years.[67] In fact, with the broad adoption of computer typesetting – desktop publishing – the traditional job profiles of printers and typesetters started to disappear in the late 1980s.[68]

Nonetheless, the computerization disputes of 1978–9 had some important consequences. For the first time, a European joint conference of journalists' and printers' unions was held, in Berlin in November 1978. It was organized in response to international corporate cooperation and brought together print workers and journalists from sixteen European countries. The delegates discussed press mergers and the results of computer technology at newspapers.[69] Four years later, a joint working group of this new union collaboration of different media professions recommended rethinking unions' technology policy and suggested opposing new technologies to some extent. In this sense, developments on the level of political actions had an impact at the discursive level.

Scholars studying workers' responses to computerization seldom consider union technology policy beyond strikes, staffing guidelines, or the option of rejecting new technologies. Yet, as historian Monika Dommann has pointed out, print shops became laboratories of union agency in times of automation.[70] One area that can be explored is unions' active engagement in technology development. Here again, the teletypesetting of the 1950s marks an important caesura. Teletypesetting had already been introduced in the interwar period, but operators still used a double-alphabet Linotype keyboard with ninety keys. Only after the Second World War was the common typewriter QWERTY-format with forty-four keys introduced to teletypesetting. To defend the union members – mainly trained Linotype operators – the American International Typographical Union (ITU) introduced the Brewer keyboard, developed by the unionist Claire N. Brewer, who had experienced the replacement of Linotype operators with typists.[71] As the ITU announced, "the Brewer Keyboard enables ITU members, trained to operate a conventional linotype keyboard, to apply their highly-developed printing skill and knowledge to the teletypsetter system of tape punching without undergoing a period of retraining to learn a different keyboard layout and a different fingering system."[72] Preserving skill in a technologically developing industry was the union's main focus. Therefore, the union itself developed a device to combine new and old technologies, thereby defending the old skills. In 1964, at least sixty-seven Brewer keyboards were in use in composing rooms throughout the United States.[73] This defensive strategy of technology development came to the fore once again when computer typesetting was introduced in the 1970s. The manufacturer Linotype-Paul developed a Linotype keyboard for the new computer typesetters. In some British printing shops, the operators could choose between the two different keyboards at the beginning of each shift. However, the machine did not become even a slight success because management and union chapters soon agreed on getting rid of the Linotype keyboard. Management sought the chance to phase out highly paid Linotype operators, whereas the union officials wanted to end the divisions between different professions within the printing industry.[74]

Only a few years later, in 1981, a Scandinavian trade union project changed its strategy, characterizing computerization as an opportunity, not a threat. The UTOPIA project – a Scandinavian acronym for Training, Technology, and Products from the Quality of Work Perspective – sought to develop new technology, in this case software, in a way that would improve the quality of work and thereby give workers the chance to develop their skills.[75] Pelle Ehn, one of the main actors involved, stated, "The UTOPIA project could hopefully contribute to changing the trade union's range of possible actions at the local level. Instead of defending the status quo, an offensive strategy was to be developed for another type of technology and improved products."[76] For a period of five years, typesetters, computer scientists, and sociologists collaborated, with the support of the Scandinavian Graphic Workers' Union, the universities of Stockholm and Aarhus, the state-owned software developer Liber, and two newspapers, to develop "skill-enhancing tools for graphic workers."[77] In retrospect, the contributors saw the project's success as related less to the actual software developed and more to the methods used: "UTOPIA showed that it is possible to design information technology based on use requirements such as work organisation, work environment, forms of co-operation and working skills."[78] However, as a critic later pointed out, the project did not produce a working system but mainly a new design approach. And it failed to become a model for international unions: to apply it, strong unions and state support were needed, but these were rare outside of Scandinavia. Moreover, software designers adopted the model only in a highly selective way. The idea of participatory design vanished and was replaced by a mere functional empowerment, which, in the end, corresponded completely with managements' need for efficiency.[79] Moreover, as Franziska Rehlinghaus's contribution to this volume shows, training on the job could serve very different purposes: the unions hoped for enhanced participation, while the entrepreneurs used "training measures to strengthen the ties and the loyalty of qualified employees."

Workers' Self-Perception: The Replacement of Skilled Industrial Workers by Knowledge Workers?

In addition to its practical aspects, the issue of skill was crucial to the workers' self-image. How, then, did the transformations caused by computerization affect workers and their self-perception? Printers' and compositors' traditional self-perception as belonging to an aristocracy of labour due to their skills and their strong position in industrial relations was not immediately threatened by computerization. In retrospect, this seems quite surprising. However, in the printing industry, workers' self-perception relied on immense pride in working with the most recent technology. Thus, even in the late 1970s, while computerization continued to emerge, the workers still shared a strong belief in technological progress. The main base for this optimism was their belief that computerization had certain limits. The workers' experience and the trade's history suggested the following narrative: skilled labour had never been replaced, and human skill would always be irreplaceable, at least to a certain degree.

In 1977, a printer being interviewed pointed out that he and his fellow workers did not worry because they were like "machine-men." They had so much sense of the machines that it would be impossible to replace them with unskilled workers.[80] At a different company, a compositor admitted to another interviewer that he and his co-workers were in fact scared of future work in a computerized environment. Yet, one thought provided consolation: they were convinced that the computer would never do better work than the skilled worker sitting in front of it.[81] This idea demonstrates that most workers understood technology as an imitation of human skills: technology might get near the human original but could never be supreme. Moreover, most workers were convinced that technological progress was limited and that most innovations had already been implemented. Even in the late 1970s – in retrospect, the start of a decade that fundamentally changed the printing industry – it was common to think that further technological developments would affect only lesser aspects of production.[82]

It is important to emphasize that workers were not surprised by technological developments: most were well informed about the most recent innovations, and many of them regularly visited the print trade fair DRUPA.[83] Of course, some workers, especially typesetters, were fully aware of the threat to their jobs. But, if they had any aversion to new technology or even daydreamed of Luddism, the workers discarded those ideas themselves. A phototypesetter told an interviewer about his bad feelings about the "silly automats" and his insight that the end of typesetting was near. Yet, the only option to make an impact was throwing those "crappy things" out of the window, which would make no difference because typesetters would "be right out of it" soon anyway.[84]

Some workers were looking forward to the new technology – even in late 1977 while the printing union prepared for a strike because the computerization of typesetting was endangering the jobs of thousands of workers. The union started an inquiry at local plants, and, while most workers were loyal to the strike, a strong minority noted that they liked working with the new technology and had no problems with computerization.[85] The works council of one printing house even asked the union not to participate in the strike actions. They feared that such strikes might convince their employer to take back the decision to introduce filmsetting.[86] In fact, no one wanted to go on working with the old technology of hot metal typesetting, which had serious hygienic problems. Here, workers were quite enthusiastically waiting for the new technology. While enthusiasm about technology surely is not the whole picture, it would be equally wrong to assume that workers in general rejected new technologies.

These findings correspond to those of the contemporary investigations of New York printers done by the sociologists Theresa Rogers and Nathalie Friedman at the end of the 1970s. How the workers assessed technological change depended on their job and age: the formerly rather low-rated machinists enhanced their status becoming technicians of the new machinery while the previously high-rated proofreaders lost status or even their jobs.[87] However, the valuations had a soft component, too: predominantly, younger typesetters emphasized that they had "always been fascinated by electronics" and therefore liked working with the new equipment, while some older typesetters missed the "romance" of hot metal and disliked the idea that a "machine tells you what to do."[88] Moreover, the new technology implied changes in employee structure: typesetter and printer jobs used to be exclusively male, but now more and more women began working as typists at the computers. In interviews, the male typewriters, for reasons of self-affirmation, stressed the difference between themselves and their "unskilled" female co-workers. It did not make any difference for these men if the women were trained typists: in their eyes, their female colleagues simply lacked the skills of typesetters. Of course, strictly speaking, experience in hot metal typesetting was no help at the computers. Yet, the men presented themselves as incorporating tacit knowledge: only experienced typesetters were able to do the job with great accuracy. One typesetter stated that, while he was "always aiming for the optimal results," his colleague, the "female typist, she does not know at all what she is typing."[89] Another typewriter at a different company claimed that "the girls" had "no inkling of what they are doing," did not care about mistakes, and had "no relationship to their work."[90] Of course, this was just the latest manifestation of traditional gender stereotypes similar to those of the interwar period.[91] By differentiating themselves from their female co-workers, the male typewriters tried to assure at least themselves (and the interviewers) that their skill was still relevant in the computer age. By conviction, the former members of the aristocracy of labour maintained a sense of supremacy over the female typists.

Not everybody was concerned about the new technology. Even in the heat of the computerization dispute in winter 1977, the print workers of the southern German city of Coburg were more interested in the issue of the impending loss of bonuses (loyalty funds) than in computer typesetting.[92] Because computers were not introduced into every German print shop immediately, workers at many print companies were not aware that job security was an urgent problem.[93]

With respect to job status, there are reasons to question the bias that assumes that automation is always a deskilling force. First, as I have demonstrated, on the subjective level, workers moving from a hot metal to a computerized environment did not always perceive themselves as deskilled. Second, on the objective level, work in a computerized environment did not necessarily prove to be less demanding. The Stuttgart Printing Centre, which was established in 1976 and was one of the most modern sites for typesetting and printing at that time in Germany, is a good example. Operating this generation of computer typesetters proved to be more complicated than foreseen. The members of the printing centre's work councils wrote a letter to the trade union paper *Druck und Papier* calling for a restoration of the old division of labour that had existed before computerization took over. In those days, for example, the editors only had to write "caption, italic" on a routing slip and the typesetters took care of the formatting. Now, working at the computers, the editors themselves had to enter skilfully a complicated combination of letters and numbers – in this case, " 'SV 153,030' 'SV339.1' 'DF12.2' Text 'DF12.0' 'CF110,2.625' 'WS' 'HO' Foto: -VXXX 'QF'."[94] In fact, this reflected what John Diebold had predicted in 1963: the "march of technology" would completely change the industry – affecting not only Linotype operators but also editors.[95]

Only after the establishment of desktop publishing beginning in 1985 did computer typesetting became simpler. However, this does not mean that this date marks the immediate end of skilled work: knowledge of computer operations was still uncommon, and new skills had to be learned. In 1995, the Bochum labour court had to decide on an issue of job grading. A former typewriter working for years with desktop publishing sued his employer to classify his job in a higher wage group. The employer argued the job could be done by anyone, but the court decided that the job was to be classified as "work with additional expertise." According to the judicial decision, the skilled typesetter had needed further training (which he actually had received) to do the work.[96] Nevertheless, the establishment of desktop publishing signified the definitive transformation of the printing industry, which finally changed workers' self-perception. In 1990, as an inquiry into the printing industry showed, most workers described their job profile by referring to a high standard of knowledge, large responsibility, and autonomy. In contrast, manual skills that were named as most important in similar inquiries during the early 1980s had lost their prominence.[97]

Thus, on the level of workers' self-perception and mentality, technological innovations did not cause an immediate transformation. For at least a decade after computerization started, continuity ruled both the workers' self-image and the union strategies.

Conclusion

I would like to suggest that historians of structural transformations since the 1970s should investigate the interconnection of computerization and globalization. These phenomena did not only affect corporations but also industrial relations and unions. It can be argued that, to some extent, the union crisis was first caused by technological change and then pushed the trade union movement's Europeanization. But it is crucial not to overlook aspects of continuity within the transformations. A linear history of innovation tends to neglect the more complicated process of implementing computers. Hot metal did not cease at once, neither did skilled typesetters disappear instantly. Old technologies such as perforators and workers' traditional mindsets with respect to technological progress were important factors related to the technological development in the late 1970s. The perspective of a history from below shows that workers' new self-perceptions within a multitude of job profiles could still rest on the skill of coping with the most recent technology. Therefore, even under transformed working conditions after the emergence of computer composition, they could still imagine themselves as being "machine-men." Such thinking reflected a concept of automation as never being total: in the context of the printing industry, any kind of automation was thought of as imitation of human skills that would never entirely replace them. This mental continuity could partially absorb the shock of structural transformation and deskilling. Therefore, workers and work councils responded even more willingly to the challenges of computerization than the leading unionists of the national printers' union.

This chapter has tried to shed light on the complicated story of technological change. Some of the common assumptions proved to be false. The workers' mindset was not always a hindrance to technological change. Furthermore, the mere focus on workers' *reactions* to technological change overlooks the crucial point that they were an active factor in these developments. Technological change is more correctly to be grasped as an interplay of entrepreneurial and political action and of the cultural frame of mind of its different actors. Also, the issue of skill is crucial. It seems reasonable to free historical research from certain presuppositions about automation and computerization. I strongly recommend questioning the still common equation of automation with efficiency, on the one hand, or with the deskilling of labour, on the other. Looking at the concrete historical practices gives a different view of what computerized workers actually did: they neither immediately lost their status as skilled workers nor did they instantly change their self-perception. Nevertheless, the next generation of print workers did not inherit their predecessors' status: no longer members of the aristocracy of labour, they became media workers. Today, much of the former work of typesetting is now done by writers themselves.

NOTES

This chapter was funded by the Deutsche Forschungsgesellschaft (DFG, German Research Council) – UH 229/2-1.

1 John Diebold, "Automation and the Editor: A Preview of Newsroom Procedures in 1973," *Problems of Journalism* (1963): 142.

2 Ibid., 149.

3 Richard Burkhardt, "Die Entwicklung der grafischen Technik im Zeitalter der Automation" paper presented at the congress of the International Graphical Federation, Vienna, October 1964, 6–7, Archive of the Social Democracy (hereafter ASD), Bonn, Germany, file 5/MEDA 112041.

4 See Andrew Zimbalist, "Technology and the Labor Process in the Printing Industry," in *Case Studies on the Labor Process*, ed. Andrew Zimbalist (New York: Monthly Review Press, 1979), 108.

5 See Harry Kelber and Carl Schlesinger, *Union Printers and Controlled Automation* (New York: Free Press, 1967), 110–11.

6 Ibid., 167.

7 See Annette Schuhmann, "Der Traum vom perfekten Unternehmen: Die Computerisierung der Arbeitswelt in der Bundesrepublik Deutschland," *Zeithistorische Forschungen / Studies in Contemporary History* 9 (2012): 249.

8 See Johannes Platz, "'Revolution der Roboter' oder, Keine Angst vor Robotern'? Die Verwissenschaftlichung des Automationsdiskurses und die industriellen Beziehungen von den 50ern bis 1968," in *Entreprises et crises économiques aux XX siècle: Actes du colloque de Metz Octobre 2005*, ed. Laurent Commaille (Metz: Centre Régional Universitaire Lorrain d'Histoire, 2009), 56–7.

9 Kathleen Ann Thelen, *Union of Parts: Labor Politics in Postwar Germany* (Ithaca, NY: Cornell University Press, 1991), 192.

10 Andrei S. Markovits, *The Politics of the West German Trade Unions: Strategies of Class and Interest Representation in Growth and Crisis* (Cambridge: Cambridge University Press, 1986), 363; see also Cynthia Cockburn,

Brothers: Male Dominance and Technological Change, rev. ed. (London: Pluto Press, 1991), 31.

11 For the Australian experience, see Jesse Adams Stein, *Hot Metal: Material Culture and Tangible Labour* (Manchester: Manchester University Press, 2016).

12 Markovits, *Politics*, 396.

13 William Willard Wirtz, "Labor and the Press," *Problems of Journalism* (1963): 138, 136.

14 Institute of Printing, ed., *Computer Typesetting Conference, London University July 1964: Report of Proceedings* (London: Institute of Printing, 1965), 84.

15 Institute of Printing, ed., *Advances in Computer Typesetting: Proceedings of the 1966 International Computer Typesetting Conference* (London: Institute of Printing, 1967); J.F. Slater, ed., *Computer-Aided Typesetting: Proceedings of an International Conference Held in London* (London: Transcripta Books 1972).

16 Institute of Printing Limited, ed. *Computer Typesetting Conference, 1964*, 69.

17 Ibid., 75, 76.

18 Ibid., 14.

19 Ibid., statement of Mr. Freiman.

20 Richard Burkhardt, *Die technische Entwicklung im grafischen Gewerbe und ihre Auswirkungen auf die Berufsausbildung und Beschäftigung: Vortrag, gehalten auf dem vierten Kongreß der Internationalen Grafischen Föderation am 19. September 1958 in München im Hause des Sports* (Heilbronn: IG Druck und Papier, 1958), 9.

21 Ibid., 12, 24, 3–4.

22 Burkhardt, "Die Entwicklung der grafischen Technik," 10.

23 Ibid., 17, 21. The German daily *Die Welt* has been producing its Essen and Berlin edition by long-distance transmission since 1957. See Hans-Helmut Ehm, *Automation, Arbeitssituation, Arbeitsmotivation: Eine empirische Untersuchung in amerikanischen Unternehmen der Druckindustrie* (Spardorf: Wilfer, 1985), 35.

24 See Hugo Reister, *Profite gegen Bleisatz: Die Entwicklung in der Druckindustrie und die Politik der IG Druck* (Berlin: Die Arbeitswelt, 1980), 117.

25 See Erwin Ferlemann, *Der technische Fortschritt und die Zukunftsaufgaben der grafischen Gewerkschaften: Referat beim IGF-Kongress vom 14. bis zum 19. September 1970 in Kopenhagen* (Stuttgart: IG Druck und Papier, 1970), 10.

26 Ibid., 22.

27 See Matthias Otto, "Die Setzmaschine in Deutschland: Beispiel für eine verzögerte und konfliktarme Technikeinführung," *Technikgeschichte* 60 (1993): 347–64.

28 Detlef Hensche, "Technische Revolution und Arbeitnehmerinteresse: Zu Verlauf und Ergebnissen des Arbeitskampfes in der Druckindustrie 1978," *Blätter für deutsche und internationale Politik* (1978): 415. My translation.

29 Musterreferat: Neue Technik. Veranstaltungen zur Vorbereitung und aus Anlass des Arbeitskampfes. Referentenmaterial der IG Druck und Papier, Hauptvorstand, No. 82/1978, 23.2.1978, p. 7, ASD, file 5/MEDA 114437.

30 IG Druck und Papier et al., "Tarifvertrag 'Neue Technik' in der Druckindustrie 1978," *Gewerkschaftliche Monatshefte* 29 (1979): 310–16.

31 See Karsten Uhl, "Maschinenstürmer gegen die Automatisierung? Der Vorwurf der Technikfeindlichkeit in den Arbeitskämpfen der Druckindustrie in den 1970er und 1980er Jahren und die Krise der Gewerkschaften," *Technikgeschichte* 82 (2015): 157–79.

32 Minutes of joint IFJ/IGF working group meeting, Bern, 30 June 1982, p. 3, ASD, IGF collection, file 138.

33 Stewart, *History of The Times*, 2, 13; John Gennard and Steve Dunn, "The Impact of New Technology on the Structure and Organisation of Craft," *British Journal of Industrial Relations* 21 (1983): 21; John Grigg, *The History of The Times*, vol. 6, *The Thomson Years, 1966–1981* (London: HarperCollins, 1995), 397, 453, 500.

34 Eric Jacobs, *Stop Press: The Inside Story of the "Times" Dispute* (London: André Deutsch, 1980), 88.

35 "Halbe Kosten," *Der Spiegel*, 30 April 1979, 115; Rosemary Collins, "Times Foreign Weekly Plan Angers Unions," *Guardian*, 21 April 1979, 24.

36 Patricia Clough, "Wie die deutschen Gewerkschaften der 'Times' den Mund verboten," *Die Welt*, 2 May 1979.

37 Albert Bechthold, "Die Auslandsausgabe einer britischen Zeitung und die Pressefreiheit hierzulande," *Stuttgarter Zeitung*, 3 May 1979; Wolfgang Borgmann, "Der Kampf um die 'Times' wird auch in Darmstadt geführt," *Stuttgarter Zeitung*, 26 April 1979; Main Executive Board of the IG Druck und Papier, Notification to the regional boards, 25 April 1979, ASD, file 5/MEDA 119007.

38 Jacobs, *Stop Press*, 91.

39 See Collins, "Times Foreign Weekly," 24. The Social Democratic Dutch printing union left the IGF as the French Communist union became a member in 1967; see Leonhard Mahlein, *Gewerkschaften international: Im Spannungsverhältnis zwischen Ost und West – aus eigener Sicht* (Frankfurt: NVG, 1984), 35–40.

40 See Collins, "Times Foreign Weekly," 24. On the same day, for instance, the *Washington Post* reported that the weekly international edition would possibly be printed in the Netherlands. See Leonhard Downie Jr., "London Times Plans International Edition," *Washington Post*, 21 April 1979.

41 "'Times'-Auseinandersetzung. Hensche: Solidaritätsstreik ist rechtlich unumstritten," *Handelsblatt*, 3 April 1979.

42 Jacobs, *Stop Press*, 97.

43 Roland Hill, "'Für uns ist das die Katastrophe': 'Times'-Erfahrungen in einer deutschen Druckerei," *Stuttgarter Zeitung*, 8 June 1979; J. Rh., "'Deutsche Setzer schaffen das Dreifache': Ein Vergleich des Chefredakteurs der 'Times'," *Frankfurter Allgemeine Zeitung*, 6 June 1979.

44 Rex Winsbury, *New Technology and the Press: A Study of Experience in the United States* (London: Her Majesty's Stationery Office, 1975), 35–6.

45 Richard Gaul, "Richter als Schlichter: Computer am Arbeitsplatz," *Die Zeit*, 19 January 1979, 19.

46 Winsbury, *New Technology*, 37.

47 Monika Goldman and Gudrun Richter, *Teleheimarbeiterinnen in der Satzherstellung/Texterfassung für die Druckindustrie* (Dortmund: Sozialforschungsstelle, 1986).

48 Jacobs, *Stop Press*, 89.

49 Borgmann, "Der Kampf um die 'Times.'"

50 Flyer addressing the solidarity rally (27 April 1979) in Zeppelinheim, ASD, file 5/MEDA 119007.

51 "Neu-Isenburg: Gegen Druck der 'Times,'" *Frankfurter Rundschau*, 28 April 1979. Afterwards, the legal dispute continued for years concerning the blockade's legal admissibility; see "Flaggschiff blockiert," *Der Spiegel*, 22 March 1981, 90–2.

52 Rainer Duhm, Letter to Walter Müller-Jentsch, n.d. [summer 1979], Archive for Social Movements (ASM), Bochum, Germany, Collection Müller-Jentsch, file 142.

53 Jennifer A. Miller, *Turkish Guest Workers in Germany: Hidden Lives and Contested Borders, 1960s to 1980s* (Toronto: University of Toronto Press, 2018), 135.

54 Gisela Mayer, "Erfolgreiche Solidaritätsaktion zeigt auch in England Wirkung," *Nahcrichten zur Wirtschafts- und Sozialpolitik* 6 (1979): 21.

55 Notice of the German news agency dpa, 30 May 1979, Griechische Presse-Gewerkschaften gegen "Times"-Druck in Griechenland (dpa 082 pl/m), ASD, file 5/MEDA 119006; see also, Zentralsekretariat des Schweizer Typographenbundes, "Times-Konflikt," *Helvetische Typographia*, 23 May (1979): 1.

56 Kim C. Priemel, "Gewerkschaftsmacht? Britische und westdeutsche Gewerkschaften im Strukturwandel," in *Die Rückkehr der Arbeitslosigkeit: Die Bundesrepublik im europäischen Kontext 1973 bis 1989*, ed. Thomas Raithel and Thomas Schlemmer (Munich: Oldenbourg, 2009), 111. However, afterwards the Wuppertal labour court ordered the German union to provide compensation; see Werner Bulla, "Solidaritätsstreiks nur mit Einschränkungen zulässig," *Druckwelt*, 1 June 1979, 744.

57 "Internationale Solidarität," *Druck und Papier* 8 (1976): 2; "Internationale Solidarität," *Druck und Papier* 9 (1976): 3.

58 Kelber and Schlesinger, *Union Printers*, 55–6.

59 Ibid., 80–1.

60 Winsbury, *New Technology*, 53.

61 International Graphical Federation, Zirkular 679, 22 May 1979, ASD, file 5/ MEDA 119006.

62 Industriegewerkschaft Druck und Papier, Resolution on tariff policy, 22 August 1977, 4, ASD, file 5/MEDA 114417.

63 Minutes of the IGF working group "action program" meeting, Bern, Switzerland, 6 March 1984, 4, ASD, IGF collection, file 138.

64 Industriegewerkschaft Druck und Papier, Minutes of the bargaining commission's second meeting, 18/20 January 1978, 8, ASM, collection Müller-Jentsch, file 8.

65 Helga Zoller, "Les Dixon: 'Wir haben die Schlacht um die neue Technik gewonnen,'" *Druck und Papier*, 3 December 1979, 11.

66 Priemel, "Gewerkschaftsmacht?," 116.

67 G.M., "Times-Konflikt in England beendet," *Druck und Papier*, 3 December 1979, 13.

68 Charlotte Schönbeck, "Kulturgeschichtliche und soziale Veränderungen durch den Wandel in der Drucktechnik," *N.T.M.* 6 (1998): 214.

69 Detlef Hensche (Industriegewerkschaft Druck und Papier board member), Press information, September 1978, ASD, file 5/MEDA 119006; International Labour Office, *New Technologies: Their Impact on Employment and the Working Environment* (Geneva: ILO, 1982), 103.

70 Monika Dommann, "Umbrüche am Ende der Linotype," *Nach Feierabend: Das Zürcher Jahrbuch für Wissensgeschichte* 12 (2016): 222.

71 Kelber and Schlesinger, *Union Printers*, 71–2.

72 International Typographical Union, *Photocomposing Machines and the Brewer Keyboard* (Indianapolis: ITU, 1954), 7.

73 Kelber and Schlesinger, *Union Printers*, 72.

74 Cockburn, *Brothers*, 99.

75 Pelle Ehn, *Work-Oriented Design of Computer Artifacts* (Stockholm: Arbetslivscentrum, 1988), 330.

76 Ibid.

77 Susanne Bødker et al., "A Utopian Experience: On Design of Powerful Computer-Based Tools for Skilled Graphic Workers," in *Computers and Democracy: A Scandinavian Challenge*, ed. Gro Bjerknes et al. (Ipswich, UK: Ipswich Book Company, 1989), 254.

78 Susanne Bødker et al., "Co-Operative Design: Perspectives on 20 Years with 'the Scandinavian IT Design Model'," in *Proceedings of the First Nordic Conference on Human-Computer Interaction*, ed. Association for Computing Machinery (New York: Association for Computing Machinery, 2000), 3.

79 Clay Spinuzzi, "A Scandinavian Challenge, a US Response: Methodological Assumptions in Scandinavian and US Prototyping Approaches," *Proceedings of the 20th Annual International Conference on*

Computer Documentation, ed. Kathy Haramundanis (New York: ACM, 2002), 209, 212–13.

80 Interview with a rotary printer, twenty-nine years old, 1977–8, in Margareta Steinrücke, *Generationen im Betrieb: Fallstudien zur generationenspezifischen Verarbeitung betrieblicher Konflikte* (Frankfurt: Campus, 1986), 196–7.

81 Claudia Weber, *Rationalisierungskonflikte in Betrieben der Druckindustrie* (Frankfurt: Campus, 1982), S. 143.

82 Interview with a bookbinder, forty-six years old, 1977–78, in Steinrücke, *Generationen*, 151–2.

83 See Steinrücke, *Generationen*, 152.

84 Weber, *Rationalisierungskonflikte*, 130, 132–3.

85 Completed questionnaire, reply after a meeting of union workplace representatives of the newspaper *Heilbronner Stimme*, 30 October 1977, ASD, file 5/MEDA 114417.

86 Report on the situation in Lower Saxony, n.d. [November 1977], ASD, file 5/MEDA 114417.

87 Theresa F. Rogers and Nathalie S. Friedman, *Printers Face Automation: The Impact of Technology on Work and Retirement among Skilled Craftsmen* (Lexington, MA: Lexington Books, 1980), 29.

88 Ibid., 48, 50.

89 Weber, *Rationalisierungskonflikte*, 119.

90 Ibid., 133.

91 Karsten Uhl, "Die Geschlechterordnung der Fabrik: Arbeitswissenschaftliche Entwürfe von Rationalisierung und Humanisierung 1900–1970," *Österreichische Zeitschrift für Geschichtswissenschaften* 21 (2010): 93–117.

92 Report on the questionnaire action in Bavaria, n.d. [November 1977], 2, ASD, file 5/MEDA 114417.

93 Evaluation of the staff meeting of the company Ditzen & Co., Bremerhaven, 3 November 1977, ASD, file 5/MEDA 114417.

94 Works council of the Stuttgart-Möhringen Printing Centre, letter to the editor, in *Druck und Papier*, 23 April 1979.

95 Diebold, "Automation," 140.

96 Judgment of the Bochum labour court, trial of Lutz Golnick against Leupenmühlen Druck GmbH & Co. KG, 22 June 1995, 14, ASM, collection Industriegewerkschaft Druck und Papier, local association Bochum, file 62B.

97 Siegfried Kempf, *Technologischer Wandel in der Druckindustrie: Gutenbergs Nachfahren zwischen beruflichem Aufstieg und innerer Kündigung* (Pfungstadt: Ergon, 1993), 202.

6 Soft Skills in an Age of Crises: Continuing Training as an Economic Coping Strategy in West German Companies

FRANZISKA REHLINGHAUS

Introduction

In German historical research about the 1970s, the oil crisis is often considered the turning point that marked a new era after the boom years of the "economic miracle."[1] Apart from the macroeconomic structural transformation, which affected especially the workers of the "old" industries and pushed forward the service sector, changes were also considered for production regimes and work organization (buzzword: post-Fordism),[2] economic thought patterns formulated in ideas of neo-liberalism,[3] social and welfare policy,[4] consumption behaviour,[5] social values and norms,[6] concepts of individuality and subjectivity,[7] body awareness,[8] and many more aspects of economic life. Even if the thesis of an all-embracing transformation during the 1970s, mainly represented by the concept of a "structural break," has been relativized and mitigated by further case studies, the hypothesis that things changed considerably at that time is still widely accepted.

One specific field in which the continuities and changes in nearly all the aspects mentioned above were bundled is the field of continuing education, especially with those measures that tried to change the mind, the character, the behaviour, and the bodies of employees. Such forms of "soft skills" training[9] were, in a certain sense, attempts to incorporate economic and social demands and personal needs into single individuals and employee groups. Continuing training could therefore be regarded as linking human resource development, social policy, and self-improvement, which were all connected to socio-economic, political, and cultural influences.

The 1970s were boom years for continuing education, especially inside those companies that became the largest providers of training seminars for adults in West Germany. Taking into account the outcomes of the economic recession, rising commodity prices, and growing international competition for customers and sales markets, this kind of countercyclical industrial investment in employees – including those companies that were under increasing pressure – is remarkable. One could interpret this development as an active, systematic, and successful industrial strategy to cope with economic and social challenges by inventing a "new spirit of capitalism."[10] Instead, I want to argue that the expansion of training investment was the result of different intertwining developments in various social fields that had started in the years before the crisis and had gained considerable and unforeseen momentum since the 1970s. First, it was the beneficiary of the educational reforms that were initiated in the 1960s and were passed forward especially by the social-liberal federal government.[11] Second, it was part of the reorganization of business structures in companies that had been affected by the first recession.[12] Third, it was a product of trade union–driven endeavours geared toward a "humanization of working life."[13] And fourth, it was the result of changing requests and desires of employees looking for career opportunities and workplace safety.[14]

The rise of continuing training was therefore more a question of reinterpretation than of reorientation, an attempt to make a virtue of the necessity that companies concentrate on personnel development and evolve into powerful actors in the areas of educational expansion and qualification in a time of economic crises. The results of this development were manifold: the continuing education sector was, and is to this day, the only part of educational policy that has remained largely unregulated politically.[15] On the one side, therefore, continuing education has obeyed market principles: the increasing demand for training offered by big companies stimulated the founding of external training institutes that became workplaces in the service industry for people of different professions (e.g., for psychologists and business administrators as well as for educators, former managers, and management consultants).[16] The history of continuing training within industry can therefore show the immediate interdependence of the industrial crisis and the rise of the service sector with its typical working conditions, like temporary employment, part-time jobs, freelance work, and so on.[17]

On the other side, it was the industries that decided upon and controlled not only the subjects of continuing education but also which groups of employees would have access to training opportunities. Consequently, the development of the concept in the 1970s laid the foundation for the relationship between skill development and career chances in West Germany, which had a strong impact on opportunities for social inclusion and, in the end, supported social inequality.[18]

In this chapter, I present continuing training as part of an industrial reaction to new challenges arising around 1970. The primary focus is thus on the perspective of the companies. To that end, the analysis concentrates on large West German enterprises that were, unlike small and medium companies, able to maintain their own training departments and to develop and offer a large choice of seminars for their employees.[19] Despite different preconditions regarding branches, legal forms, the social structure of staff members, corporate culture, and the degree to which they were affected by structural changes and the economic crisis, several companies reformed their continuing training concept in the mid-1970s in a similar way. We can thus speak about a general trend in this field. This chapter therefore emphasizes similarities in greater detail than differences and will sketch the development in that time regarding five aspects of such training. The first section will examine the interdependence between political and economic arguments for continuing training. The second section will present the improvement in cost calculation while the third will focus on the integration of continuing training in personnel development. The fourth section examines seminar topics, and the final section will analyse the practices of evaluation.

Continuing Training and Education Policy

Unlike primary school, secondary school, and higher education, the continuing education sector in West Germany had not been regulated by law since the late 1960s.[20] After the Second World War, the initiatives for an education system for adults beyond vocational training in the proper sense had been taken from the American and British occupation forces, the adult education centres, the trade unions, and private industry.[21] The Western victorious powers, the adult education centres, and the trade unions had been primarily focused on political re-education and on workers' and general education.[22] But the occupying powers, as well as several companies and employers' organizations, quite soon developed specific training programs that initially covered questions of leadership and rationalization measures and later the whole set of soft skills training that implemented psychological and communicative knowledge for business purposes. Since the 1950s, a growing number of continuing education institutes were founded that provided their services and programs for different companies.[23] Altogether, the adult education sector was a largely unregulated, dynamic market where several agents competed for contracts and potential clients.

It was the social-liberal government led by Willy Brandt that started an educational initiative designed to include the continuing education sector in 1969. The so-called Sputnik shock in 1957, the education programs of the Organization for Economic Co-operation and Development that were dedicated to lifelong learning starting in 1961, the debates over Georg Picht's "educational catastrophe" in 1964, and Ralf Dahrendorf's reply that education had to be a citizen's right[24] all encouraged a reform climate that was also influenced by the first significant economic recession in 1966–7.[25] In Brandt's government statement in 1969, he proclaimed education policy as one of the main tasks of the new government to "mobilize the performance reserves of society and to improve the chances of every individual."[26] The reforms in the continuing education sector were thus to serve several purposes. First, the government declared continuing education as an adequate instrument to compensate for the injustices of the school system that perpetuated social inequalities. The idea here was mainly to open new life chances for poorly educated people to whom continuing education would offer career opportunities and social advancement. Second, especially left-wing political movements and the trade unions demanded continuing education as an instrument for political emancipation.[27] Therefore, the social-liberal government promised a law that committed employers to granting employees educational leave with continued payment of wages.[28] Finally, lifelong learning was seen as a strategy "for maintaining welfare and national competitiveness in a knowledge-based economy,"[29] based on specific, economically valuable skills.

These three sources of impetus resulted in several legislation processes that were meant to professionalize and incorporate continuing education as the fourth pillar of the West German educational system. The German Education Council (Deutscher Bildungsrat) published in 1970 an Education Structure Plan (*Strukturplan für das Bildungswesen*) that emphasized continuing education as an integrative power for the cohesion of society.[30] In concrete terms, the government tried to regulate access to training courses, to standardize certificates, to extend state control of training providers, and to facilitate codetermination in continuing education questions.

It is not surprising that corporations eyed these ambitious political efforts critically and ultimately did not support them. In particular, those firms that had been active in the field of continuing education since the 1950s dreaded political interference in their internal affairs. Companies like Bayer and Siemens feared not only the potential costs but also the loss of control of the content of the training: the integration of job-specific training and general and political education was considered to risk companies' economic success because it undermined the upskilling of employees exclusively for business purposes. From this point of view, the companies were also anxious about competition from training offerings outside the companies, which, moreover, could figure into future state support.

In June 1970, the Confederation of German Employers' Associations (Bundesvereinigung der deutschen Arbeitgeberverbände) formulated some "ideas" about adult education that were sent to the federal Ministry for Education and Science, the political group chairs of the federal parliament, the prime ministers and the state ministers of education and the arts of the German *Länder* (states), and the group chairs of the regional parliaments.[31] The confederation's paper emphasized that the business sector was willing to take responsibility in continuing education and that companies had always been an important driving force in educational politics. Employers argued for a new view on the training sector, which should, first and foremost, be regarded as a meaningful and productive future investment. Consequently, they warned against the risks of overregulation. The creation of training institutes, the curriculum design, the nature of employment, and the training of instructors had to remain the free responsibility of the training providers. This would be the only way to realize an adult education system that was also consistent with a democratic state. Such a rationalistic and functional conception, which regarded the education system as a function of shifting economic requirements, corresponded to a logic that sought equilibrium of industrial demand and supply of skills as a perfect market situation where governmental regulations seemed to be irrelevant and inadequate.[32]

The employers' reservation and doubts could not prevent a codetermination and consultation right for works councils regarding training activities of employees, which was the most important change in the formal and legal structure of continuing training in industry. Since 1972, works council representatives decided jointly with the employers about the execution of training measures and had a right to recommend employees as participants.[33] In practice, however, the role of the works councils appeared to be to "rubber-stamp" decisions that had already been made by human resources (HR) departments.[34]

Apart from these new regulations, which were codified in the Works Constitution Act (*Betriebsverfassungsgesetz*), the largest part of the political reforms concerning the advanced training sector were interrupted by the oil crisis in autumn 1973, which suddenly limited the financial basis for further action. Nonetheless, the Education Master Plan (*Gesamtplan für das Bildungswesen*) that was presented by the federal government in December 1973 had set ambitious targets for the continuing education sector, including the foundation of local-regional cooperation bodies, the development of standardized curricula according to a modular system, the building of continuing education centres, the creation of 40,000 places for short-term training (in addition to an estimated 160,000 places planned by 1985) and 95,000 places for full-time training by 1985, the qualification of thousands of full- and part-time instructors, and finally, the step-by-step implementation of training leave.[35] Whereas the master plan remained extremely vague regarding potential costs of the planned measures, the Edding Commission, which was set up by the federal government in 1970 to analyse the expenditures and the financing of informal occupational education, presented in 1974 the potential costs for its implementation. Even the expenses for an educational leave of two weeks for 15 per cent of all employees were estimated at 200 million DM in the set-up phase through 1985, and thereafter at 4,738 billion DM per annum.[36] In a debate in the Bundestag a few days after the publication of the Edding report, the governing parties as well as the parliamentary opposition subordinated realization of the Education Master Plan to future economic development. The Christian Social Union delegate Albert Probst demanded therefore a "waiver of reformist excessiveness" regarding the current economic situation.[37]

The result was that only a few *Länder* (Berlin, Bremen, Hamburg, Hessen, and Niedersachsen) passed laws on educational leave during the 1970s. The last serious attempt to regulate the continuing training sector by a new Vocational Training Act failed in 1976 due to the resistance of the *Länder*. Obviously the political willingness to invest huge sums in the reorganization of the continuing training sector was shrinking or, rather, was constricted by the cost explosion in the unemployment insurance system.[38] Thus even the educational policy was affected by the "great disillusionment" that followed the reforming zeal of the late 1960s.[39]

At the same time, industrial decline made the question of continuing education more urgent than before: less-educated workers, among them women and migrants, in the secondary economic sector were particularly affected by unemployment, and the service sector also possessed great potential for labour-saving measures through computer technology, as Karsten Uhl's chapter in this volume has shown for the printing industry.[40] In light of the economic crisis, the political arguments for continuing education changed fundamentally: instead of pursuing the integration of general and vocational education under state control, politicians of all parties emphasized again the necessity of differentiating between adult and occupational training and appealed to the responsibility of the employers.[41] So it came to pass that the policymakers handed the interpretation of continuing training as a method for labour market qualification over to private industry. But, confronted with rising staff costs, rising commodity prices, and declining growth rates, economic demands had changed too.

Data Collection and the Question of Costs

For a long time, the statistical recording of training measures inside companies had included only the number of single training events and the number of participants. Usually, these data were published in the companies' personnel and social reports, often incomplete, which made it difficult to compare them over a longer period of time. Around 1970, West German companies started collecting data on the costs of training activities. Inspired by the work of the Edding Commission, the companies implemented new cost-finding models to gain an overview of the share of training costs in total personnel costs.

The first problem facing the data collection was that the concept of "continuing training" was itself unclear and therefore highly disputable. Even if several companies adopted the definition that was coined by the Vocational Training Act in 1969, which subsumed all measures that were to conserve, enlarge, or adjust the skills of employees or enable them to improve their professional status,[42] the concrete understanding differed from company to company. In 1968, Bayer, for instance, had defined continuing training from both an idealistic and a functional perspective: continuing training was to provide a space for the professional and mental "self-unfolding" of employees and was meant to strengthen their "intellectual and character skills." The overarching objective was to integrate staff into the company's system and increase their professional competences.[43] In 1974, the company's committee for personnel development complained that several divisions and departments listed even work meetings and recurring specialist conferences in their educational planning. In order to prevent future misunderstandings, the HR department was given the task of defining the concept of "continuing training" with a legal, organizational, and educational meaning. One-day events were not to be recorded.[44]

At Bertelsmann, the purpose of establishing a special "training model" in 1973 made it necessary to gain insights into the status quo of training activities. From that point on, the profit centres were invited to fill in a detailed form on all training activities during the past year and future educational planning, including the subject, aims, methods, duration, and costs of training courses.[45] Leaving aside the fact that the director of the publishing group, Rudolf Wendorff, regarded the survey as a bureaucratic waste of time,[46] the responses from the profit centres showed a broad interpretation of the concept of "continuing training": whereas "political and cultural" or "simple information events" were not considered as training,[47] internal meetings or participation in work fairs were subsumed under the term. Accordingly, ten out of sixteen employees who took part in "continuing training" in 1975–6 at the Orbis Company merely visited a book fair.[48] Clearly, continuing training served as a catch-all term for several activities, and statistical recording of it remained difficult.

Despite these problems, the firms pushed the statistical recording forward, because they were especially interested in one particular factor: apart from the direct costs for instructors, board and lodging, rooms and materials, the HR departments began to collect data about the time employees spent participating in training and, therefore, not working. The conversion from training hours to training costs was complex, because it required additional information about the number of participants, their occupational status, and their salary per hour. For developing a convincing calculation model, the companies exchanged information and experiences. Siemens especially was considered to be a pioneer regarding these questions: a specialist for cost accounting in the company had been a member of the Edding Commission.[49] In 1979 companies like Bertelsmann, IBM, BASF, and Siemens agreed to use the same calculation model for direct and indirect training costs,[50] thus making the data comparable.

There were several reasons why these data in particular became so important. First, the total expenditure in training had been unknown so far, but was now discovered as a field with cost-saving potential, which became extremely important in the context of the economic crisis. The reduction of training hours, the companies hoped, would affect the remaining working time as well as the payment of the instructors and the costs of rooms. Second, the companies searched for substantial arguments against a right to paid educational leave, which probably would affect their productivity. Whereas the trade unions argued that employees needed opportunities for continuing education according to their personal and career needs without being afraid of any financial disadvantages,[51] companies feared additional costs and the loss of control in training questions. With reference to the statistical data, the firms could now argue that they were already financing several training days, including the continued payment of wages.

The last reason for the professionalization of the computational models was that the expenditure in training became an argument in internal debates about policies with human capital. In 1975, Bayer's Education Department formulated a paper with "arguments for in-company initial and continuing training."[52] The paper took clear aim at plans of the management board to significantly reduce expenditures in training. The Education Department argued instead that the training costs should be considered as investments in human capital even if it was impossible to ascertain their valuations for future earnings. The argument was that a high level of training expenditure was a decisive factor in the competition for talent. Aside from the fact that young qualified graduates considered training offerings as a factor when determining the attractiveness of a potential employer, the company itself had an interest in qualifying its workforce: skills like cooperation and communication were decisive for Bayer's leadership concept. And training itself contributed to greater motivation and job satisfaction.

Accordingly, the HR department pointed to training investments of large industrial companies: Bayer's training costs per employee in the past had been significantly lower than the expenditures of firms like BASF or Siemens and increased only slightly. Therefore, a reduction of offerings was apparently inappropriate.[53] As in Bayer, several other HR departments used the comparison in training hours and costs with other firms as an internal argument to legitimate their commitment to education despite the difficult economic circumstances. In interpreting continuing training as a benchmark, as a marker of progressiveness, the HR departments countered arguments that were focused on cost saving. The result was that the offerings and the expenditures for training activities grew remarkably during the 1970s, promoted by promises of a better workforce and higher productivity. The Institute of the German Economy (Institut der deutschen Wirtschaft) calculated in 1977 that private industry had increased its training expenditure since 1971 by 42 per cent to 17.35 billion DM.[54] Companies therefore spent twice as much as the federal government had expended for education, sciences, and research together and conducted 44 per cent of all training seminars that took place in Germany.[55] Apart from the fact that the figures also included costs of apprenticeships, which had declined in the same period, they showed that the industry's strategy had changed over the course of the decade.

Continuing Training as Part of a Substantial HR Policy

The oil crisis occurred at a time when reorganization processes in several companies were well underway. The strong competitive pressure of the international market, caused by changes in demand patterns and the pace of technological innovations, resulted in new business strategies to move into new products and markets. Many companies needed to find growth opportunities outside their core business, and diversification was one possible answer. In the late 1960s, several of the biggest German companies adopted a divisional structure in their business organization. Siemens deployed a divisional structure in 1969, as did Bayer in 1970; Friedrich Krupp AG was converted into a limited-liability company after the death of its proprietor, Alfried Krupp von Bohlen und Halbach, in 1967. These reorganizations were often preceded by generational changes in management and were therefore also connected with a change in managerial attitudes and a redistribution of responsibilities.[56] Several companies used not only the expertise of business consultants to master the formal questions of organization,[57] but also the offerings of training providers to influence the behaviour of employees in a desired direction. It is therefore not surprising that the companies' reorganization was also connected to a restructuring of HR departments and their subdivisions that were responsible for education and training.

Around 1970, a variety of new commissions and institutions inside the companies were established that were meant to map and coordinate training activities, to test external offerings, and to prevent overlapping of responsibilities and doubling up of work. Single centralized departments for training under the direct responsibility of the head of personnel, the designation of education officers for every central unit, board staff for manager training, and joint education committees with representatives from the employers' and employees' side were only some of the organizational innovations during the 1970s at Bayer, Bertelsmann, United Electric Power Plants Westphalia (Vereinigte Elektrizitätswerke Westfalen – VEW), Rhenish-Westphalian Power Plant (Rheinisch-Westfälisches Elektrizitätswerk AG – RWE), and Krupp.[58] From an organizational point of view, there was a general trend to centralize and to differentiate the management of training in all companies.

Differentiation meant also that a growing number of employees were regarded as trainable: besides masters, foremen, middle and upper management, and secretaries who had been participants in continuing training since the 1950s, purchasers and salespeople, engineers, administrative staff, members of the works council, and many more became new subjects of training measures.[59] The voluntary training offers of the former years became obligatory courses in the 1970s. They became part of detailed development plans for different groups of employees that pinpointed the training that should be completed at certain career levels. Bertelsmann, for instance, initiated a working group in 1973 to create an advanced training model for the company.[60] Bayer started with a training plan for factory managers and went on with plans for the executive staff in production and distribution, for scientists, for engineers, for the staff of the HR department, and for foremen.[61]

The result was that, in many cases, participation in training became a precondition for individual career advancement. Accordingly, many companies documented training activities from the 1970s on in their personnel records and annual performance reviews. Siemens, Bayer, and Bertelsmann developed special promotion file cards, where promotion objectives and past and future training activities were to be recorded,[62] the former as documentation of skills that could be relevant for future staffing, but also as an indicator of personal engagement and the individual willingness to learn, the latter as measures to be taken for compensating any deficit and as individual promotion-related tasks. Human resource development was to be individualized, and also to activate everyone's largely untapped potential that was waiting to be exploited by the employer. Usually, it was the superior who decided which seminar would be appropriate. Even when an employee asked to participate in special training, the permission of the boss was required.

This rightsizing attempted to rationalize human resource policy and to supervise the optimal exploitation of the workforce inside the companies. Instead of looking for the right person in the right place – a principle of Taylorist and Fordist economies – the new strategy to tailor the workforce to the job requirements seemed to be promising and more efficient. Moreover, it fitted with psychological convictions at this time, that attitudes and behaviours were principally changeable.[63] Thus, systematic training promised to turn wrong personnel selections – which had been understood as bad investment – into modifiable and improvable human capital, provided that the employer kept control over the teaching and learning process.

Consequently, employers considerably restricted the latitude for individual choice. Employers refused permission for educational leave even in those *Länder* where it had been guaranteed by law. There were several lawsuits in the labour courts where trade unions and companies disputed the admissibility of those refusals during the 1970s.[64] In some cases, employees had to pay afterwards: the coffee-roasting facility Eduscho, for instance, refused to pay the total Christmas bonus for those employees who had taken their education leave in 1976. Eduscho justified its decision by saying that the Christmas bonus "had to be earned first" and that the attendance of the employees "played a crucial role" in that.[65] Training wants and training needs were therefore two distinct matters.

The ambivalent relationship between individualization of training on the one side and standardization and discipline on the other was also reflected in the seminar planning process. Even before the Works Constitution Act regulated the codetermination in training questions, several companies conducted training needs analyses "to ensure that task-based, operationally necessary, and business objectives are supported and employees receive assistance through their participation."[66] As of 1972, surveys were conducted periodically and systematically, including questionnaires and open interviews, as the basis for decision making.[67] The strategy was to determine the respective needs of certain employee groups, to develop an appropriate training program for them, and to teach them all step by step in the following years until new desires and requirements became evident and were identified in a follow-up study. This kind of future-oriented arrangement of training in the style of a "five-year plan" shows that continuing education itself had become a response strategy for dealing with future challenges facing the economy. Whereas in the political sphere the planability of the future became highly questionable since the oil shock in 1973,[68] companies still believed that training obeyed the logic of supply and demand and could therefore be predicted and calculated like other items in the economic sphere.

The involvement of employees in training decisions did not, in fact, mean that companies were more responsive to individual needs and suggestions. In 1974, for instance, Bayer started an analysis of training requirements for engineers. The different categories of training measures – technology, chemistry, interpersonal skills/leadership, work safety, cost calculation, computing, working methods, information about the company, and labour law – were predetermined, and were to be hierarchized according to the answers employees gave to a survey. The formulation of the questions shows that the employer was not really interested in the personal training interest of each single engineer but mainly in the supra-individual and job-related requirements. Accordingly, the engineers as well as their superiors were asked "which kind of continuing training or additional information a young graduate engineer needs to fulfill his duties in a certain position optimally."[69] Those interviewed were asked to distribute one hundred points across the given skill areas. The results of the survey were in a certain sense problematic. The interviews had shown that each engineer formulated different desires and had not been able to separate from his or her own experience, and so the meaning of the given categories was highly disputable. The training department concluded that the requirements of the job positions as well as the needs of the engineers differed to such an extent that it did not make any sense to create a single training program for all engineers.[70]

In the following years, the company tried to meet different needs and preferences by substantially expanding its training offerings. Leadership training, for instance, was conceptualized for different employee groups at various stages of their careers with changing thematic priorities: "leadership and motivation," "leadership and conference management," "leadership behaviour," "leadership and negotiation techniques," to name just a few. Similar developments can be observed in other companies.

The result was that not only the expenditure in training grew in the 1970s, but also the number of courses and participants. Nevertheless, not everybody benefited from the boom in continuing training. The distribution of training participation strongly depended on particular positions in the work context.

The Perfect Employee

In 1977, Kurt Johannson, education expert at the Industrial Union of Metalworkers (IG Metall), published an article in the *Gewerkschaftliche Monatshefte* in which he discussed the development of continuing training inside companies since the economic crisis.[71] It was remarkable, he wrote, that the private sector had not reduced but, rather, had substantially expanded training offerings in the past few years. What were the companies' strategies regarding this issue? Johannson revealed that the investment aspect had gained enormous relevance in educational thinking: the investment in continuing education had to pay off. The result was that those employees who benefited most from training were primarily the ones who were already privileged – that is, highly skilled white-collar professionals, masters, and sometimes skilled workers. The unskilled workforce, which was most affected by the outcomes of the economic crisis, did not have the opportunity to participate. Johannson emphasized that the expansion of training inside the companies was anything but a successful and reasonable educational policy instrument to cope with the economic downturn and to combat cyclical unemployment. Instead, it was an instrument to achieve political conformity and individual loyalty of the workforce.

Johannson referred to a study that had been conducted by the Institute for Social Research (Institut für sozialwissenschaftliche Forschung – ISF) in 1976. The ISF had identified the criteria for an educational policy that would lessen the effects of the difficult labour market situation in Germany:[72] continuing education had, in particular, to promote the qualification of those employees who were facing the threat of unemployment, meaning women, unskilled and semi-skilled workers, migrants, and young workers. Continuing training as a full-time measure therefore ought to be used as an instrument to bridge economic downturns, and the time ought to be devoted to ensuring the qualification of these vulnerable employee groups given the requirements of the labour market. That meant primarily a general and broad qualification, including retraining measures that were certified and thus requested and usable at different working places in various companies. Flexibility had to be the overarching aim.

In fact, a representative survey among almost two thousand firms had shown that the employers did the opposite:[73] because they did not know if the economic downturn was a short-term cyclical weakness or the outcome of a long-term structural crisis, they were reluctant to invest in employees who would eventually not be needed any more. The oversupply of labour made it more profitable to hire and fire less-educated employees as needed. On top of this, the employees in precarious jobs themselves did not dare to ask for further qualifications, being afraid of losing their jobs.[74] The result was that companies deliberately refused continuing education to vulnerable workers in order to avoid raising false hopes of job security and occupational advancement.[75] In its place, employers used training measures mainly to strengthen the ties and the loyalty of qualified employees by providing skills that were specific to the product, workplace, or company and were not formal qualifications.[76]

In his argument, Johannson pointed to precisely these aspects of training measures to assert that continuing education in companies represented, first and foremost, social engineering. Due to reorganization processes since the late 1960s, with the decentralization of decision-making processes, mechanization and automatization, and the reinforcing of employee rights, employers had to establish new forms of rule making. "Apparently, instructions are not enough to guarantee assent; instead, special methods of manipulation through leadership techniques are needed that have to be learnt."[77] In order to nip potential opposition in the bud, companies needed more and more executives who were psychologically trained. But also their employees had to internalize methods of self-control. The most needed "skills" were diligence, persistence, flexibility, satisfaction with working conditions, and loyalty to the interests of the company and its management – virtues that were exclusively usable inside the company but did not mean a qualification for better opportunities in the labour market.

Johannson demonstrated the role of training in this context with the example of the growing number of conflict-management courses: participants were systematically taught that conflicts in the workplace were caused by individual behaviour and not by structural deficiencies.

Such an individualization of problems and their exclusive psychological treatment meant also that the economic crises and coping with its consequences were loaded onto the individual employee. The aim was to solve any kind of problem in the best interest of the company, while accepting and supporting the erosion of solidarity among the workforce. The companies wanted to neutralize the pressures of change that came up in society. Therefore, continuing education was a serious challenge that also undermined the bargaining power of the trade unions.

Johannson's article was symptomatic of a repoliticization of trade unions' educational strategy during the 1970s that warned against the societal consolidation of hierarchical power structures through continuing training and demanded educational concepts that were oriented toward practical work inside the companies.[78] Their arguments included the appeal to works council members to boycott training measures that were organized by the employer's side.[79] Thus, the trade unions strongly emphasized the sociopolitical impacts of in-company training. Those observations were verified by several scientific studies,[80] but also by the companies' own documentation. Paradigmatically, the yearly training reports at Bertelsmann documented in great detail the distribution of continuing education with respect to aspects like gender, status, and topics. The reports revealed that a significantly higher proportion of salaried employees than waged workers participated in continuing training. In 1978–9, for instance, the proportion was about 30.4 per cent of all white-collar employees to 3.4 per cent of all blue-collar employees.[81]

Taking a look at the seminar programs in the 1970s, the increase of company-specific, behaviour-orientated seminars for the skilled workforce becomes evident. One reason for that development was that restructuring processes were often accompanied by the implementation of new leadership principles that became part of several seminars in the following years. Bayer adopted in 1969 the management model of the Academy of Managers (Akademie für Führungskräfte), and, as early as 1970, the institute conducted fifty-four courses on this model,[82] with the number of courses increasing in future years. At the same time, the company formulated binding principles of leadership. Between 1973 and 1979, the preparation and formulation as well as the implementation of these principles took place in the form of several training sessions for different leading employee groups that were part of the general training program of the company. Accordingly, in January 1978 alone, twenty-eight seminars with the theme "conversation on leadership" took place at Bayer, with over 400 participants.[83]

In 1974, Bertelsmann likewise published a new corporate constitution with principles of leadership that included fourteen "commandments" about the behaviour required of managerial staff.[84] The "principles of leadership" and the corporate constitution became the most important subjects of management training and made up more than half of the training days that were foreseen in the central management-training plan of 1979.[85]

Besides such in-house training, which was focused mainly on company-specific rules of conduct, companies substantially expanded their repertoire of behaviour training, in addition to that offered by external providers. Here again, the claim was to suggest a program that was tailor-made for the company's own staff, in contrast to the external continuing education institutes and instructors that often presented the same seminars to several companies. The alignment with company-specific demands was brought about by close consultation and the discussion of case studies from everyday working life. In 1971, for instance, the Krupp executive board planned to implement training for all salespeople in the company and therefore employed a working group to test the training offerings of several providers, including the Academy of Sales Management (*Verkaufsleiter-Akademie*) in Bad Nauheim with its training about "leading salesmen actively."[86] The working group concluded that the training would be appropriate for the Krupp employees but demanded an alignment to Krupp-specific requirements. A general scepticism toward external instructors, who were able to teach the "how" but not the "what,"[87] led to the academy's proposal to perform a field study beforehand: to enable instructors to get to know the concrete working process and specific problems inside the company, selected staff would be accompanied for two days. This kind of concession was due to the strong competition among, in this case, seven other providers,[88] and Krupp planned to invest no less than 1.5 million DM for the first training period of eighteen months, besides the costs for rooms, travel, and accommodations.[89]

The Academy of Sales Management was one among many providers in the 1970s that used special methods of team building and group dynamics, adopting a trend that had arisen earlier in the United States. Whereas training in the 1960s and before seems to have improved primarily the skills of "lone fighters" – by rationalizing, for example, their reading and writing skills or their time management – group-dynamic learning processes were taught in order to enhance the working atmosphere as well as to detect and improve hidden capabilities of individual employees. Founded in 1970 in Cologne, the Institute for Applied Creativity (Institut für angewandte Kreativität) became an important training provider in this field in the following years, binding together the topics of creativity, problem-solving skills, and group dynamics in an innovative manner.[90] The education departments of the companies themselves proved the value of new teaching methods inspired by the human potential movement and Gestalt psychology, including "mini-lab," "switching-chair," and "hot-seat" exercises.[91] The purpose here was, just as Johannson supposed some years later, to raise self-awareness of individual conflicts and communication difficulties and their specific preconditions.[92] Although such forms of sensitivity training were harshly criticized in the 1980s, they were highly popular during the 1970s.

At the same time, seminars about problem solving and decision making according to the Kepner-Tregoe system found their way into several companies.[93] The purpose was to teach employees how to find solutions for potential technical and strategic problems by applying strictly systematic thinking patterns and questioning methods.[94] Developed by two former participants of the RAND Corporation, Charles Kepner and Benjamin Tregoe, the system promised to cut costs significantly. It was offered as a "train-the-instructor" concept, so that companies could adopt the system by teaching in-house instructors through Kepner-Tregoe experts and obtaining a licence for the teaching material. The broad introduction of Kepner-Tregoe seminars in the 1970s is especially interesting because it was, in a certain sense, the counterpoint to sensitivity training, in emphasizing primarily a structured and rationalistic approach to problems at the workplace. Even if Kepner-Tregoe and group-dynamic seminars demanded completely different behaviour patterns of the participants, both were presented to the same target groups at the same time. This simultaneity makes evident that the companies' training strategies were not as systematic and target-oriented as one might think. The decision to apply a certain measure was often based on experience reports and recommendations of other companies that were published in management magazines or mentioned in informal exchanges. Therefore, the seminar choice was a question of trial and error, as criteria were uncertain and first needed to be developed.

Cost-Benefit Analyses

The expansion of training offerings and the growing interest in cost recording shows that training activities had to meet new demands. The purpose of training in the 1950s and even in the 1960s had been to develop the workforce inside the company that was necessary to economic reconstruction and consolidation. Generally, training had been seen as a form of fringe benefit and therefore as a special form of labour relations that was not influenced by the works council.[95] Accordingly, the costs of continuing training in big companies were usually recorded as social expenditures.[96] The overwhelming aim to meliorate the working atmosphere as a part of "human relations"[97] changed fundamentally in the 1970s. By that time, companies were first and foremost interested in the outcome of the courses, which were seen as an investment in human capital.[98] Obviously the training expenditures could not be treated like investments in research or plant engineering, but nevertheless the question of cost-benefit analyses became urgent, and different methods to measure input and outcome were discussed and tested.

The change in perspective becomes obvious when we look at the development of evaluations. In the first years after the Second World War, when a coherent training system inside the companies was still to be developed, organizers and supervisors asked from time to time for impressions from the training group or demanded short personal experience reports from selected participants. Some engineers at Krupp took this opportunity in 1961 to complain about the in-house psychologist Mr. Becker, who had given a seminar about "psychology and leadership": they saw Becker's presentation as lowbrow and primitive, and as inappropriate for engineers. Respondents labelled it therefore a waste of time and money, which should not be used for "experiments of a theoretician who had never seen iron and steel works from the inside."[99] The focus of written reports – which were, for instance, systematically collected in the Rhenish lignite mining industry, especially in the late 1950s – was primarily input-orientated: the participants assessed the performance of the instructor, the clarity and comprehensibility of the presentations, and the training atmosphere.[100]

Whereas the formalized validation of training measures had been a part of business discourse in the United States since the 1950s,[101] German companies started conducting official evaluations no earlier than the late 1960s. The first evaluations that were normally handed to employees at the end of a training seminar mirrored the company's desire to gain insight into the quality of training by asking for personal impressions. The satisfaction of the employees became the main criterion assessing for seminars' value, and, accordingly, evaluation forms asked systematically about the quality of rooms and material, the schedule, the organization, and the expertise and personality of the instructor. In a very concentrated form, Bayer used a questionnaire up into the 1970s that was limited to four items: "Did the seminar meet your expectations? Would you say that time and effort paid off? Overall judgement. Comments."[102]

Focusing on the quality of the seminar input, the participants gained a strong position as critical commentators of the instructors and, moreover, were able to identify problems and sought to formulate improvement suggestions.[103] They became experts on their own learning process. The instructors on the other side relied on positive ratings. The background for this reversal of roles was that the shortage in the German labour market during the 1960s had led to an expansion of training offers inside the companies to improve the qualification of the existing workforce. The growing demand made it necessary to award contracts to external training providers, which, on the one hand, guaranteed greater innovation and flexibility in planning but, on the other hand, were much more expensive than the internal offerings. In the companies' view, evaluations became necessary to determine whether the training providers matched the companies' objectives. The evaluation forms that were conceptualized at that time were typical for this approach: the central aspect in which HR departments were interested was if the expectations of the participants had been met. It is evident that the growing variation in training formats and design during this time can be regarded as a result of an idea of competition for the participants' favour.

As we have seen, the objectives of training changed in the wake of the oil crisis. Accordingly, the evaluations that had been established just a few years before no longer met the purposes of the management boards, which were demanding evidence of training success in terms of effective benefits for the company. Especially regarding soft skills training, the question arose whether training experiences led to behavioural changes of the participants and how these could be measured. Even the HR experts realized that training resembled a black box: employees went in, were taught, and went out without anybody knowing what, if anything, had happened to them.

Debates about the effectiveness of training measures led to a scientification of evaluation knowledge in Germany. The Wuppertaler Kreis, as umbrella organization of several German continuing training institutes, ran a meta-study in 1974 about evaluation practices in German, European, and American companies to receive insights into the status quo.[104] The results regarding Germany were disappointing. The study revealed several methodological weaknesses and problems with the evaluation process itself: the forms that were currently in use were not suitable for "translating" subjective training experiences into objective criteria. The reason was that the companies were themselves unclear about the criteria of "success": the scale ranged from profit maximization to much more vaguely defined values, such as the happiness of the employees or their liberation from performance pressure. The adoption of these objectives through a training course did not depend solely on the personality of the participant. Moreover, evaluators could not be sure if workers were only simulating acceptance of the recommended values – that is, paying lip service because of their fear that resistance would affect their personal appraisal, their status, and their job security. Instead, an adequate evaluation had to inquire as to the behaviour, the knowledge, and the performance of an employee before the course and after. But, here too, it was hard to predict in which situation a learning effect would appear in the workplace, alongside the fact that a change in behaviour could not be linked to a single training experience but was often the result of a variety of influencing factors.

However, particularly HR experts did not give up hope that a rationalization of evaluation was possible. HR consultants such as Klaus Schindler, Rolf Th. Stiefel, Hans-Jürgen Kurtz, Anja Marcotty, and Peter A. Döring developed ambitious models that were to serve as an orientation for business practice.[105] Döring, for instance, demanded evaluations before, during, and after a seminar. He recommended the implementation of interviews, role-playing exercises, games, and other formats as supplements to questionnaires; he also suggested medium- and long-term evaluations after specific time periods and experimented with test and control groups.[106] Proposals of this type were sophisticated and complex: their focus was on applicability at the workplace and thus basically met the economic demands of employers. Nevertheless, they were never fully executed in the continuing-training practices of the companies. The reason was simple: their systematic implementation would have made it necessary to create entire departments responsible for nothing else but evaluating the growing number of seminars. In other words, controlling would have become more expensive than training.

As early as 1971, Walter Thurner, head of training at Ford, presented a mathematical calculation model that promised to generate with less effort valid data about the returns on training measures.[107] After the potential targets of continuing training measures were valuated and qualified, input and output of training could be compared by using the following formula: "rate of return = value - costs/costs × 100." Training measures were considered profitable if the percentage was greater than 100. The Thurner model was discussed in several companies, including Krupp in 1972, where the German Society for Human Resources (Deutsche Gesellschaft für Personalführung) started a working group to confer about new approaches of training validations.[108] The model was an adaptation of human capital theories, which had led to the formulation of mathematical methods for "human resource accounting," especially in the United States. Inspired by economists such as Gary S. Becker, Jacob Mincer, and Theodor W. Schultz – who had emphasized that training was "a process of capital formation in people" that showed its returns in the process of labour[109] – Eric Flamholtz, Lee Brummet, William Pyle, and others used mathematical formulas for calculating the investment in continuing education.[110] Widely discussed during the 1970s, those formulas were in the end rarely implemented in the training organization process. The companies adopted only a few of the proposals and instead experimented with new formulas that were much more oriented to the output of training by asking questions about its benefits and applicability. The focus thus shifted from the performance of the instructor to the performance of the participants. In doing so, the evaluation process itself was discovered as a possible way to influence the behaviour of the employees, as the following example might illustrate.

In 1979, fifteen management trainees of Bertelsmann AG attended a three-day seminar about "personal working methods" to learn about how to deal with "stress, work overload, and hecticness." The seminar was conducted by the Institute of Management Development (Institut für Management Entwicklung), and at the end the participants had to fill in a form that had been designed by the institute.[111] Looking at the results, one might think that the participants had visited several different seminars: the range of grading differed not only concerning the instructor but also concerning such "objective" elements like the quality of the seminar room. Several participants added personal reflections and also expressed their anger frankly: there had been too many flies in the room, the seminar had been superficial, the timetable had not been met, the instructor had not been interested in feedback, and so on.

It was a common practice at Bertelsmann that the HR department asked for the results of the evaluation and passed them on to the participants, their bosses, and the management board. Two weeks later, all these parties received a letter from the HR department in which the results of the evaluation were discussed.[112] Interestingly, the personnel manager did not respond to the participants' critique. Instead, he passed the ball back to the participants themselves, noting, "the training and consolidation of new and more effective working methods on the basis of the seminar discussions and exercises can only happen at the individual workplace."[113] He announced a survey a few months later in which the medium-term results of the seminar were to be evaluated again – a clear message of what was expected from the employees.

Apparently, the intentions of the employees who had filled in the forms deviated significantly from the motives of the company: the former had articulated their impressions as feedback for the organizers in the hope that the future design of the seminar would be changed. The HR department, by contrast, used the evaluation to ensure that the participants were receptive to the training contents and thus made them responsible for their learning success. In other words, the evaluation was reinterpreted as an instrument for controlling the attitudes of the participants, with improving their self-reflexivity as a starting point for behavioural changes. In doing so, evaluations themselves became a substantial part of the intended learning process instead of "measuring" the concrete impact with respect to the company's benefit.

The failure and reinterpretation of cost-benefit analyses show that the advancement of continuing training in the 1970s was neither the product of a philanthropic qualification offensive nor a systematic and successful strategy to submit employees to the logic of the market economy. Even if companies attached great hopes to the effects of continuing education, the investment in training remained a factor of uncertainty.

Summary

In West German political, economic, and educational debates, continuing education and training became a magic formula for coping with the manifold challenges facing society during the 1970s. Its rhetorical advancement as the fourth pillar of the German educational system cannot hide the fact that political regulation failed in the end.

As a result of funding problems, qualification issues were left to the "market," which meant to private industry. The employers who had feared political intervention during the reform climate around 1970 regained the authority over training in a situation in which they were themselves struggling with the outcomes of structural transformations and the oil shock. In response to increasing unemployment figures, the companies were taken at their word, that they would educate and qualify those employee groups that were generally most threatened. Indeed, private industry expanded offerings of and expenditures on training during the 1970s, but it set its own focus. In public debates, the companies pointed to the huge amount of money that they were already investing, arguing against a right to paid educational leave for everybody; in internal discussions, the payment for training was reinterpreted as investment in human capital. This reinterpretation was itself a crisis response strategy: soft skills training became an alternative to downsizing the skilled core workforce that should have been rehired and qualified under better economic circumstances. Soft skills training in particular became a method to cultivate employees' individual loyalty and bonds to the company, even because it could be offered as part of a joint union-and-state program on "humanization of working life." Training therefore promised to prevent labour disputes and state interventions. Furthermore, it became a marker of progressiveness, which itself became an economic factor under international competitive pressure. Finally, training could be interpreted as a form of prevention with respect to future crises: from an organizational point of view, the training sector seemed to provide the greatest possible flexibility in coordinating demand and supply of skills. Moreover, it pretended that training itself enabled the workforce to learn how to deal better with economic challenges.

The result was that in-house training was restructured, firmly anchored, and thereby strengthened in the companies' organization. Processes of professionalization, especially regarding cost-benefit considerations, led to an implementation of training needs analyses, standardized staff development plans, and output-oriented evaluations. The advancement of training as part of professionalized HR development meant that training activities were no longer an individual, voluntary surplus, but became a common part of the occupational lives of especially those employees who were, due to their position in the working context, already beneficiaries of occupational and technical development during this period. In a broader context, the distribution of training opportunities inside the companies exacerbated social inequalities.

Even if skilled employees were involved in training decisions through training needs analyses, evaluations, and the consultation rights of the works councils since 1972, it is hard to speak about a unilineal process of individualization. In a time that is always considered to be the origin of neoliberal self-technologies – that is, in which personal freedom and responsibility became an instrument for economic policy – access to continuing education and its organizational structure became more regulated than ever before. Nevertheless, the appeal to participate and to put the acquired knowledge into practice was controlled and documented for every single employee and thus became the condition for individual career advancement.

Trade union–driven critiques addressed not only the injustices concerning access and participation but also the concentration on seminars that promoted soft skills in favour of a single company rather than certified qualifications for the labour market. "Productivity and loyalty" were the overwhelming objectives of training within industry;[114] and even the contents of training measures showed that company-focused leadership seminars, behaviour training, and problem-solving exercises tied up a large part of the money that was dedicated to continuing education in the 1970s. However, companies' educational strategies were not as elaborate as one might think. Contradictory seminar subjects and the failure of evaluations suggest that the general offering of training opportunities and the willingness to learn and to change one's own behaviour were much more important than the concrete course contents.

The advancement of industrial continuing education in an age of crises can thus also be explained by path dependencies and a competitive pressure that resulted from comparisons with other companies. Moreover, large companies especially could not escape public and political expectations, so that the expansion of training implied several promises: the promise of avoiding political and trade union interference in internal affairs, of gaining and maintaining autonomy and sovereignty in educational questions, of educating employees who would work toward the best interest of the company, of preventing brain drain of qualified staff, and of meliorating the working atmosphere, and the promise that the investment would pay off in the long run.

That this strategy was subject to many uncertainties is reflected in an aphorism that has been used till today to open the discussion in training seminars at Bayer: "Someone asked the CEO: 'What will happen if we invest a lot of money in the education of an employee and he leaves us?' And the CEO answered: 'What will happen if we do not invest anything and the employee remains?' "[115]

NOTES

1 Anselm Doering-Manteuffel and Lutz Raphael, *Nach dem Boom: Perspektiven auf die Zeitgeschichte seit 1970*, 3rd ed. (Göttingen: Vandenhoeck & Ruprecht, 2012); Morten Reitmayer and Thomas Schlemmer, eds., *Die Anfänge der Gegenwart: Umbrüche in Westeuropa nach dem Boom* (Munich: Oldenbourg, 2014); Knud Andresen, Ursula Bitzegeio, and Jürgen Mittag, eds., *"Nach dem Strukturbruch"? Kontinuität und Wandel von Arbeitsbeziehungen und Arbeitswelt(en) seit den 1970er-Jahren* (Bonn: Dietz, 2011).
2 Knud Andresen, Ursula Bitzegeio, and Jürgen Mittag, "Arbeitsbeziehungen und Arbeitswelt(en) im Wandel: Problemfelder und Fragestellungen," in *"Nach dem Strukturbruch,"* ed. Andresen, Bitzegeio, and Mittag; Winfried Süß and Dietmar Süß, "Zeitgeschichte der Arbeit: Beobachtungen und Perspektiven," in *"Nach dem Strukturbruch,"* ed.

Andresen, Bitzegeio, and Mittag; Joachim Hirsch and Roland Roth, *Das neue Gesicht des Kapitalismus: Vom Fordismus zum Post-Fordismus* (Hamburg: VSA-Verlag, 1986); Sabine Fromm, *Formierung und Fluktuation: Die Transformation der kapitalistischen Verwertungslogik in Fordismus und Postfordismus* (Berlin: wvb Wissenschafts-Verlag, 2004); Max Koch, *Arbeitsmärkte und Sozialstrukturen in Europa: Wege zum Postfordismus in den Niederlanden, Schweden, Spanien, Großbritannien und Deutschland* (Wiesbaden: Westdeutscher Verlag, 2003).

3 Thomas Lemke, "Neoliberalismus, Staat und Selbsttechnologie: Ein kritischer Überblick über die Governmentality Studies," *Politische Vierteljahresschrift* 41 (2000): 31–47; Ralf Ptak, *Vom Ordoliberalismus zur Sozialen Marktwirtschaft: Stationen des Neoliberalismus in Deutschland* (Opladen: Leske Budrich, 2004); Andreas Wirsching, "'Neoliberalismus' als wirtschaftspolitisches Ordnungsmodell? Die Bundesrepublik Deutschland in den 1980er Jahren," in *Der Staat und die Ordnung der Wirtschaft*, ed. Werner Plumpe (Stuttgart: Steiner, 2012), 139–50; Philipp Ther, *Die neue Ordnung auf dem alten Kontinent: Eine Geschichte des neoliberalen Europa*, 2nd ed. (Berlin: Suhrkamp, 2014).

4 Winfried Süß, "Sozialpolitik nach dem Wirtschaftswunder," in *Willy Brandt: Neue Fragen, neue Erkenntnisse*, ed. Bernd Rother (Bonn: Dietz, 2011), 207–18; Thomas Raithel and Thomas Schlemmer, eds., *Die Rückkehr der Arbeitslosigkeit: Die Bundesrepublik Deutschland im europäischen Kontext 1973 bis 1989* (Munich: Oldenbourg Wissenschaftsverlag GmbH, 2009).

5 Sina Fabian, *Boom in der Krise: Konsum, Tourismus, Autofahren in Westdeutschland und Großbritannien, 1970–1990* (Göttingen: Wallstein, 2016); Axel Schildt and Detlef Siegfried, *Between Marx and Coca-Cola: Youth Cultures in Changing European Societies, 1960–1980* (New York: Berghahn Books, 2006).

6 Andreas Rödder and Wolfgang Elz, *Alte Werte – Neue Werte: Schlaglichter des Wertewandels* (Göttingen: Vandenhoeck & Ruprecht, 2008); Bernhard Dietz and Jörg Neuheiser, eds., *Wertewandel in der Wirtschaft und Arbeitswelt: Arbeit, Leistung und Führung in den 1970er und 1980er Jahren in der Bundesrepublik Deutschland* (Munich: de Gruyter, 2016).

7 Maik Tändler and Uffa Jensen, eds., *Das Selbst zwischen Anpassung und Befreiung: Psychowissen und Politik im 20. Jahrhundert* (Göttingen: Wallstein, 2012); Sabine Maasen et al., eds., *Das beratene Selbst: Zur Genealogie der Therapeutisierung in den "langen" Siebzigern* (Bielefeld: Transcript, 2011); Maik Tändler, *Das therapeutische Jahrzehnt: Der Psychoboom in den siebziger Jahren* (Göttingen: Wallstein, 2016).

8 Peter-Paul Bänziger, "Fordistische Körper in der Geschichte des 20. Jahrhunderts: Eine Skizze," *Body Politics* 1 (2013): 11–40; Martin Lengwiler and Jeannette Madarász, eds., *Das präventive Selbst: Eine Kulturgeschichte*

moderner Gesundheitspolitik (Bielefeld: Transcript, 2010); Ulrike Thoms, "Der dicke Körper und sein Konsum im Visier von Wissenschaft und Politik in der DDR und der BRD," *Comparativ* 21, no. 3 (2011): 97–113; Stephan Theilig, *Historische Konzeptionen von Körperlichkeit: Interdisziplinäre Zugänge zu Transformationsprozessen in der Geschichte* (Berlin: Frank & Timme, 2011); Jürgen Martschukat, *Das Zeitalter der Fitness: Wie der Körper zum Zeichen für Erfolg und Leistung wurde* (Frankfurt am Main: S. Fischer, 2019).

9 See Paul G. Whitmore and John P. Fry, "Soft Skills: Definition, Behavioral Model Analysis, Training Procedures," paper presented at the United States Continental Army Command Soft Skills Training Conference, Fort Bliss, TX, 12–13 December, 1972.

10 Luc Boltanski and Ève Chiapello, *Der neue Geist des Kapitalismus* (Konstanz: UVK-Verlags-Gesellschaft, 2003).

11 Franziska Meifort, "Liberalisierung der Gesellschaft durch Bildungsreform: Ralf Dahrendorf zwischen Wissenschaft und Öffentlichkeit in den 1960er Jahren," in *Universität, Wissenschaft und Öffentlichkeit in Westdeutschland,* ed. Sebastian Brandt (Stuttgart: Steiner, 2014), 141–59; Armin Kremer, "Entwicklungslinien und Verlauf der Bildungsreform: Bilanzierung in kritischer Absicht," in *1968 und die neue Restauration,* ed. Armin Bernhard and Wolfgang Keim (Frankfurt am Main: Peter Lang, 2009), 189–208; Sven Bergmann, "Die Diskussion um die Bildungsreform in der Nachkriegszeit (Georg Picht)," in *Gesellschaftspolitische Neuorientierungen des Protestantismus in der Nachkriegszeit,* ed. Norbert Friedrich (Münster: Lit, 2002), 101–26; Alfons Kenkmann, "Von der bundesdeutschen 'Bildungsmisere' zur Bildungsreform in den 60er Jahren," in *Dynamische Zeiten: Die 60er Jahre in den beiden deutschen Gesellschaften,* ed. Axel Schildt, Detlef Siegfried, and Karl C. Lammers (Hamburg: Hans Christian Verlag, 2000), 402–23.

12 Brigitta Bernet, "Vom 'Berufsautomaten' zum 'flexiblen Mitarbeiter': Die Krise der Organisation und der Umbau der Personallehre um 1970," in *Wertewandel in der Wirtschaft und Arbeitswelt: Arbeit, Leistung und Führung in den 1970er und 1980er Jahren in der Bundesrepublik Deutschland,* ed. Bernhard Dietz and Jörg Neuheiser (Munich: de Gruyter, 2016), 31–54; Susanne Hilger, *"Amerikanisierung" deutscher Unternehmen: Wettbewerbsstrategien und Unternehmenspolitik bei Henkel, Siemens und Daimler-Benz (1945/49–1975)* (Stuttgart: Steiner, 2004), 212–24; Christian Kleinschmidt, *Der produktive Blick: Wahrnehmung amerikanischer und japanischer Management- und Produktionsmethoden durch deutsche Unternehmer 1950–1985* (Berlin: Akademie-Verlag, 2002), 260–75; Toshio Yamazaki, *German Business Management: A Japanese Perspective on Regional Development Factors* (Dordrecht, NL: Springer, 2013), 175–210.

13 Werner Fricke, "Drei Jahrzehnte Forschung und Praxis zur Humanisierung der Arbeit in Deutschland – eine Bilanz," in *Wirtschaft, Demokratie und soziale Verantwortung: Kontinuitäten und Brüche*, ed. Wolfgang G. Weber (Göttingen: Vandenhoeck & Ruprecht, 2004); Anne Seibring, "Die Humanisierung des Arbeitslebens in den 1970er Jahren: Forschungsstand und Forschungsperspektiven," in *"Nach dem Strukturbruch?,"* ed. Andresen, Bitzegeio, and Mittag, 107–26; Nina Kleinöder, "Literaturbericht zum Forschungsprogramm zur Humanisierung des Arbeitslebens," Working Paper no. 8, Hans-Böckler-Stiftung, February 2016, accessed 5 November 2019, https://www.boeckler.de/pdf/p_fofoe_WP_008_2016 .pdf; Nina Kleinöder, Stefan Müller, and Karsten Uhl, eds. *"Humanisierung Der Arbeit": Aufbrüche und Konflikte in der rationalisierten Arbeitswelt des 20. Jahrhunderts* (Bielefeld: Transcript, 2019).

14 Wilke Thomssen, "Arbeiterbildung zwischen betriebsdemokratischem Bewußtsein und Aufstiegsorientierung," *Gewerkschaftliche Monatshefte* 11 (1974): 671–81.

15 Apart from those measures that resulted in a professionally qualifying degree like master craftsman training.

16 Eckhard Emminger and Wiltrud Gieseke, "Professionalität der in der Weiterbildung Tätigen," in *Lernen – ein Leben lang: Vorläufige Empfehlungen und Expertenbericht*, ed. Arbeitsstab Forum Bildung (Bonn: Forum Bildung, 2001), 190–207.

17 Ina Krause, "Arbeitsmarkt und Arbeitsverhältnisse in der Weiterbildung: Segmentationstheoretische Überlegungen und empirische Befunde," in *Das Personal in der Weiterbildung: Im Spannungsfeld von Professionsanspruch und Beschäftigungsrealität*, ed. Rolf Dobischat, Arne Elias, and Anna Rosendahl (Wiesbaden: Springer, 2018), 309–27.

18 Alexander Yendell, *Soziale Ungleichheiten in der beruflichen Weiterbildung* (Wiesbaden: Springer 2017).

19 These include Bayer AG, Bertelsmann AG, Rheinische Braunkohlenwerke AG, Vereinigten Elektrizitätswerke Westfalen AG, Krupp AG.

20 One exception here is the Adult Education Law of North Rhine Westphalia from 1953, which regulated the funding of the adult education centres: "Gesetz über die Zuschußgewährung an Volkshochschulen und entsprechende Volksbildungseinrichtungen," *Gesetz- und Verordnungsblatt für das Land Nordrhein-Westfalen* 7, no. 21 (21 March 1953): 219; Martina Wennemann, *Bildungspolitik und Bildungsentwicklung: Gesetzgebung und ihre Auswirkung in der Jugend-, Erwachsenen-und Weiterbildung* (Wiesbaden: VS Verlag für Sozialwissenschaften, 1999), 100–7.

21 Horst Siebert, "Erwachsenenbildung in der Bundesrepublik Deutschland: Alte Bundesländer und neue Bundesländer," in *Handbuch*

Erwachsenenbildung/Weiterbildung, ed. Aiga Hippel and Rudolf Tippelt, 4th ed. (Wiesbaden: VS Verlag für Sozialwissenschaften, 2010), 59–88.

22 Günther Wolgast, *Zeittafel zur Geschichte der Erwachsenenbildung: Mit einem Kurzabriss "Geschichte der Erwachsenenbildung im Überblick"* (Berlin: Luchterhand, 1996); Elke Gruber, Ekkehard Nuissl, and Christiane Schiersmann, eds., *Geschichte der Erwachsenenbildung* (Bielefeld: Bertelsmann, 2010); Josef Olbrich and Horst Siebert, *Geschichte der Erwachsenenbildung in Deutschland* (Opladen: Leske + Budrich, 2001), 331–52.

23 An overview is given by Siegfried Fassbender, *Überbetriebliche Weiterbildung von Führungskräften: Der Wuppertaler Kreis und seine Mitglieder* (Essen: Girardet, 1969).

24 Regula Bürgi, *Die OECD und die Bildungsplanung der freien Welt: Denkstile und Netzwerke einer Internationalen Bildungsexpertise* (Berlin: Barbara Budrich, 2017); Vera Centeno, *The OECD's Educational Agendas: Framed from Above, Fed from Below, Determined in Interaction: A Study on the Recurrent Education Agenda* (Frankfurt am Main: Peter Lang, 2018); Georg Picht, *Die deutsche Bildungskatastrophe: Analyse und Dokumentation* (Olten: Walter, 1964); Ralf Dahrendorf, *Bildung ist Bürgerrecht: Plädoyer für eine aktive Bildungspolitik* (Hamburg: Nannen, 1966); Sven Bergmann, "Die Diskussion um die Bildungsreform in der Nachkriegszeit (Georg Picht)," in *Gesellschaftspolitische Neuorientierungen des Protestantismus in der Nachkriegszeit*, ed. Norbert Friedrich and Traugitt Jähnichen (Münster: Lit Verlag, 2002), 101–26; Meifort, "Liberalisierung der Gesellschaft durch Bildungsreform."

25 Brigitta Bernet and David Gugerli, "'Sputniks Resonanzen': Der Aufstieg der Humankapitaltheorie im Kalten Krieg – Eine Argumentationsskizze," *Historische Anthropologie* 3 (2011): 433–46; Wolfgang Lambrecht, "Deutsch-deutsche Reformdebatten vor 'Bologna': Die 'Bildungskatastrophe' der 1960er-Jahre," *Zeithistorische Forschungen* 4, no. 3 (2007): 472–7; Peter Massing, "Konjunkturen und Institutionen der Bildungspolitik," in *Bildungspolitik in der Bundesrepublik Deutschland: Eine Einführung*, ed. Peter Massing (Schwalbach am Taunus: Wochenschau-Verlag, 2003), 19.

26 Willy Brandt, "Abgabe einer Erklärung der Bundesregierung," *Deutscher Bundestag*, 6th election period, 5th sess. (10 October 1969), accessed 5 November 2019, http://dipbt.bundestag.de/doc/btp/06/06005.pdf.

27 "Forderungen des DGB zur beruflichen Bildung (verabschiedet vom DGB-Bundesvorstand im April 1972)," *Berufliche Bildung – Politik des DGB: Programme, Dokumente, Fakten*, ed. Wolfgang Bartels (Frankfurt am Main: Nachrichten-Verlag, 1976), 16–26.

28 "Sozialbericht 1971 der deutschen Bundesregierung," *Deutscher Bundestag*, 6th election period, Drucksache VI, 2155 (12 May 1971), 29–30, accessed 5 November 2019, http://dipbt.bundestag.de/doc/btd/06/021/0602155.pdf.

29 Christian H. Jorgensen, "Three Conceptions of Changing Relations between Education and Work," in *Knowing Work: The Social Relations of Working and Knowing*, ed. Leena Koski, Liv Mjelde, and Markus Weil (Bern: Peter Lang, 2009), 187.

30 Deutscher Bildungsrat, *Empfehlungen der Bildungskommission: Strukturplan für das Bildungswesen* (Stuttgart: Ernst Klett Verlag, 1970), 54–7.

31 Bundesvereinigung der deutschen Arbeitgeberverbände, Grundgedanken zur Erwachsenenbildung, Cologne 1970, Bayer Archiv Leverkusen (hereafter BAL) 62–4, vol. 1.

32 Jorgensen, "Three Conceptions of Changing Relations," 191–2.

33 "Betriebsverfassungsgesetz," *Bundesgesetzblatt Teil I* 2 (1 January 1972), § 96–8, 32.

34 Mira Maase, Werner Sengenberger, and Friedrich Weltz, *Weiterbildung: Aktionsfeld für den Betriebsrat? Eine Studie über Arbeitnehmerinteressen und betriebliche Personalpolitik* (Cologne: Europäische Verlags-Anstalt, 1975), 143.

35 "Unterrichtung durch die Bundesregierung, Bildungsgesamtplan," *Drucksache 7/1774* (10 December 1973), 36–40, accessed 5 November 2019, http://dipbt.bundestag.de/doc/btd/07/014/0701474.pdf.

36 Friedrich Edding, *Kosten und Finanzierung der außerschulischen beruflichen Bildung (Abschlussbericht)* (Bielefeld: Bertelsmann, 1974), 231.

37 Albert Probst, Deutscher Bundestag, 86. Sitzung (15 March 1974), 5617, accessed 5 November 2019, http://dipbt.bundestag.de/doc/btp/07/07086.pdf.

38 Georg Altmann, *Aktive Arbeitsmarktpolitik: Entstehung und Wirkung eines Reformkonzepts in der Bundesrepublik Deutschland* (Stuttgart: Steiner, 2004), 207–12.

39 Tim Schanetzky, *Die große Ernüchterung: Wirtschaftspolitik, Expertise und Gesellschaft in der Bundesrepublik, 1966 bis 1982* (Berlin: Akademie Verlag, 2007); Konrad Jarausch, ed., *Das Ende der Zuversicht? Die siebziger Jahre als Geschichte* (Göttingen: Vandenhoeck & Ruprecht, 2008).

40 Christoph Boyer, "Schwierige Bedingungen für Wachstum und Beschäftigung," in *Die Rückkehr der Arbeitslosigkeit: Die Bundesrepublik Deutschland im europäischen Kontext 1973 bis 1989*, ed. Thomas Raithel and Thomas Schlemmer (Munich: Oldenbourg, 2009), 15.

41 See, for example, Landtag Nordrhein-Westfalen, 7. Wahlperiode, 93. Sitzung am 24.1.1974, 3689, 3702.

42 Continuing training was defined as follows: "Die berufliche Fortbildung soll es ermöglichen, die beruflichen Kenntnisse und Fertigkeiten zu erhalten, zu erweitern, der technischen Entwicklung anzupassen oder beruflich aufzusteigen." See "Berufsbildungsgesetz," *Bundesgesetzblatt Teil I* 75 (14 August 1969), § 1, Abs. 3, 1112.

43 Weiterbildung bei den Farbenfabriken Bayer (1967), BAL 334/14.

44 Protokoll der 2. Sitzung des Ausschusses Personalförderung (4 April 1974), BAL 388/193.

45 Bestandsaufnahme der Fortbildungsaktivitäten in den Bertelsmann-Unternehmen (16 February 1973), Unternehmensarchiv Bertelsmann AG (hereafter UA BAG) 17/159.

46 Rudolf Wendorff, Fortbildungsaktivitäten der Bertelsmann-Unternehmen. Rundschreiben von Herrn Dr. Strobel (22 February 1973), UA BAG 17/159.

47 Erfassung der Weiterbildungsmaßnahmen vom 1.7.1975–30.6.1976 (5 August 1976), UA BAG 17/161.

48 Bertelsmann Weiterbildung. Statistischer Auswertungsbogen, Firma Orbis (10 September 1976), UA BAG 17/161.

49 Moko-Protokoll (25 March 1974), BAL 388/192.

50 Erfassung Weiterbildungskosten, hier: Bewertung der Ausfallszeiten (30 August 1979), UA BAG 17/165.

51 "Forderungen des DGB zur beruflichen Bildung," 23.

52 Zentrales Bildungswesen, Argumente für betriebliche Aus-und Weiterbildung (3 October 1975), BAL 341/14.

53 Zentrales Bildungswesen, Umfang und Aufwand der Fortbildung der Bayer AG (23 April 1975), BA, 388/193.

54 "Wirtschaft steigert Bildungsangebot. Bildungsaufwand jetzt über 17 Mrd. Mark," *Handelsblatt* (21 July 1976), 1–2.

55 "17 Mrd. DM für Bildung. Starkes Engagement der Wirtschaft," *Handelsblatt* (21/22 January 1977), 15.

56 Yamazaki, *German business management*, 180ff.

57 Christian Marx, "Die Vermarktlichung des Unternehmens: Berater, Manager und Beschäftigte in der westdeutschen Chemiefaserindustrie seit den 1970er-Jahren," *Zeithistorische Forschungen / Studies in Contemporary History* 12, no. 3 (2015), accessed 5 November 2019, https://zeithistorische -forschungen.de/3-2015/5266.

58 "Bericht aus dem Personal- und Sozialbereich," *Unsere VEW* 48, no. 2 (1974): 7; Bayer AG, Zentrales Bildungswesen. Jahresbericht 1972, BAL 74–7.

59 Jörg Mönninghoff, "Gesellschaftspolitische Konsequenzen betrieblicher Bildungsprogramme," *Arbeit und Leistung* 25, no. 11 (1971): 213.

60 Rundschreiben von Dr. Strobel über "Fortbildungsaktivitäten der Bertelsmann-Unternehmen" (19 February 1973), UA BAG 17/159. The central continuing education program, *Zentrales Weiterbildungsprogramm für Führungskräfte*, was finalized in 1979 (1 August 1979), UA BAG 58/17 (2).

61 Fortbildungssystem für leitende Angestellte und Betriebsleiter der Bayer AG (12 November 1973), BAL 341/2.

62 Erfahrungsaustausch über Personalentwicklung und Bildungsplanung zwischen Farbenfabriken Bayer AG und Siemens AG (5 March 1971), Anlage 13, BA, 220/6; Beurteilungsbogen für Führungskräfte, UA BAG 58/17 (2).

63 See Tändler, *Das therapeutische Jahrzehnt*.

64 "Bildungsurlaub: Einfach abgebügelt," *Der Spiegel* 17 (1977): 36–41.

65 "Bitterer Kaffee," *Der Spiegel* 51 (1976): 104.

66 "… um sicherzustellen, daß aufgabenbezogene, betrieblich notwendige sowie unternehmenspolitische Zielsetzungen unterstützt und Mitarbeitern durch die Teilnahme Hilfestellungen geboten werden." Personalberichte 1980/81, UA BAG 17/56.

67 Protokoll der Beiratssitzung über das Fortbildungswerk Rheinbraun (20 October 1964), Historisches Archiv RWE Power 373/2.

68 Fritz W. Scharpf, *Planung als politischer Prozeß: Aufsätze zur Theorie der planenden Demokratie* (Frankfurt am Main: Suhrkamp, 1973), 73–113.

69 Zentrales Bildungswesen, Analyse des Fortbildungsbedarfs in Ingenieur-Abteilungen der Bayer AG, 8 (25 March 1974), BAL 388/173.

70 Zentrales Bildungswesen, Analyse des Fortbildungsbedarfs in Ingenieur-Abteilungen der Bayer AG, 2 (25 March 1974), BAL 388/173.

71 Kurt Johannson, "Anpassung als Prinzip: Die Bildungspolitik der Unternehmer im Betrieb," *Gewerkschaftliche Monatshefte* 28, no. 5 (1977): 302–9.

72 Mira Maase and Werner Sengenberger, "Wird Weiterbildung konjunkturgerecht betrieben? Über die Vereinbarkeit von betrieblicher Personalplanung und öffentlicher Arbeitsmarktpolitik," *Mitteilungen aus der Arbeitsmarkt-und Berufsforschung* 9, no. 2 (1976): 166–73.

73 Jürgen Sass, Werner Sengenberger, and Friedrich Weltz, *Weiterbildung und betriebliche Arbeitskräftepolitik: Eine industriesoziologische Analyse* (Cologne: Europäische Verlags-Anstalt 1974).

74 Maase and Sengenberger, "Wird Weiterbildung konjunkturgerecht betrieben?"

75 Friedrich Weltz and Gerd Schmidt, *Arbeiter und beruflicher Aufstieg: Eine Auswertung von statistischem Material und Befragungsergebnissen* (Munich: Institut für sozialwissenschaftliche Forschung, 1971), accessed 5 November 2019, https://www.isf-muenchen.de/pdf/isf-archiv/1971-weltz-schmidt -arbeiter-aufstieg.pdf.

76 Sass, Sengenberger, and Weltz, *Weiterbildung*. See also Enno Schmitz, *Leistung und Loyalität: Berufliche Weiterbildung und Personalpolitik in Industrieunternehmen* (Stuttgart: Klett-Cotta 1978), 11.

77 "Folgebereitschaft läßt sich offenbar nicht mehr allein durch die bloße Anweisung erzeugen, sondern bedarf besonderer Methoden der Manipulation. Diese Manipulation der Arbeitenden durch Führungstechniken ergibt sich nicht von selbst, sie muß erlernt werden." Johannson, "Anpassung," 306.

78 Peter Faulstich, *Interessenkonflikte um die Berufsbildung: Das Verhältnis von gesellschaftlichen Interessenstrukturen und staatlicher Bildungspolitik* (Weinheim: Beltz, 1977), 142.

79 Protokoll der Sitzung des Ausschusses für Bildung (May 1972), Archiv der sozialen Demokratie (AdsD) DGB-Archiv 5/DGAV001322.

80 *Daten zum Weiterbildungsverhalten: Ergebnisse einer Befragung von Infratest/ Sozialforschung im Auftrag des Bundesministeriums für Bildung und Wissenschaft. Soziale Indikatoren – Bildung*, ed. Institut für Sozialwissenschaftliche Forschung e.V. (Munich, 1973), 10, accessed 5 November 2019, http://nbn -resolving.de/urn:nbn:de:0168-ssoar-246895; Dirk Axmacher, "Qualifikation und imaginäre Bildungsreform," in *Bildungsarbeit mit Erwachsenen: Handbuch für selbstbestimmtes Lernen*, ed. Klaus Bergmann (Reinbek bei Hamburg, DE: Rowohlt, 1977); Maase, Sengenberger, and Weltz, *Weiterbildung*; Fritz Böhle and Norbert Altmann, *Industrielle Arbeit und soziale Sicherheit: Eine Studie über Risiken im Arbeitsprozeß und auf dem Arbeitsmarkt* (Frankfurt am Main: Athenäum, 1972).

81 ZP Personalbericht 1978/79, UA BAG 17/32 (2).

82 Jahresbericht 1970 Personal- und Sozialwesen, BAL 221/3, vol. 4.

83 Jahresbericht 1978 Zentralbereich Personalwesen, Anhang, 1, BAL 221/3, vol. 4.

84 Leitsätze für die Führung des Hauses Bertelsmann, Beiträge zur Erläuterung (1974), UA BAG 3/17–3.

85 Zentrales Weiterbildungsprogramm für Führungskräfte (1 August 1979), UA BAG, 58/17 (2).

86 Historisches Archiv Krupp (HA Krupp), WA 51/4273.

87 Aktenvermerk der Krupp Maschinenfabriken zum Arbeitskreis "Fortbildung im Betrieb" (12 February 1971), HA Krupp WA 51/4273.

88 Protokoll vom 27.1.1971 der 6. Sitzung des Konzern Arbeitskreises "Fortbildung im Verkauf" (25 January 1971), HA Krupp WA 51/4273.

89 Vorstandvorlage (8 June 1971): Vorstandsvorlagen: Fortbildungsmaßnahmen für Mitarbeiter im Betrieb an die Stabsabteilung Führungskräfte und Stabsabteilung Verkauf Inland, HA Krupp WA 51/4273.

90 Friedrich H. Quiske, Stefan J. Skirl, and Gerald Spiess, *Denklabor Team: Konzept für kreative Problemlösungen in Forschung, Verwaltung und Industrie* (Stuttgart: Deutsche Verlags-Anstalt, 1973).

91 Bayer AG, Zentrale Weiterbildung, Fortbildungsveranstaltungen externer Institute, I. Quartal 1974, BAL 388/173 (1974).

92 Ibid.

93 Fortbildungsprogramme, HA Krupp WA 230 v 562; ZB, Besprechung über Beurteilung der Kepner-Tregoe-Methode am 10.4.1975, 11 April 1975, BAL 388/193; Rheinische Braunkohlewerke AG Cologne, Hefte zur Fortbildung, Nr. 1: Problemlösung und Entscheidungsfindung, 1979, Historisches Archiv RWE Power 373/10.

94 Charles H. Kepner and Benjamin B. Tregoe, *Management-Entscheidungen vorbereiten und richtig treffen* (Munich: Management-Buchclub, 1970).

95 Karin Büchter, "Betriebliche Weiterbildung: Historische Kontinuität und Durchsetzung in Theorie und Praxis," *Zeitschrift für Pädagogik* 48, no. 3 (2002): 338.

96 See, for example, Personal- und Sozialwesen. Jahresberichte der Wohlfahrtsabteilung bzw. der Sozialabteilung, 1951–1963, BAL 221/3.

97 Kleinschmidt, *Produktive Blick*, 173–203.

98 Sabine Donauer, *Faktor Freude: Wie die Wirtschaft Arbeitsgefühle erzeugt* (Hamburg: Edition Körber-Stiftung, 2015), 58–75.

99 Correspondence with Günter Klotzbach about "Erfahrungen mit dem ersten Ingenieur-Gespräch am 16. Februar 1961 im Ausbildungswesen" (1 March 1961), HA Krupp WA 78/450.

100 For instance, the collected experience reports in Historisches Archiv RWE Power, 1717/1 and 882/11.

101 For example, Daniel M. Goodacre, "Experimental Evaluation of Training," *Journal of Personnel Administration and Industrial Relations* 2 (1955): 166–73; Clyde E. Blocker, "Evaluation of a Human Relations Training Course," *Journal of the American Society of Training Directors* 9, no. 3 (1955): 7–8; Thomas A. Mahoney, Thomas H. Jercike, and Abraham Korman, "An Experimental Evaluation of Management Training," *Personnel Psychology* 13, no. 1 (1960): 81–98; Norman Maier, "An Experimental Test of the Effect on Discussion Leadership," *Human Relations* 6, no. 2 (1953). See, as an overview, Donna M. Mertens, "Institutionalizing Evaluation in the United States of America," in *Evaluationsforschung: Grundlagen und ausgewählte Forschungsfelder*, ed. Reinhard Stockmann (Wiesbaden: VS Verlag für Sozialwissenschaften, 2000), 41–56.

102 Evaluation forms about behavioural training, 1974, BAL 341/14.

103 Many forms adopted scoring systems that employees had already known from school: the participants had to decide whether the instructor's performance had been "very good," "unsatisfactory," or something in between: Siegfried Faßbender, *Die Beurteilung von Weiterbildungskursen durch die Teilnehmer*, Führungskräfte fördern (Cologne: Hanstein, 1974), 84ff.

104 Ibid., 1–4.

105 Klaus Schindler, *Wirkung und Erfolg der Weiterbildung: Zu Fragen der Effizienzmessung* (Cologne: Deutscher Instituts-Verlag, 1979); Klaus Schindler, ed., *Evaluierung betrieblicher Bildungsarbeit: Erfolgskontrolle im Lern- u. Funktionsfeld*, 2nd ed. (Deutenhausen, DE: Münchener Bildungsforum Seifert, 1979); Hans-Jürgen Kurtz, Anja Marcotty and Rolf T. Stiefel, eds., *Neue Evaluierungskonzepte in der Management-Andragogik* (Munich: Edition Academic, 1984); Peter A. Döring, *Erfolgskontrolle betrieblicher Bildungsarbeit* (Frankfurt am Main: RKW, 1973); Rolf Th. Stiefel, *Grundfragen der Evaluierung in der Management-Schulung* (Frankfurt am Main: RKW, 1974).

106 Döring, *Erfolgskontrolle betrieblicher Bildungsarbeit*, 30–1.

107 Presentation of W. Thurner mentioned in Horst Groenwald, "Bericht über den 24. Deutschen Betriebswirtschafter-Tag," *Arbeit und Leistung* 25, no. 1 (1971): 20.

108 "Protokoll einer Besprechung der Arbeitsgruppe, die sich mit den möglichen Formen der Ertragsmessung von Bildungsveranstaltungen befaßte" (30 May 1972), HA Krupp WA 230 v 562.

109 Jacob Mincer, "On-the-job Training: Costs, Returns, and Some Implications," *Journal of Political Economy* 70, no. 5 (1962): 50; Gary Stanley Becker, *Human Capital: A Theoretical and Empirical Analysis, with Special Reference to Education* (New York: National Bureau of Economic Research, 1964); Pedro N. Teixeira, "Gary Becker's Early Work on Human Capital: Collaborations and Distinctiveness," *IZA Journal of Labor Economics* 3, no. 1 (2014): 1–20.

110 Eric Flamholtz, Lee Brummet, and William Pyle, "Human Resource Measurement: A Challenge for Accountants," *Accounting Review* 43, no. 2 (1968): 12–15.

111 Seminarauswertungen Persönliche Arbeitstechniken (10–12 June 1979), UA BAG 0059/11.

112 Correspondance of Eberhard Pfeuffer about the seminar "Arbeitstechniken" (28 June 1979), UA BAG 0059/11.

113 "Das Erproben und Festigen neuer und effektiverer Arbeitsweisen kann, auf der Basis der Seminardiskussionen und-übungen, nur am jeweiligen Arbeitsplatz selbst erfolgen."

114 Enno Schmitz, *Leistung und Loyalität: Berufliche Weiterbildung und Personalpolitik in Industrieunternehmen* (Stuttgart: Klett-Cotta, 1978).

115 Walter Strotkötter, Bayer Business Services GmbH, interview by Franziska Rehlinghaus, 18 April 2016, audio 01:38:11–01:38:27, from private collection.

SECTION THREE

(Dis-)Continuities

7 Deindustrialization and the Globalization Discourse in France since 1980

ANDREAS WIRSCHING

"Deindustrialization" is a central concept when it comes to the perception of structural transformation in Western industrialized countries. The term was first coined in the United States around 1980, where domestic industrial decline was viewed as a serious economic, political, and social problem.[1] The term was used in a consistently pejorative sense: the 1970s with all of its factory closings and the sharp downturn in economic growth reflected "economic despair" and an "inability to compete in the global marketplace." This use of the term had thus already been established in the contemporary narrative on the time "after the boom."[2] The same applies to its cognitive connection to the overall process of internationalization and later "globalization." These terms are connected and suggest a narrative of loss, ending in decline, factory closures, and unemployment.

Recent developments in trade disagreements between the United States, fanned by its president, Donald Trump, and the "rest of the world" point to an ongoing continuity in this regard. The wish to protect one's own industries or even to reindustrialize the United States expresses a longing for a return to an earlier, easier-to-comprehend social world. One can therefore increasingly link complaints about deindustrialization and connected recriminations to the clichés used in populist propaganda. It is all the more important to submit known linear narratives of deindustrialization to a critical eye, since the underlying narrative framework of a time "after the boom" has become outdated. More time has now passed since the "structural shift" of the final third of the twentieth century than the number of years the "boom" or the "*Trente Glorieuses*" themselves lasted. And this subsequent period has now also lasted longer than the era of the world wars as well. It therefore no longer suffices, as a means of understanding recent history, to semantically construct a "post"-history that derives its standards from the previous era. One would then be in danger of falling for a self-referential history of decline. The topic of deindustrialization, which is closely connected to the process of globalization, instead needs to be relativized in this vein. At its core, deindustrialization is a phenomenon that has affected just a few regions in the United States, Canada, northern Italy, and Northwestern Europe.[3] In global terms, the period since 1970 has in fact been marked by a massive expansion in industrialization. First the "tigers" in Taiwan, South Korea, Singapore, and Hong Kong, and then especially China and India, but also Vietnam, Bangladesh, and others, have developed a high level of industrial production, one that continues to grow dynamically. The term "deindustrialization" hence reveals a connected epistemic centredness on the "West" and Western industrial countries. The narrative of loss that is evoked here is actually, from a global perspective, a micro-narrative inviting us to expand our scope to the macro level. When we connect the two levels, the extent to which deindustrialization and industrialization are dependent upon each other becomes clear; they are indeed simultaneous phenomena. One can take it to the next level and say – to apply Talleyrand's turn of phrase: deindustrialization is practically a metaphysical idea. It means approximately the same thing as industrialization.

Now that over four decades have passed since the end of the boom period, we can no longer speak only of a history of factory closings,[4] but instead of a history of deindustrialization "beyond the ruins",[5] to the inclusion of a political, mental, and cultural framework for the phenomena in question, all within the context of an overarching transformation process. France is worthy of particular attention in this connection. As France was a relative latecomer to industrialization, crisis phenomena in traditional industries combined there with national fears of decline, strong impulses toward modernization, and syndicalist union traditions. France can thus serve as a strong paradigm for the social, political, and cultural substance of the deindustrialization narrative. Starting with a discussion in section I of the empirically graspable phenomena of deindustrialization in France, we will then look the second section into the political-social reaction to this and then into that reaction in terms of memory culture. The third section examines the cognitive intertwinement of deindustrialization with globalization (*mondialisation*) discourse, which is particularly prevalent in France. Finally, the results will be placed in a more comprehensive context in the concluding section.

I

As in all other Western industrialized countries, loud alarmist voices abounded in France around 1980 with regard to the state of domestic industry.[6] As early as the 1960s, people saw the expansion of global trade and growing international competition as a threat to French industry. The continuing rise in direct foreign investment on the part of French multinational companies was accompanied, in return, by an increase in imports and the presence of foreign capital within the domestic market.[7] At the same time, the percentage of workers in the secondary sector sank, falling from 38.5 to 22 per cent of the total workforce between 1974 and 2007, with the figure for the manufacturing industry decreasing from 23.4 per cent in 1970 to 12.9 per cent in 2007.[8] These trends involved primarily three main regions, which were home to the majority of industrial jobs: eastern and northern France as well as the Île-de-France region. In 2006, still over every fifth member of the workforce in these regions was employed in industrial jobs. Particular regions such as Lorraine and Nord-Pas-de-Calais were dominated by the iron and steel industry, which has seen an unparalleled decline since the 1970s. Lorraine, Île-de-France, and Franche-Compté were and continue to be centres of the French automotive industry, which has been hit by crises time and again. Alsace-Lorraine and the north, in particular, witnessed a secular decline in the textile industry.[9]

The debate over "deindustrialization" in France took place mostly within these regions with their relevant industries.[10] Even before 1973, many of those industries and companies were under massive competitive pressure and, in part, did not keep up with technological innovations. One symbolic example was the last production of a new train steam engine at the world-famous Graffenstaden machine plant near Strasbourg in 1964. At the same time, the number of jobs began to fall precipitously, and by the beginning of the 1980s, the company completely imploded.[11] Even more dramatic was the 1973 collapse of the globally renowned Besançon-based watch and clock manufacturer, Lip, which apparently did not keep up with the competition posed by electronic watches, especially from Japan, and which had to file for bankruptcy. In the subsequent scandal, the syndicalist traditions of France came into play, and the local factory shutdown became a national affair and the centre of the media's attention. The following months saw a series of factory occupations, mass demonstrations, and violent clashes.[12]

The situation in the steel industry was particularly symptomatic of this trend. The steel crisis hit France palpably, as it did all other Western industrialized countries beginning in the mid-1960s. Overcapacities, economic troughs, heightened international competition, and dwindling productivity profits combined for a syndrome that threatened the industry's very existence.[13] Streamlining, specializing, and direct state subsidies were the instruments of choice in tackling this crisis, as were French mergers like that of several companies to form the steel giant Creusot-Loire in 1970. Following what was often considerable investment, the European steel industry was hit particularly hard by the economic crises of 1973 and 1978. The European Commission introduced a quota system based on the European Coal and Steel Community (ECSC) Treaty, a system that was meant to help bring about more reliable production quantities. The system, in its fundamentals, was extended six times and continued through 30 June 1988. At the same time, a practical subsidy and intervention spiral[14] emerged from uncoordinated aid and bailouts on the part of individual governments, which still did not end when the commission introduced a "subsidy codex" in 1980 and 1981.[15] Economists in 1983, in any event, announced that there were only two alternatives for the steel industry, which was characterized as a globally "mature" sector: "international stabilization through some form of innovative organization, or chronic industry sickness."[16] The iron and steel industry in France and Western Europe has in fact been completely restructured since then. The much-diminished industry adapted to the global market through innovations of both entrepreneurial and technological nature as well as a considerable rise in productivity. This adaptation has brought about new and largely crisis-proof jobs. In Lorraine, for example, around 8,000 people still work in the iron and steel industry, which once employed 100,000 workers.[17]

The situation in the French textile industry was nearly as dramatic. Between 1962 and 1974, the number of companies in that sector fell by nearly half, from 6,667 to 3,716, while the number jobs decreased from 470,405 to 347,878 over the same period of time.[18] As this industry was traditionally driven by (frequently female) low-wage workers, who were readily available in threshold and developing economies, the Western European textile industry succumbed to strong international competition at a relatively early date. By the mid-1970s, the industry was on the road to decline, with no return. Between 1972 and 1990, the number of jobs in France in this sector decreased again from just under 370,000 to 140,917 and the number of companies from over 4,000 to 2,000.[19]

The situation in the particularly cyclical automotive industry was more complicated. The industry's centres were found in the east of France (Peugeot-Talbot) and in the Île-de-France region (Renault and

Citroën). As of the late 1960s, the industry was already in the midst of a serious crisis. Some traditional brands had disappeared from the market (Panhard) or had been taken over by other companies (Talbot, Simca). Over the course of 1968, the weakening giant Renault had been affected by strikes, demonstrations, and factory occupations in the name of *autogestion*, or worker self-management, while Citroën was on its way into its own final crisis – that company went bankrupt in 1974 and was taken over by Peugeot at the initiative of the government.

We can in fact speak of a kind of "globalization" during the period before 1970 in the automotive industry, which was undergoing constant change.[20] With global production steadily rising and world trade expanding just as dynamically, a new global player came to the fore in Japan, which posed serious competition within a short period of time. In less than a decade (1963–71), the number of cars manufactured in Japan soared from a few thousand to almost four million.[21] This sudden international competition coincided with a high employment rate in the automotive industry in traditional manufacturing countries such as France, West Germany, the United Kingdom, and the United States. In France, for example, job numbers had been rising steadily beginning in the early 1950s, reaching a historic peak with 350,000 workers in 1978 (as a total of full-time jobs or their equivalents).[22] This high level of employment was aided by migration from the countryside to urban areas and the immigration to France of unskilled and semi-skilled workers from other countries. The streamlining and job-cutting measures precipitated by the crisis therefore chiefly came without warning. They also cast doubt, and abruptly so, on the industry-based lifestyle of the working class, which had only recently been viewed and pursued as a great opportunity.

The outcome of the deindustrialization trend in France between 1970 and 2007 had a clear impact on employment structure. Nearly two million industrial jobs were lost, falling by half to around 11 per cent of total jobs.[23] In this, France did not depart from the trends in other Western industrialized countries. The same applies, of course, to the other underlying trend of "deindustrialization," which was also to be observed across industrialized countries: the reduction in the number of jobs ran counter to trends of higher productivity and added value in industry. Between 1974 and 1989, the French industrial economy's net value added increased from 223 to 282 billion euros.[24] The focus was hence no longer on the expansion of production in sheer numbers: this would, indeed, not have been feasible in times of market saturation and overcapacity. The goal was instead that of increasing productivity, which helped raise the value of capital while diminishing that of labour.

A portion of the gross national product thus shifted from wage earners to holders of capital, both in France and in the other industrialized countries of the West.[25] Deindustrialization was always accompanied by shifts in participation in the gross domestic product, contributing to the growth of social inequality since the 1980s.

II

In the years between the second oil crisis of 1978 and the mid-1980s, the economic crisis fully took hold of the affected industrial sectors. It came to an initial head with the change of government in 1981 under François Mitterrand, who initially forged a Socialist-Communist coalition. As soon as his government took office, the serious social and political problems deriving from the economic crisis, deindustrialization, and job loss intensified. Any industrial policy program would thus have to be equal to the task. In order to stop deindustrialization or even to unleash a countervailing trend, French industry would have to become more competitive, while, at the same time, the international entanglement of the French economy would have to be limited. Instruments to be used to this end were derived from a mixture of neo-Keynesian expansion and classical statist measures such as the assumption of debt and the expansion of state ownership in the crisis-ridden sectors. In the face of persistently poor economic conditions, massive budgetary problems, and the repeated forced devaluation of the French franc, however, the political consensus supporting the Socialist program collapsed very quickly.[26]

It was in this context that the Creusot-Loire steel conglomerate collapsed spectacularly in 1984.[27] Le Creusot was considered a paradigmatic *ville-usine par excellence*, and the company was the "jewel in the crown" of the iron-processing industry in France.[28] In 1984, however, bankruptcy would become unavoidable, despite considerable rescue efforts, and the largest French steel producer disappeared from the scene virtually overnight.

The case of Creusot-Loire rapidly became a political symbol of change and of the weakness of the French left. In the midst of an economic crisis, a century of proud French industrial tradition could no longer be salvaged. Previously, no left-wing French politician would have dared to accept the truth of the market and leave a huge but insufficiently competitive international company with 14,000 employees to its fate. The closure of Creusot-Loire thus became "a veritable electroshock, a spectacular admission of the powerlessness of the state in industrial matters."[29] It became a symbol for the ideological reorientation of French

Socialists under Mitterrand and Laurent Fabius after 1983, which led to considerable frustration in left-wing camps. The debates over how to understand Creusot's collapse were accordingly bitter: was it in fact the management's fault, or perhaps more so that of politicians, who did not intervene strongly enough?[30]

The fact that the French state did not save Creusot-Loire was in part due to the immense debt – one to two billion francs – the emerged from the bankruptcy proceedings. The case, moreover, symbolized a turning point in the French way of dealing with the problem of deindustrialization – a shift from an active, interventionist industrial policy to a passive job market and social policy. In terms of fighting against deindustrialization and unemployment, it no longer seemed to be the method of choice to use subsidies to prop up unproductive jobs, but instead to soften the blow through social policy measures. Not long after their victory in the 1981 elections, the government led by Prime Minister Pierre Mauroy introduced several measures to redistribute the (industrial) jobs that were becoming scarcer. It introduced a fifth week of paid vacation and reduced the number of weekly working hours from forty to thirty-nine. The decisive step would then follow in February 1983: the immediate lowering of the retirement age from sixty-five to sixty was a decision that would have consequences. While softening the social blow of deindustrialization, it would become a massive burden on the French state and usher in a long-term shift in mentality.[31]

In September 1981, Prime Minister Mauroy already described what would become the country's future policy. He addressed workers in a speech in Lille, his own political home base where he had been mayor for three decades, and a city particularly affected by deindustrialization:

> I would like to address myself to those who are the most senior, to those in this region who have spent their lives working ..., and when the hour of retirement comes, you will retire in order to give work to your sons and daughters. This is what I am asking of you. The government will enable you to retire at 55 years. Leave at 55 with your head high, proud of your life's labor. This is what we will ask of you. This is our contract of solidarity. Let the older workers, those who have worked, leave, and make room for the youth so that everyone may have work.[32]

The early retirement policy, which was introduced in a similar fashion in other industrialized countries such as West Germany,[33] would have a strong influence on the job market for two decades. Within a very short period of time, the employment rate among older workers fell precipitously, with nearly no active workers left over 65, and the rate falling for men between 60 and 64 years of age from 65.7 per cent in 1969 to 16.5 per cent in 1993. Employment dropped for 55–9 year-olds from 82.5 to 68.9 per cent over the same period of time, with the average retirement age falling from 62 to 58 within those twenty-five years.[34]

This "shutdown" of the male workforce was the lowest common denominator that those involved could agree to: it was easy for the state and entrepreneurs, unions and the workers themselves, to meet the job shortage situation, brought about by deindustrialization and structural change, and to deal with the costs involved by passing them on to the social insurance system. This situation allowed a *culture de la préretraite* to develop, which affected mentalities in the long run. This culture was based on a fixation on the model of (male) industrial full-time jobs that considered the retraining of laid-off workers over the age of fifty to be just as impossible as their reintegration into the job market.[35] Deindustrialization therefore also entailed an end of a familiar way of life as well as a crisis of masculinity. The idea that a family's means depended on the income of one individual (male) breadwinner had already begun eroding well before 1989. The concept of a one-earner family had held great influence as a normative model into the 1970s. Beginning in the 1980s, however, it neared its end, with deindustrialization playing a decisive role in the process. Between the mid-1970s and the end of the 1980s, the economic basis for the single-wage-earner model, the stable, life-long, "Fordist" industrial job – was lost to accelerated structural change. As a result, the normal male employment timeline began to disintegrate, with the significant decrease in men's employment as a result.[36]

While the goal of *retraite* as a new way of life of individual freedom and tranquillity took centre stage in the long run,[37] in the short term, experiences of loss held sway. The sharp reduction in the male employment rate was connected to the experience of a generation of people for whom the market economy, with its rapidly changing labour market, offered no new opportunities. For those of the older generations, who were not able to adapt to the new conditions, the transition to early retirement usually entailed a sort of masked unemployment and an interruption of their working lives. The same was true of those who had, only recently, been lured into work in factories during the "boom" and the connected rural exodus. Immigrant, unskilled, and semi-skilled workers especially ran the risk of losing their jobs.

The dispute intensified with particular acrimony at the Talbot automotive factory in Poissy near Paris, which had recently been acquired by Groupe PSA. When the company's management announced a plan to lay off more than four thousand workers in 1983, a month-long strike was held in response. In the end, however, there was a kind of tacit consensus among the companies, trade unions, the state, and workers. Migrants accepted financial support from the government in return for voluntarily returning to their countries of origin.[38] Other immigrants and unskilled workers had to accept gaps in their careers as well as losses in income, at least for a period of time. Many had to look for new jobs in other industries, which were mostly to be found in the expanding service sector.[39]

While skilled workers between the ages of thirty-five and fifty still had relatively good prospects of keeping their jobs in the swirl of deindustrialization and structural change, this did not indeed apply to older, immigrant, and less-qualified workers. By 1995, over a million jobs had been lost,[40] resulting in a shift in the age structure of the industrial workforce. Whereas highly qualified middle-aged workers continued to serve as the core of their companies' staff, fewer young workers were being hired, as was reflected in the high level of youth unemployment in France. In Longwy, for example, a centre of the Lorraine iron and steel industry, the children of steelworkers struggled to find new job prospects,[41] as they underwent the shift from a clearly structured collective proletarian culture that was based on industrial jobs to a highly differentiated context in which individual "employability" had the last word when it came to hiring and promotion.[42]

As Jean-Luc Deshayes examined in detail in the case of Longwy, the key issue related to deindustrialization was in fact a matter of culture and by no means only a question of how workers were able to secure their material existence. Of course, the structural change of the 1980s and 1990s had a great effect on the income of the recipients of wages and social benefits. And, as mentioned above, the share of wages in the gross domestic product shifted in favour of the owners of capital during this period. Nevertheless, unemployment benefits, early retirement, and the dynamic development of jobs in the service sector in the midst of the deindustrialization process all provided a sufficient range of alternative sources of income. This was the case even if the emerging service jobs were often "bad jobs" that provided low wages and poor working conditions. The pressure on workers and their families to adapt in terms of culture and everyday life would be far more consequential in the long run. The frequently invoked "individualization" process – that is, the emergence of the individual from a traditional context anchored in a specific type of work, conventions, and hierarchies – was linked to the process of deindustrialization. In this view, the factory was a centre of social cohesion and a workplace that shaped people's identities while allowing for their personal "agency."

As a large "family," the factory provided meaning and form for the life-worlds of many industrial workers. The closing of factories upended the workers' lifeworld coordinates, leading to a great deal of nostalgia derived from looking back at these "lost worlds."[43] In this light, deindustrialization was not just a matter of losing one's economic basis, but also of losing one's very identity.

This process was also reflected in gender relationships and hierarchies. Deindustrialization threatened (white) male workers most with regard to their economic stability and social position. Just as men over fifty began to see their employment come under threat, the female employment rate began to rise significantly. An increasing number of married women and mothers began to take up regular employment during the 1980s and 1990s, not least due to the erosion of the typical male work pattern. While the average number of working years sank for men, it increased for women. This change in the employment structure had many causes,[44] but was essentially linked to the process of deindustrialization. This process and the end of the "Fordist" working career was thus linked to the end of the classical gender-specific division of labour with a sole male earner married to a housewife.

These developmental processes can be observed to various degrees in all of the regions affected by deindustrialization in Europe and North America. The comparatively generous early retirement schemes and the way in which French workers and trade unions reacted to impending factory closures were particularly characteristic of France. There, a particular syndicalist-localist tradition came into play, one that was both site-centred and strident. The factory served as the centre of its identity, as a place that linked work, economic resources, and social life. This particularly long-standing tradition in France produced radical and quantitatively significant social movements as a response to bankruptcies and factory closures. They explain the frequently acrimonious and often vehement conflicts over the consequences of deindustrialization on the local stage. One can follow a clear thread from the factory occupation during the Lip scandal to the closures of Creusot-Loire and Moulinex and the "boss-napping" that took place ahead of the imminent closure of a Sony cassette factory in Bordeaux in March 2009.[45]

III

Deindustrialization in France has thus, on the one hand, been a phenomenon central to the overarching structural changes underway in all Western industrialized countries beginning in 1970. These changes affected a handful of industrial regions and chiefly concerned low-skilled, immigrant, and older men. This groups was most frequently at risk of losing their jobs, which entailed a variety of consequences, ranging from early retirement and long-term unemployment to often laborious career changes, or even having to leave the country in the case of immigrants. Deindustrialization was a process generally affecting only certain groups and areas and limited in its scope. On the other hand, deindustrialization came with the loss of lifeworlds and familiar and easily navigable social and economic structures. Those affected faced an increasingly complex, mobile, and individualized world, with an economic base found chiefly in the service industries. These provided both new "bad jobs" and jobs that required a high level of qualification – too high for many former industrial workers. Deindustrialization and its being viewed as a "world we have lost" thus also constituted a cultural complex.[46]

It is this context that led to specific perceptions, and indeed fears, of "globalization," a phenomenon that has been met with a great breadth of descriptions and analyses. Nearly no other contemporary topic has been the subject of so many different, even contrary, views. This range reflected less the emergence of completely new developments than it did the rapid quantitative increase of essentially known phenomena. The various characteristics of globalization – the intensification of the international division of labour, the growth of world trade and foreign production, the expansion of capital investment and financial markets, and the opening of borders and increase in migratory movements – were not all new. But they came together in the final third of the twentieth century in a hitherto unknown dynamic.[47]

This phenomenon coincided in France with concerns about the industrial decline of the country and the aforementioned fears of losing traditional lifeworlds. And the discourse on globalization provided the political-cultural language needed to articulate these concerns. There have been two camps on this issue: those who, as it were, "blamed" globalization for the problems in France, along with those who diminished it as just a buzzword – as Pierre Bourdieu said, while the word does not say particularly much, it does work as a pseudo-argumentative means of discursively pushing through neoliberally defined socio-political interests.[48] On the other side of the issue, modernizers in the political and economic realms actually used the globalization argument as a lever to achieve domestic reform. They argued against what they saw as the presumptuousness and calcification of the French economic system and its predominant mentalities.

By the 1960s, the expansion of world trade and growing international competition were already perceived as threats to the French industrial economy. Imports and foreign capital increased on the domestic market along with greater foreign direct investment of French multinational companies.[49] Parallel to this, efforts began in the late 1960s to strengthen potential crisis regions in the north and east of France through particular restructuring and reindustrialization measures. The regional commissions run by the central Délégation à l'Aménagement du Territoire et à l'Action Régionale (DATAR) would, however, prove ineffective, as they acted chiefly as representatives of local economic interests. Just as these activities did little to increase the competitiveness of local industries, Mitterrand's regional structure policy also aimed only at softening the blow of the new realities and mollifying the workers by increasing social and temporary unemployment benefits.[50]

These measures reflected long historical traditions and path dependencies in the mentality of entrepreneurs as well as state officials. They expressed themselves in a certain way that could be regarded as "specifically French."[51] The emergence of a strong central state, which, in a long historical process, had largely absorbed any intermediary levels of governance, promoted interventionism as well as the (excessive) self-identification of officials with the state. This favoured a practically "parasitic" relationship between the French bourgeoisie and the state, as was reflected in the predominant type of French entrepreneur. It established a protectionist vicious circle in which the state promoted the type of investors who were willing to act entrepreneurially only if the state protected them from the risks. This bourgeois bloc, consisting of representatives of companies and the state, came across as authoritarian and exclusive. This is one major reason for the long-term, anti-capitalistic radicalism of the French workers' movement. Excluded from the political nation in the nineteenth century, the movement regarded the bourgeois state-industrial complex as its ongoing adversary and pressed for placing curbs on capitalism. After 1945, it was in fact the unions that demanded that the state protect endangered companies.

It was only toward the end of the *Trente Glorieuse* period that this constellation gradually began to change as a result of rapidly growing international competitive pressure and the increased influence of a new class of entrepreneurs who were connected to multinational corporations. These developments resulted in great changes to the French economy and society. The pressure to adapt and a desire for political reform strongly countered the traditional state-centred *dirigisme* into the 1990s. With traditional French industries now either abandoned or thoroughly modernized, as in the case of the automotive sector, France is quite competitive on the international market today, a situation that has benefited many in the country.[52]

In this context, the modernizers' discourse aimed to make existing French industry more competitive. As the École nationale d'administration alumnus, politician, and entrepreneur Francis Lorentz urged in 1981, competitiveness would have to become the most important goal in order to stop industrial decline in France: "For this the industrialists have to change: They need to think in terms of the global market. This change is far from becoming a reality and has yet to begin in earnest."[53] In this vein, as the banker Bernard Esambert explained in January 1984, all reforms, be they institutional, social, financial, or territorial, had to be accelerated: "They now need to anticipate needs and maintain industrial development at a high level to enable the French economy to maintain its rank in international competition."[54] According to the Commissariat général du Plan, the international competitiveness of French industry and its capacity to innovate, and in particular its ability to establish production sites abroad, had to be a top priority, notwithstanding "internal constraints that may call it into question, particularly in the field of employment and land-use planning."[55]

These reformist views were widespread among French business and administrative elite in the 1980s. Together with the shift in policy under Mitterrand in 1983, such views led to the tendency for the state to withdraw increasingly from the market, instead of pursuing an active industrial policy within the framework of the state's plan, as had previously been the case. A gradual change would follow in France's economic policy and corporate culture as it focused more on international competition and how to face the challenges it entailed.[56]

This reorientation toward meeting the realities of international competition has been and continues to be opposed by those who view globalization as the source of all ills, as it were. Globalization would soon become a "big excuse" for all problems affecting the French economy. With the considerable involvement of French intellectuals, an image of an American-driven *mondialisation* process was constructed, one that is fundamentally opposed to French culture and history.[57] This resulted in a majority remaining sceptical of global integration to this day. Such scepticism is to be found most among the civil service and trade unions, which are particularly strong in France. Herein lies the heart of the French anti-globalization discourse and it is where the *entrepreneurs de morale* fight against "liberalism" for the sake of the *défense du service public*.[58] This sort of polarization reflects the deep divisions in French society. The legacy of deindustrialization, including its perception as the cause of an unjustly lost world, plays an important role in this regard. It provides a vision of a seemingly clear-cut world of days gone by, characterized by collective norms and structures, a world that is now being defended in the public sphere and in the few remaining private-sector arenas.[59]

This traditionalist stance, which emerged from the trauma of deindustrialization, seems to have recently been carried forward by new voices: groups of young people who have no "industrial" past of their own but who are against the idea of an open, liberal France owing to their unemployment, personal immigration background, or other cultural experiences of marginalization. As the journalist Alexandre Devecchio summarized the results of a study of his, "the young people today in France are more protectionist than their parents because they are the main victims of globalization ... For the young, globalization means closing factories, moving them abroad. De-industrialization. It's not a positive thing."[60] Such views also open the door for the Front National and enhances the pull of populism. At a time when deindustrialization, as described in this chapter, has already come to pass, the Front National has been reactivating the rhetoric of deindustrialization. It "explained" France's high unemployment figures in 2013 as "the consequence of the government's obstinacy in pursuing a policy of deindustrialization in France. The first cause of this deindustrialization is the choice of completely opening our economic and financial borders. It is an option for the European Union at all cost."[61] The deindustrialization narrative has now become a standard topic in the appeals used by the populists.

IV

This chapter has pointed to how strongly the experience of deindustrialization has begun to affect cultural memory in France. It can be cognitively linked to the question of how globalization should be viewed and what consequences it has for the country, which brings us back to the departure point of this chapter. The recent history of France provides an excellent example of how the historical narrative of development "after the boom" has lost its power of persuasion. More than twenty years of precipitous economic, social, and cultural change have entailed a profound transformation for French society.[62] The same is true for French industry, which has since gone through a restructuring process, with technological modernization, much greater productivity, new international value chains, and a major contribution to French exports.[63] It is no longer the same today as it was in the mid-1980s. As a microhistorical subject, viewed from the perspective of global history, deindustrialization in France is first and foremost about a culture of memory. It is characteristic that the topic was discussed in France almost exclusively as a purely national matter and that analytical glimpses at a European, transatlantic, or overall global process tend to remain the exception. Sociological and historical research is also often limited to descriptions of local and regional situations, thus creating the impression that deindustrialization is a phenomenon specific to the regions studied.[64] As recent research on the United States and the United Kingdom has highlighted, it is crucial how the loss of the familiar industrial working world is interpreted locally. Such interpretations are decreasingly tied to the people directly affected by the phenomenon in the 1980s and 1990s. Rather, the ongoing importance of deindustrialization is borne out in the way its interpretation shapes the political-cultural identity of places, regions, and entire countries. Beyond economics and structural change, deindustrialization entails the inscription of the process onto the collective memory as well as "representation and remembrance."[65] The intergenerational sense of structural and social exclusion brought about by deindustrialization corresponds with the need to conserve in one's cultural memory the lost and seemingly clear-cut world of industrial work. These processes offer potential as tradition-minded bulwarks against the demands of a post-industrial, highly individualized society, which is anchored in education and competition, flexibility and performance.

For historians, the deindustrialization narrative and related phenomena, with their long-term cultural impact, are of particular significance. Historical research should not itself, however, be allowed to become a source of such identity constructions. A focus on the local context would epistemologically narrow the scope, as it is bound to repeatedly reconstruct a narrative of linear decline following the *Trente Glorieuses*. This, in turn, would largely prevent any other perspectives from developing and cannot therefore lead us out of the impasse of a self-referential history of decline.

NOTES

I want to thank David Dichelle for translating this article.

1 For a classic study, see Barry Bluestone and Bennett Harrison, *The Deindustrialization of America: Plant Closings, Community Abandonment, and the Dismantling of Basic Industry* (New York: Basic Books, 1982). In the late 1980s, many argued that the process was even more serious than had been thought or had been suggested by official statistics: Lawrence R. Mishel, "The Late Great Debate on Deindustrialization," *Challenge* 32 (1989): 35–43.

2 Anselm Doering-Manteuffel and Lutz Raphael, *Nach dem Boom: Perspektiven auf die Zeitgeschichte seit 1970* (Göttingen: Vandenhoeck & Ruprecht, 2008); on deindustrialization, see especially 34–42.

3 This claim holds for this purpose, if we leave out the problem of deindustrialization in post-communist European countries. We do this in the following discussion, since completely different conditions applied. In terms of productivity, it is well known that industry was not competitively viable in communist countries.

4 Factory closings continue to be the general focus of Pierre Lamard et al., eds., *1974–1984, une décennie de désindustrialisation?* (Paris: Editions Picard, 2009); see, for instance, the contribution in that volume by Michel Hau, "Les grands naufrages industriels français," 15–35.

5 Jefferson Cowie and Joseph Heathcott, eds., *Beyond the Ruins: The Meanings of Deindustrialization* (Ithaca, NY: Cornell University Press, 2003).

6 Guy Di Méo, "La crise du système industriel, en France, au début des années 1980," *Annales de géographie* 93 (1984): 326–49. For a comprehensive survey and analysis of the global economic position of French industry, see Christian Stoffaes, *La grande menace industrielle*, 2nd ed. (Paris: Calmann-Lévy, 1980); Bertrand Bellon and Jean-Marie Chevalier, (eds., *L'industrie en France* (Paris: Flammarion, 1983).

7 See Méo, "La crise"; for an American point of view, see Bennett Harrison and Barry Bluestone, *Deindustrialization of America* (New York: Basic Books, 1982), 141–7.

8 Pierre Lamard and Nicolas Stoskopf, "Introduction," *1974–1984*, ed. Lamard et al., 7; Leif van Neuss, "The Economic Forces behind Deindustrialization: An Empirical Investigation," working paper, University of Liège, 2 August 2016, 43, accessed 7 June 2018, DOI: 10.13140/RG.2.1.4081.4325, https://www.researchgate.net/publication/305789585.

9 Stefan Lindner, *Den Faden verloren: Die westdeutsche und französische Textilindustrie auf dem Rückzug (1930/45–1990)* (Munich: C.H. Beck, 2001).

10 For a comprehensive overview of the development, see Alain Chatillon, *Rapport d'information fait au nom de la mission commune d'information sur la désindustrialisation des territoires* (Paris: Sénat, 2011).

11 Luc Jeanvoine, "Le dépérissement de l'usine de Graffenstaden," *Entreprises et histoire* 27, no. 1 (2001): 44–54.

12 Xavier Vigna, "Lip et Larzac: Conflits locaux et mobilisations nationales," in *68, une histoire collective (1962–1981)*, ed. Philippe Artières and Michelle Zancarini-Fournel (Paris: La Découverte, 2008), 487–94; Xavier Vigna, *Histoire des ouvriers en France au XXe siècle* (Paris: Perrin, 2012), 262–7. For the social and political context, see Xavier Vigna, *L'insubordination ouvrière dans les années 68: Essai d'histoire politique des usines* (Rennes: Presses universitaires de Rennes, 2007).

13 For a comparative European perspective, see the articles in Yves Mény and Vincent Wright, eds., *The Politics of Steel: Western Europe and the Steel Industry in the Crisis Years (1974–1984)* (Berlin: de Gruyter, 1987); Philippe

Mioche, "La sidérurgie Française de 1973 à nos jours: Dégénérescence et transformation," *Vingtième siècle: Revue d'histoire* 42 (April–June 1994): 17–28.

14 See Helmut Wienert, "Gelungene Umstrukturierung? Eine Zwischenbilanz der Anpassungsbemühungen der europäischen Stahlindustrie," *RWI-Mitteilungen* 40 (1989): 253–4.

15 On the subsidies and the connected European discussion, see Dieter Alexander, "Die Krise der Deutschen Stahlindustrie. Darstellung, Ursachenanalyse und theoretisch-empirische Überprüfung strategischer Konzepte der Krisenbewältigung" (PhD diss., Würzburg, 1992), 241–5.

16 W.H. Frost, "Interpreting the Mature Industry Situation," *International Studies of Management and Organization* 13, no. 4 (Winter 1983/84): 71.

17 Pascal Raggi, "Industrialisation, désindustrialisation, ré-industrialisation en Europe: Le cas de la sidérurgie lorraine (1966–2006)," *Rives méditerranéennes* 46 (2013): 11–28.

18 Figures from Lindner, *Den Faden verloren*, 79.

19 Ibid.

20 Th. Méot, "L'industrie automobile en France depuis 1950. Des mutations à la chaîne," in *L'économie française, comptes et dossiers*, ed. Institut national de la statistique et des études économiques (Paris: INSEE, 2010).

21 Ibid., 116.

22 Ibid., 123.

23 Denis Clerc, "Des salaires aux dividendes. Les changements de la répartition de richesse en France depuis 1970," *L'économie politique* 41 (2009): 16; van Neuss, "Economic Forces," 45; Chatillon, *Rapport d'information*, 23–6.

24 Clerc, "Salaires," 16. The prices are adjusted for inflation.

25 van Neuss, "Economic Forces," 44.

26 See Vincent Wright, "Socialism and the Interdependent Economy: Industrial Policy-making under the Mitterrand Presidency," *Government and Opposition* 19, no. 3 (summer 1984): 287–303, which also emphasizes the strong continuity in industrial policy with the Raymond Barre government under Giscard d'Estaing. On industrial policy in France during that period, see Jack E.S. Hayward, *The State and the Market Economy: Industrial Patriotism and Economic Intervention in France* (Brighton, UK: Wheatsheaf Books, 1986), esp. 212–36; Elie Cohen, *L'état brancardier: Politiques du déclin industriel, 1974–1984* (Paris: Calman-Levy, 1989), esp. 311–16; Vivien A. Schmidt, *From State to Market? The Transformation of French Business and Government* (Cambridge: Cambridge University Press, 1996), esp. 94–131.

27 A detailed analysis of the Creusot-Loire case can be found in Cohen, *État bracandier*, 25–66. See also Catherine Vuillermot, "Creusot-Loire: Naissance et mort d'un groupe industriel français à travers sa revue interne (1970–1984)," in *1974–1984*, ed. Lamard, 65–77.

28 Philippe Braunstein, review of Octave Debary, *La fin du Creusot ou l'art d'accommoder les restes: Restes d'une visiteau musée, Annales. Histoire, sciences sociales* 60, no. 6 (2005): 1385.

29 Louis Bouret, "La rigueur en débat?" *Esprit* 145, no. 12 (December 1988): 151.

30 Claude Beaud, "Le drame de Creusot-Loire: Échec industriel ou fiasco politico-financier," *Entreprises et histoire* 10 (June 2001): 7–23; Claude Beaud, "Heurs et malheurs de la grande braderie de Creusot-Loire (1985–2001)," *Entreprises et histoire* 32, no. 1 (June 2003): 152–62. We cannot here go further into the role of the clear-cut mismanagement of the shady Belgian CEO Édouard-Jean Empain, who became well known especially after to his abduction in 1978.

31 See the contemporary analysis by Xavier Gaullier, *L'avenir à reculons: Chômage et retraite* (Paris: Éditions ouvrières, 1982).

32 Address of Pierre Mauroy in Lille, 27 September 1981, quoted in Timothy B. Smith, *France in Crisis: Welfare, Inequality and Globalization since 1980* (Cambridge: Cambridge University Press, 2004), 111–12.

33 See Andreas Wirsching, *Abschied vom Provisorium: Geschichte der Bundesrepublik Deutschland 1982–1990* (Munich: DVA, 2006), 258–60.

34 Xavier Gaullier, "Retraites, préretraites et temps de la vie," *Gérontologie et société* 25, no. 102 (2002–3): 69. See also Lutz Raphael, "Arbeitsbiografien und Strukturwandel 'nach dem Boom': Lebensläufe und Berufserfahrungen britischer, französischer und westdeutscher Industriearbeiter und –arbeiterinnen von 1970 bis 2000," *Geschichte und Gesellschaft* 43 (2017): 44–5.

35 Gaullier, "Retraites," 77. On the connection between deindustrialization and early retirement, see also Cornelius Torp, *Gerechtigkeit im Wohlfahrtsstaat: Alter und Alterssicherung in Deutschland und Großbritannien von 1945 bis heute* (Göttingen: Vandenhoeck, 2015), 270–4.

36 For the British case, see Linda McDowell, *Redundant Masculitinies? Employment Change and White Working Class Youth* (Oxford: Blackwell, 2003).

37 Gaullier, "Retraites," 77.

38 Vincent Gay, "Fighting to Leave or to Stay? Migrant Workers, Redundancy and Assisted Return Programs during the Talbot Dispute, 1983–1984," *Travail et emploi*, special issue (2015): 7–30. On the experience of immigrants during France's deindustrialization crisis, see also the chapter by Michael Kozakowski in the present volume.

39 Examples in Raphael, "Arbeitsbiografien," 47–9.

40 Ibid., 43.

41 Jean-Luc Deshayes, *La conversion territoriale Longwy (1978–2010): Le salariat entre paternalism et mondialisation* (Nancy: Presses universitaires de Nancy, 2010), 159–75.

42 Jean-Luc Deshayes, "Une double mise à distance sociale et spatiale des sidérurgistes et de leurs enfants dans le Longwy des années 1980," *CIST2014 – Fronts et frontières des sciences du territoire* (March 2014): 160–5.

43 See Jackie Clarke, "Closing Time: Deindustrialization and Nostalgia in Contemporary France," *History Workshop Journal* 79 (2015): 107–25. The focus there is on interviews that the author carried out with female workers with the Moulinex kitchen machine manufacturer, which went bankrupt in 2001. Most of those factories were closed. See also, in general, Cowie and Heathcott, introduction in *Beyond the Ruins*.

44 See Andreas Wirsching, "Erwerbsbiographien und Privatheitsformen: Die Entstandardisierung von Lebensläufen," in *Auf dem Weg in eine neue Moderne? Die Bundesrepublik Deutschland in den siebziger und achtziger Jahren,* ed. Thomas Raithel, Andreas Rödder, and Andreas Wirsching (Munich: Oldenbourg, 2009), 83–97.

45 See Andreas Wirsching, *Der Preis der Freiheit: Geschichte Europas in unserer Zeit* (Munich: C.H. Beck, 2012), 264.

46 Along the lines of the well-known book by Peter Laslett, *The World We Have Lost: Further Explored,* 4th ed. (London: Routledge, 2005).

47 George Ritzer, ed., *The Blackwell Companion to Globalization* (Oxford: Blackwell, 2007); David Held and Anthony McGrew, eds., *The Global Transformation Reader: An Introduction to the Globalization Debate,* 2nd ed. (Cambridge: Polity, 2003).

48 Pierre Bourdieu, *Gegenfeuer: Wortmeldungen im Dienste des Widerstandes gegen die Neoliberale Invasion* (Konstanz: Univ.-Verl. Konstanz, 1998), 39–52. A useful overview of the state of globalization critique is provided by Chamsy el-Ojeili and Patrick Hayden, *Critical Theories of Globalization* (Basingstoke, UK: Palgrave Macmillan, 2006).

49 See Guy Di Méo, "La crise du système industriel, en France, au début des années 1980," *Annales de géographie* 93 (1984): 326–49.

50 Sharon Zukin, "Markets and Politics in France's Declining Regions," *Journal of Policy Analysis and Management* 5 (1985): 40–57.

51 The following is in accordance with Henri Weber, "Cultures patronales et types d'entreprises: Esquisse d'une typologie du patronat," *Sociologie du travail* 30 (1988): 557.

52 For a comprehensive view, see Smith, *France in Crisis,* 54–87.

53 Quoted in Michel Raimbault and Jean-Michel Saussois, "L'organisation des rapports État-Industrie en matière d'emploi," *Sociologie du travail* 23, no. 2 (April–June 1981): 160.

54 Bernard Esambert, "La Politique industrielle de Georges Pompidou," *Revue des deux mondes* (January 1984): 60.

55 "Redéploiement de l'industrie française, concurrence internationale et aménagement du territoire," Rapport du groupe Redéploiement industriel de la commission Aménagement du territoire du VIIIe Plan, M. Philippe Lescanne, April 1980, quoted in Raimbault and Saussois, "L'organisation," 151.

56 Typical recent examples include Pierre Dockès, *L'enfer, ce n'est pas les autres! Bref essai sur la mondialisation* (Paris: Descartes, 2007) and Jean Arthuis, *Mondialisation: La France à contre-emploi* (Paris: *Calmann-Lévy*, 2007).

57 Philip H. Gordon and Sophie Meunier-Aitsahalia, *The French Challenge: Adapting to Globalization* (Washington DC: Brookings, 2004), 41–64.

58 Jean-Michel Denis, "Les syndicalistes de SUD-PTT: Des entrepreneurs de morale?" *Sociologie du travail* (2003): 318.

59 See Sophie Béroud et al., *La lutte continue? Les conflits du travail dans la France contemporaine* (Bellecombe-en-Bauges, Fr: Éditions du Croquant, 2008), 43–9.

60 Quoted in Stephen Beard, "French Voters Increasingly Question Globalization," Marketplace, accessed 1 June 2018, https://www.marketplace .org/2017/04/21/world/french-voters-increasingly-reject -globalization. See also Alexandre Devecchio, *Les nouveaux enfants du siècle, Djihadistes, identitaires, réacs: Enquête sur une génération fracturée* (Paris: Cerf, 2016).

61 Press release of the Front National, 24 July 2013, accessed 21 June 2018, https://www.rassemblementnational.fr/terme/desindustrialisation/.

62 For a comprehensive overview, see Pepper D. Culpepper, Peter A. Hall, and Bruno Palier, eds., *La France en mutation 1980–2005* (Paris: Presses SciencesPo, 2006).

63 See OFCE, *L'industrie manufacturière française* (Paris: La Découverte, 2010); Lionel Nesta, "Désindustrialisation ou mutation industrielle?" *Économie et statistique* 438–40 (2010): 297–301.

64 See, in particular, the work by Jean-Luc Deshayes, *La conversion territoriale Longwy (1978–2010): Le salariat entre paternalisme et mondialisation* (Nancy: Presses universitaires de Nancy, 2010).

65 See Tim Strangleman, James Rhodes, and Sherry Linkon, "Introduction to Crumbling Cultures: Deindustrialization, Class, and Memory," *International Labor and Working-Class History* 84 (December 2013): 7–22.

8 Look to the Future, Embrace Your Past: Regional Industrialization Policies and Their Aftermath

BART HOOGEBOOM AND MARIJN MOLEMA

At the end of the 1960s, the European economy entered a stage of structural change. Many sectors became saturated with technological innovation, while markets also became saturated.[1] Moreover, the rise in public prosperity propelled loans so that labour, as a production factor, became more expensive. This situation especially affected labour-intensive workplaces, for example shipyards, steel plants, and sites of textile production, which were scaled down or even completely vanished during the late 1960s and the 1970s. "Deindustrialization" has become a widely used concept in attempts to grasp this process and give the structural economic changes a proper place in contemporary history. However, we should use the term with caution to avoid over-generalization. The German economic historian Werner Abelshauser for example, points to the close interplay between industrial activities and the service sector in the economies of the twenty-first century.[2] A division between the "secondary" and "tertiary" sectors may, on many occasions, be arbitrary, such that the notion of a solitary rise of the service sector does not correspond with economic reality.

In addition to the *sectoral* nature of industry, we should pay attention to the *geographical* aspects of structural economic change. Deindustrialization, in its metaphorical sense, evokes images of abandoned production plants, large empty factory spaces, rusting pipes, and motionless hoisting cranes. Andreas Wirsching, in the preceding chapter, emphasizes the regional character of stereotypical industries such as steel and textiles, and analyses how economic changes within these regions have impacted the "narrative of deindustrialization." Industrial development was indeed concentrated in certain places, which remain, or were, the core regions of our modern economy. Alongside those core regions, and between the national centres of production, there are also places in which industrial development lagged behind. With the help of infrastructural programs and industrial premiums, many states envisaged a postwar process in which these regions would catch up. It is still debated whether European states succeeded in this endeavour.[3] Some studies emphasize the success of regional industrialization plans, while others stress the failure of regional industrial politics. The process of deindustrialization – or, more precisely, our thinking about "deindustrialization" as an influential process – is not a neutral or external factor in the debate about the success or failure of regional industrialization policies. As Wirsching does in his chapter, we also want to emphasize the time-specific circumstances in which the narrative of deindustrialization was constructed, and unveil the political dimension of the term. Critical assessments are implicitly or explicitly nurtured by the idea that industry lost its growth dynamics from the 1970s onwards. The new rising sector was perceived to be services and, as a matter of fact, regional areas were again perceived as lagging behind. Moreover, as critics of regional policies emphasized, the development of the real economy showed that states could not solve the regional problem.

Evidence supporting such opinions frequently relied on overgeneralizations and was not based in any quantitative or qualitative analysis. Therefore, we could argue that negative appraisals of regional industrialization policies were partly driven by the mere *idea* of deindustrialization. Historical analysis should add a critical evaluative dimension to this debate. On this basis, our chapter will embark on a history of regional economic policies and the interplay between developments at the macro and micro levels. It will scrutinize changing ideas about, and institutions of, regional development and will analyse its effects by looking at one specific region in the north of the Netherlands. This micro case study is crucial to grasping the influence of economic development and policy on the ground. Here, "on the ground" means a focus on the level at which the interventions were targeted, which in this instance was a region consisting of a few municipalities. Thus, this contribution moves from the global to the local, with a guiding research question that inquires into how, from the end of the 1960s onwards, regions were affected by two aspects that might be thought of as two sides of the same coin: structural transformations in the economy and the political responses to these transformations. The analysis is based primarily on policy documents, interviews with policymakers, statistics, and secondary literature. It will limit its in-depth analysis to the period up to 2008, which marks a recent crisis in the Dutch economy. In the concluding section, however, we will briefly address these past ten years and link our research back to global developments.

The Regional Industrialization Model

While the postwar period in Europe is often characterized as golden years of economic growth, many regions experienced only a faint glow. These areas could not keep up with rapid macroeconomic developments, resulting in relative higher unemployment numbers and outward migration. In comparison with the United States, European governments took a more central role in trying to solve the regional problem. In the United States, the initiative was left much more to private investors, and a form of territorial competition was taken for granted. In Europe, however, equal levels of development became a core issue in national economic policies. Another reason for the differences between the United States and Europe is to be found in their respective political systems. Territorial politics, in the sense that regions politicize their own interests, are to be found in both. However, as Kevin Cox has shown, European countries have more mechanisms through which local or regional concerns can be represented at a national level.[4] Exchange between the national and subnational levels is promoted by state structures found in these European countries, or through political parties that safeguard local/regional interests.

A European politics of regional development started in the United Kingdom.[5] Infrastructure such as roads, harbours, and industrial parks, but also investment premiums, had to attract manufacturing companies and stimulate the "normal" development of backward regions. Following the British example, countries on the continent created laws and launched programs in the 1950s. Regional policy in Germany started in 1951, with the selection of "emergency areas" that received extra funding. In the mid-1950s, the French identified "assisted areas." Other examples can be found in Denmark and Belgium, where a Regional Development Act (1958) and "Expansion Laws" (1959), respectively, were adopted. Once embedded in administrative structures, regional industrialization policy reached its heyday in the 1960s. The basic idea was that the state should help shape the preconditions for the industrial take-off of these regions. The French economist François Perroux, among others, legitimated this concentration on regional centres.[6] His growth-pole theory envisaged the agglomeration of the economy, which he considered was often the result of some large companies stimulating the growth of small and medium enterprises as suppliers.

In the Netherlands, the first step toward an encompassing regional policy was taken in 1951, when the Development Plan for Southeast Drenthe was approved. This plan was financed partly by aid delivered through the Marshall Plan. In order to convince the Americans of its relevance, planners emphasized the political instability that high unemployment would cause. The Dutch government argued that "poverty and discontent provide fertile soil for communism."[7] This plan became a model for eight other regions across the country. One of these development areas was Oostelijk Friesland (Eastern Friesland), located in the northern province of Friesland. We will turn to this specific region, and northeast Friesland in particular, in more detail further below.

Current Planning Concepts and Their Origins

Historians Jan Luiten van Zanden and Richard Griffiths have emphasized the discursive effects of postwar industrial policy, arguing that its function was to change the economic self-image of the Netherlands.[8] We believe that abstract concepts and spatial models have a significant impact on public investment decisions, strategic planning, zoning laws, and the behaviour of civil servants and entrepreneurs. Thus far, this story of spatial-economic policies quite closely reflects the historical literature about planning. Planning is thought to have reached its zenith during the period of "high modernity," roughly from 1890 to 1970.[9] From the 1970s, neoliberal ideas challenged the paradigm of strong state intervention. A recent work has pleaded for new historical research in which the mechanisms of political interventions should be analysed in the light of neoliberal principles and ideologies.[10]

As far as regional policies are concerned, new planning concepts envisaged the responsibilities of local and regional actors themselves. Conceptual developments were stimulated by the structural economic transformations of the 1970s. The end of growth driven by postwar reconstruction and industrialization undermined the basic assumptions underlying regional policies. Industrial employment declined rapidly on a national level. This stimulated critique of regional policies as being too much the result of top-down policies that projected the same industrial logic onto all regions regardless of location. In contrast, new ideas about regional development became more heterogeneous.[11] They emphasized geographical differences in economic and social relations, with the specific hallmarks of a region to be the point of departure for renewed regional development policy. Those who embraced these ideas argued that, because local actors knew their own region better than did central governments, the political initiative should be given to the regions.

This paradigmatic change started in the mid-1970s, developed further in the 1980s, and was supported by new economic theories in the 1990s. Economists and other scholars from the United States were the main source of inspiration, one of whom, Paul Krugman, had championed ideas on the self-enforcing growth effects of agglomeration economies.[12] Another was Michael Porter, who hypothesized that related companies would enjoy positive externalities when clustered in proximity to each other.[13] Agglomeration and cluster theories were popular insofar as they offered a practical guide to stimulating regional economic development. However, these theories were applied not only in economically vulnerable regions. Core economic regions were also reinventing themselves with the help of these new economic ideas, and, in fact, they were much more successful than the regions in using these ideas to attract new companies and investment.

These new ideas favouring agglomeration and clustering turned into a new orthodoxy by the early 1990s. The 1970s and 1980s can thus be seen as a period of transition, in which economic policy entailed a balancing act between neoclassical growth theory, Keynesian coordination policies, and stimulating Schumpeterian innovation. This meant that economic policy expanded in scope but at the same time reduced its ambitions. A letter from 1992, issued by the Dutch minister of economic affairs and former European Union commissioner Frans Andriessen, illustrates this perspective very well: "The right dose of all of these ingredients depends on time and place. Neglect of one or more ingredients can, as economic history has taught us, in the end administer considerable economic damage. The economy remains a fragile system, we cannot mould it but we can break it."[14]

This holistic view of economic policy and bottom-up initiative not only arose out of new theoretical insights or past failures but was also strongly related to European integration. National competences, such as fiscal policy, private sector subsidies, competition policies, trade policies, and market regulations, were influenced by Brussels. Moreover, the completion of the Common European Market in 1992 and the fall of the Iron Curtain warranted a more outward-looking view of the Dutch economy. Concerns about the competitive position of the Netherlands in a united Europe became front and centre in Dutch debates on economic development. These debates furthered the vision of the Netherlands as a "distribution country" (*Nederland Distributieland*), its economic faith closely tied to ensuring exceptional connections between the "main ports" – the port of Rotterdam and Amsterdam Airport Schiphol – and the European hinterland.[15]

This "main port strategy" was combined with theoretical insights concerning economic concentration. In part, the state accepted the concentration of employment as a natural phenomenon. As the secretary of economic affairs asserted in the Dutch national parliament in 1990, "There is a tendency in business to concentrate ... Do not let us think that we can fully compensate more or less natural processes by going against the grain."[16] In addition, economists such as Porter and Krugman were used to emphasize not only "natural tendencies" but also their favourable economic effects. This analysis steered policy away from attempting to boost development in peripheral areas, with policymakers instead focusing on reinforcing development in already dynamic sectors and geographical clusters.

In the 1990s, the government prioritized Dutch investment in physical infrastructure and stimulated development along transportation corridors. In some ways, this vision of the Netherlands as a "trading nation" was a return to the past. Manufacturing has been only of modest importance throughout Dutch history, with the postwar period being the exception. At the height of industrial employment in the Netherlands, around 1963, approximately 1.45 million workers were employed in manufacturing, with this number dwindling to a mere 900,000 in 2008, although the working population expanded significantly during these decades.[17] Here, we see the same economic transformation as that which occurred in other modern countries, a transformation that is often referred to as deindustrialization and involves the decline of traditional industries after the economic boom of the 1960s and 1970s.[18]

We argue that spatial-economic policies, inspired by economic theory, had a real impact on the geographic and sectoral composition of the economy. Whereas the old spatial model emphasized evenly spread industrial development, the new model was particularly unfavourable to peripheral regions, especially regions attempting to boost development in sectors that were not seen as promising in a remote location. From a national perspective, the northern Netherlands was often viewed as a region for recreation and rural living. The complementarity between the industrious west and the sedated north of the country became part of almost utopian thinking on the separation of functions across space. As one liberal parliament member asked the minister of transportation in 1997: "To live and engage in recreation in Friesland [one of the three provinces of the northern Netherlands], to work in the main port, this would be a solution to many problems, and provide space for everyone without degradation of the living environment, indeed it would even be improved. What is the vision of the minister?" To which the minister of transportation and fellow liberal, Annemarie Jorritsma, replied, "Personally, I can fully agree with this vision. You have before you someone who wants to make it a reality."[19]

Policies Seen from the Micro Perspective

In the remainder of this chapter we will report on an in-depth inquiry into a former development area in the north of the Netherlands. This region is called northeast Friesland, which until 2018 comprised six municipalities in the northeast of the province of Friesland (Fryslân).[20] In 2008, at the end of our research period, the region had about 125,000 inhabitants. During the period investigated, northeast Friesland received a lot of governmental attention, resulting in the construction of industrial zones within the regional centre (the city of Dokkum) and along the main canal in the region (the towns of Burgum and Kootstertille). These two towns as well as Dokkum were targeted as centres for industrial development in the 1950s. While these policies were relatively successful, northeast Friesland remained economically vulnerable. During the recession of the 1980s, the region suffered from unemployment levels well above 20 per cent,[21] and a regional coalition sought to revive the area's economy from the mid-1980s onwards.[22] The key project within the regional Action Program was the realization of a motorway running from the south to the north of the region called the "Central Axis." This ambition set the region on a collision course with provincial politicians who embraced corridor-based development in the south of the province.

We argue that the new orthodoxy on development policy in the 1990s was not only at times one dimensional and disconnected from economic reality, but also disrupted the consensus-based politics in regional planning. The devolution of development policy to regional and local authorities stimulated competition between the core and periphery for public investments at all geographical levels. While the provincial core areas used new ideas to lobby for large projects, peripheral municipalities united into regional coalitions arguing that development in their regions was not a lost cause and not without reason. Although employment was concentrated in core locations, this did not mean that the rural areas remained tranquil commuting zones. Today, there is still considerable employment in northeast Friesland, although there were about 170 fewer jobs for every 1,000 inhabitants than the Dutch average in 2008 (see figure 8.1). However, if we look more closely at the regional economy, we see differences in sector composition. Obviously, the agricultural sector remains overrepresented; however, the manufacturing and construction sectors are as prominent in northeast Friesland as they are in the Netherlands generally. This is a significant structural change since 1950, when the region hosted the equivalent of only half

Figure 8.1. Number of jobs in different sectors per 1,000 inhabitants (2008)

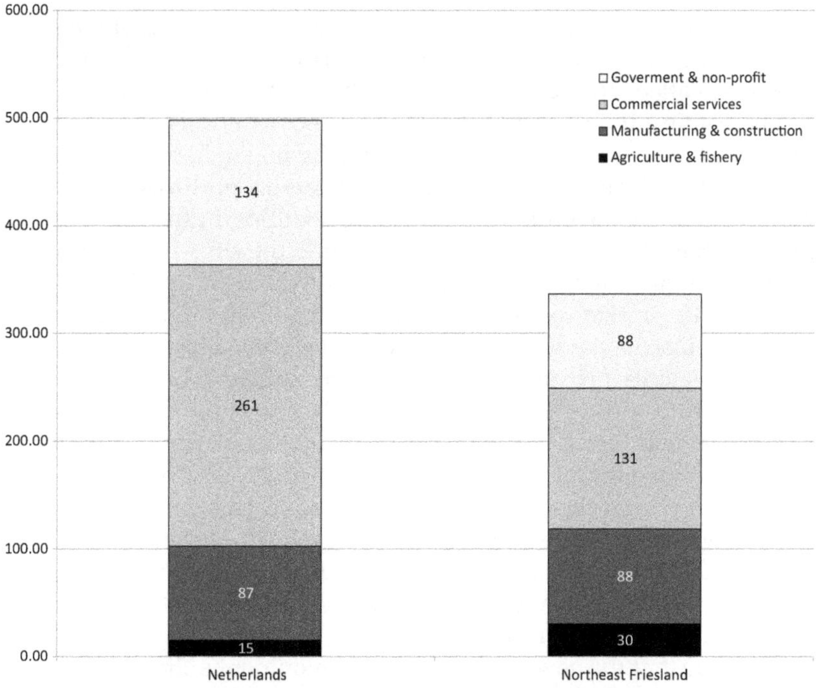

Source: Province of Friesland, Landelijke informatie van Arbeidsplaatsen en Vestigingen, 2008.

the average industrial concentration (see figure 8.2), and is related to both the late industrialization of the region and its less rapid deindustrialization after the 1970s. More importantly, taking the underdeveloped commercial service sector into consideration, the importance of industrial employment becomes even more apparent. In addition, the concentration of public facilities in the core economic areas means that considerably fewer non-profit organizations and government institutions are located in regions such as northeast Friesland.

A Closer Look at Regional Policy

In order to understand the structure of the region's economy, we should take a closer look at regional industrialization policies. The first phase, between 1952 and 1959, targeted eastern Friesland as a whole. This was traditionally a poor region, with people living in shacks made of peat

Figure 8.2. Number of secondary jobs per 1,000 inhabitants

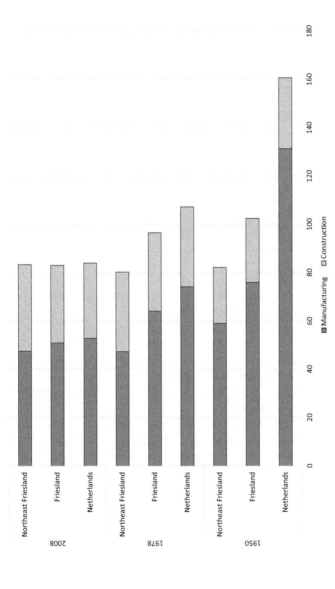

Note: The number of secondary jobs is slightly smaller than in figure 8.1 because jobs that entail fewer than fifteen hours per week were excluded from these data.

Source: Statistics Netherlands (CBS), Bedrijfstelling 1950, 1978; Werkgelegenheidsregister, Landelijke informatie van Arbeidsplaatsen en Vestigingen 2008; CBS population data 1950, 1978, 2008.

and clay well into the twentieth century. The structural reason for this level of poverty was the peat soil, which limited agricultural opportunities. Eastern Friesland was the largest of nine development areas in the Netherlands, both in terms of geographical size and financial appropriation.[23] The main policy objective was to reduce the high levels of unemployment caused by dwindling agricultural employment and steep population growth. To reach this goal, regional industrial policies were combined with policies stimulating outward migration to other parts of the Netherlands and abroad. The most important policy instrument, apart from major investments in infrastructure and industrial parks, was a subsidy on building costs for manufacturing firms.[24]

After 1959, the objectives expanded considerably. Overpopulation and congestion in the west of the Netherlands were now considered to be the principal policy problems, solvable only by deconcentration on a macro scale.[25] Large sections of the Netherlands were labelled "problem areas," including the three northern provinces (Friesland, Groningen, and Drenthe) in their entirety.[26] In line with the goal of deconcentration, policies no longer stimulated, but rather attempted to reverse, migration flows to the Randstad area in the western Netherlands, one of Europe's largest conurbations. An important additional instrument was the Investment Premium Arrangement (*Investeringspremieregeling* – IPR) of 1967. This was a general subsidy on capital investments, which continued to be operational until 2011.

Industrial policies in Friesland lacked geographical focus despite the leading principle of dispersal through regional concentration championed by the national government. Within the small province of roughly half a million, no fewer than eleven towns and cities were selected as development centres, both in the first phase and subsequently. This breadth was not only related to the balanced settlement structure, involving more small- and medium-sized towns, in comparison to the settlement in adjacent provinces of Groningen and Drenthe, but it also reflected the egalitarian views on development held by the Frisian population. With the idea of *Fryske eigene*, a concept used in public discourse to capture Frisian identity, the numerous small cities, towns, and villages were considered to be an inalienable part of Friesland. The idea that this settlement structure should not be altered too much by "regional concentration" was a powerful one. When the Ministry of Economic Affairs sought to reduce the number of development centres after 1964, considerable protest ensued.[27] In the end, smaller towns such as the village of Kootstertille were able to maintain their status as centres of industry.[28] This tradition of balanced development remained in place up to the early 1990s.[29]

Policy Successes

The effects of these policies can be demonstrated by looking at the relative concentration of manufacturing firms in the Netherlands. When regional industrialization policies were first introduced around 1950, about 1.6 per cent of manufacturing workers were employed in the eleven targeted municipalities in Friesland, which were home to around half of the Frisian population. In 1978, this percentage had increased to 2.6 per cent (see figure 8.3). The fact that the share of manufacturing employment remained relatively stable in the Frisian municipalities that were not targeted by industrialization policies shows that policy did influence the structure of the regional economy (see table 8.1). Between 1945 and 1959, 105 companies moved to Friesland, employing 5,000 workers in 1959.[30] In the 1960s, growth slowed, but even between the 1960s and 1978, seventy-five companies migrated to the province, employing 2,500 workers.[31] The most prominent example of a manufacturing firm relocating to Friesland was a Philips subsidiary, which moved to Drachten in 1950. In 1963, this subsidiary employed more than 2,300 workers.[32] The growth of this factory contributed to a steep population increase in Drachten, from around 10,000 in 1950 to about 35,000 in 1975.

The availability of surplus space, cheap labour, and inexpensive locations created an important competitive advantage for northeast Friesland, when compared to the scarce labour and congestion in the Randstad area. These conditions stimulated industrial deconcentration, especially of labour-intensive subsidiaries in the metals sector.[33] This process was largely completed by the end of the 1960s, when economic growth began to slow and labour market conditions normalized. A variety of companies from other regions were drawn to the centres of industry in northeast Friesland. The largest included a raincoat factory, RIA, in Zwaagwesteinde (1950); a steel-bridge producer in Burgum (1957); the textile manufacturer Parley in Dokkum (1959); and loading-dock producer Stertil in Kootstertille (1963).[34] Other medium-sized production locations were joint ventures with Anglo-Saxon corporations, including the heating system company Biddle from London and water heater producer Rheem from Pittsburgh, which opened subsidiaries in Kootstertille (1963) and Burgum, respectively (1966). This exogenous industrialization was reinforced by local entrepreneurship. Several local manufacturers were able to expand their business in traditionally strong sectors such as agricultural machinery, food production, and construction. The most iconic entrepreneur was Pier Prins, who started building farm vehicles from a shed in Dokkum during the

Figure 8.3. Regional industrialization policies in Friesland, 1959–94

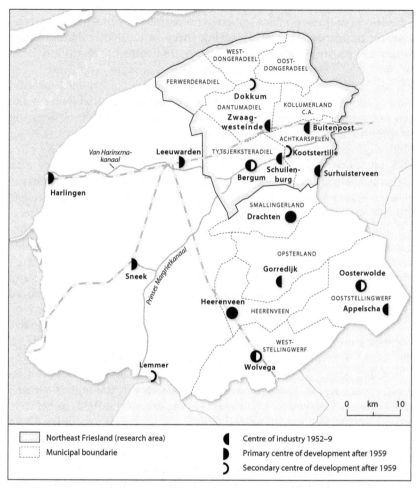

Source: Based on J.H. Zoon, *Friesland Tussen Hoop en Vrees: Enige beschouwingen over de invloed van de industrialisatie gedurende de periode 1950–1964 op de Friese Welvaart* (Drachten, NL: Laverman, 1969), drawn by UVAKaartenmakers.

Second World War and expanded to a 22,000-square-metre plant with around five hundred employees by the late 1970s.[35] Other examples are the Spinder brothers from Harkema, who produce steel fittings and dairy equipment, and the Hellema family, operating two biscuit factories in Hallum.

Table 8.1. Number of jobs in manufacturing in Friesland and the share of Dutch manufacturing employment, 1950–78

Area	1950		1963		1978	
	Number of jobs	% of jobs in Dutch manufacturing	Number of jobs	% of jobs in Dutch manufacturing	Number of jobs	% of jobs in Dutch manufacturing
Targeted municipalities	20,941	1.59	29,323	2.03	26,296	2.55
Other Frisian municipalities	14,423	1.09	14,861	1.03	10,434	1.01
Friesland	35,364	2.68	44,184	3.05	36,730	3.56

Source: Statistics Netherlands, Bedrijfstellingen 1950, 1963, 1978.

Structural Effects on the Region's Economy

The long-term effects of regional industrialization policies on northeast Friesland can be observed by taking a more systematic view of regional economic development. Figure 8.4 shows that employment in the manufacturing and construction sectors remained relatively resilient over the long term after an initial burst up to 1963 and then a steady decline until the late 1980s. There are no clear signs that deindustrialization continued afterwards, although both of these sectors are prone to recession. Moreover, although there has been a rise in service-sector employment, it was unlikely that many high-quality service jobs would relocate to the area. Most of the service industry caters to the local population, including a growing health sector for an aging population.

There has been a decline in several industrial branches, most notably textiles and clothing (see table 8.2). However, a decline in terms of employment does not necessarily signal deindustrialization. The food sector, for example, was once dominated by small dairy factories supplied by nearby farmers. Today, the most dominant companies in this sector are a few technologically advanced biscuit factories with international operations that make up a small cluster around the rural village of Hallum. These advanced plants are not locally oriented in supply or demand, but are tied to the village because they are owned by a local family. Similar changes have occurred in the metals sector, once a sector employing unskilled labour but now struggling to find qualified workers with advanced vocational training or a college degree. Paradoxically, this is also the case for Biddle and Stertil, companies that moved to the area in the 1960s in search of cheap unskilled labour.[36] Nonetheless, the fact that these companies are still thriving more than four decades after their relocation does not support the idea that industrial policies missed their mark or offered only a temporary solution.

The structural economic changes marked a clear change in the development of the region. Although industrial decline might not be the right concept for explaining the development path of the northeast Friesland economy, the consequences of the economic downturn were considerable. Most pressing was a steep increase in unemployment numbers during the 1980s. The regional economy depended to a large extent on construction and industries related to this sector. Construction is generally among the hardest-hit sectors during a recession. In addition, the RIA raincoat factory, the Parley textile factory, and the Rheem water heater manufacturer filed for bankruptcy in 1976, 1981, and 1983, respectively. Finally, it is important to mention the consequences of concentration, automation, and rationalization in the dairy industry.

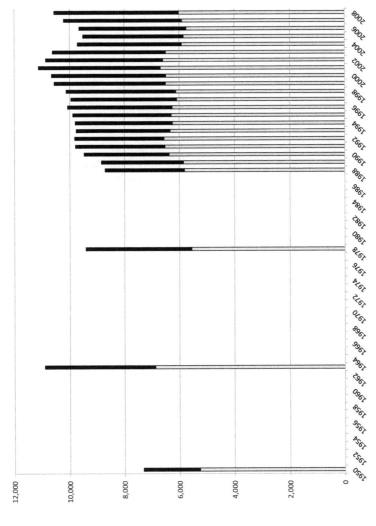

Figure 8.4. Total number of jobs in the secondary sector, Northeast Friesland

Source: Statistics Netherlands, Bedrijfstelling 1950, 1963, 1978; Province of Friesland.

Table 8.2. Total employment by sector in manufacturing and construction in Northeast Friesland

Economic sector	1950	1978	2008
Food industry	2,281	1,242	1,219
Metals	1,564	2,333	1,544
Building materials	174	530	370
Textiles and clothing	555	381	179
Wood and furniture industry	256	451	526
Rubber and plastics	179	205	438
Chemicals	70	45	113
Other manufacturing sectors	153	368	1,622
Total manufacturing	5,232	5,555	6,011
Construction	2,056	3,870	4,540
Total secondary sector	7,288	9,425	10,551

Sources: Statistics Netherlands, Bedrijfstellingen, 1950, 1978; Werkgelegenheidsregister Landelijke informatie van Arbeidsplaatsen en Vestigingen, 2008.

Transportation costs are of great importance in this sector and put a peripheral region such as northeast Friesland at a serious disadvantage. Since the dairy factory in Burgum closed down in 2003, there has been only one dairy factory operating in the region, while in 1950 there were nineteen such factories employing more than eight hundred workers.[37]

Policy Shifts on a National Level

Scholars, politicians, and policymakers criticized the system of spatial planning, regional policy, and structural policies from the second half of the 1970s. It was perceived as too complex and inefficient and as relying on postwar industrial growth. Implicitly, policymakers took this growth for granted by tasking themselves with the support of weaker regions (and sectors) while attempting to slow growth in other areas. As stated above, new economic ideas overtook these older notions. Policy papers underscored the relevance of emerging rather than declining sectors.[38] The idea of stimulating innovation in well-grounded and competitive industries became more concrete when a commission led by Gerrit Wagner, a former CEO of Shell, published a report titled *A New Industrial Impetus* (1981). Wagner identified several "main areas of attention" ("hoofd aandachtsgebieden"), which included sectors such as the food industry, but also spatial clusters such as the economic activities related to Schiphol Airport and the country's harbours.[39]

A few years later, the Goudswaard Commission developed a similar analysis. Its ideas were embraced by the new centre-right cabinet led by the Christian Democrat Ruud Lubbers (1982–6). This government was very receptive to arguments of entrepreneurs on social and economic policy. The recommendations of the Wagner and Goudswaard commissions were revitalized a few years later when the ideas of Harvard economist Michael Porter were used to reinforce already existing lines of thought in Dutch economic policy. A study commissioned by the Dutch government called *The Economic Strength of the Netherlands* (1990) operationalized the theoretical framework used in Porter's book *The Competitive Advantage of Nations* (1990).[40] The report proposed policies that supported the strongest sectors by resolving development issues related to the physical and knowledge infrastructure that transcended the interests of individual firms. The clusters the authors identified were specific sectors within agriculture and food production, the chemical industry, electronics, and transportation. Ultimately, Porter was used extensively, not to actively back strong sectors, but rather to strengthen the overall business climate, particularly the knowledge and physical infrastructure.[41] In hindsight, policymakers took one recommendation especially seriously: "The most important competitive advantage, on which a large part of the Dutch economy depends, is the location of the Netherlands along crucial transportation corridors. The importance of a well-functioning infrastructure cannot be stressed enough."[42]

The emphasis on spatial economic development and infrastructure came to dominate spatial planning in the 1990s. In the Fourth Report on Spatial Planning (1988) and the Fourth Report on Spatial Planning Extra (VINEX, 1991), significant emphasis was put on the spatial implications of an internationally competitive Dutch economy. The reports especially lauded the "main ports" – Schiphol and the port of Rotterdam – and their connection with the German hinterland through corridors in the centre of the Netherlands. Moreover, they conceptualized rural regions such as northeast Friesland as areas where nature preservation and the concentration of public facilities were the most urgent problems.[43] At the heart of these plans was the idea of the separation of different functions in space to create complementarity between different regions.

A committee of civil servants from five different ministries took a central role in the translation of these ideas into concrete policy measures. The task of this Interdepartmental Commission on the Strengthening of Economic Structure (ICES) was to prioritize infrastructure projects based on their merit for national growth. The funds would be supplied by the Fund for Strengthening the Economic Structure (FES), which would transform the capital earned from natural gas, or "underground capital," into "above-ground capital" in the form of a knowledge and physical infrastructure. In total, around 33 billion euros was spent from the fund between 1995 and 2010, of which 80 per cent went to transportation infrastructure.[44] Most of these funds were spent on two huge infrastructural projects: a high-speed railway connection between Amsterdam and Brussels and a freight train connection between the port of Rotterdam and the German hinterland.

These developments undermined the Dutch spatial planning system, traditionally organized in a way that balanced the spatial implications of the various interests of different policy domains.[45] The idea of evenly spread development championed up to the 1980s was replaced by corridor-based development, which concentrated investment in the economic heartland and caused considerable urban sprawl in proximity to the infrastructure. Moreover, it was difficult to realign with other policy priorities, such as the compact city, nature preservation, and the rejuvenation of depressed economic areas.

Discord and Consensus in the Region

How did all these new economic development ideas and their political translation into new policy measures affect northeast Friesland? We see both a willingness to embrace the new ideas and implement them on a regional level, as well as an active fight against the shifting policies. Projects that aimed to strengthen the knowledge infrastructure in the region clearly indicate that regional policies also shifted in northeast Friesland. Between 1988 and 1993, a Business Support Station (*Steunpunt Bedrijfsleven*) was established in the region, with a former executive of a medium-sized manufacturing firm, Peter Danz, chosen to lead the organization. Its goals were to provide accessible consultancy services to regional firms, support start-ups, and attract new enterprises from outside the region. According to annual reports, its services were in demand. Although the project was co-financed by European, national, and provincial funds, with the municipalities asked to pay only a modest share of the cost, local politicians decided to discontinue the project. According to Danz, they acted "penny wise, pound foolish."[46]

The region disapproved of the spatial-economic ideas; moreover, at a higher political level, the province of Friesland excluded the region from the corridor concept. In the Regional Plan Friesland of 1994, the province was divided into three zones: urban zones, natural and cultural landscapes, and agricultural zones. Small-scale farming, recreation, and tourism would be concentrated around the more attractive landscapes; more intensive agriculture would be concentrated in the fertile clay area in the north of the province; and in the urban zones, more export-oriented manufacturing and services would be stimulated. According to provincial planner Anne Dijkstra, provincial administrators wanted to override the agricultural image of the province by attracting multinationals to the urban zones.[47] The newly developed International Business Park Friesland (IBF) in Heerenveen would become the primary location for such companies.

Massive infrastructural projects in the Randstad were also criticized. Northern politicians, as well as business leaders and union representatives, invoked an image of a central government with little regard for or faith in the periphery. Such criticism sparked the creation of the Langman Commission in 1998, chaired by former minister of economic affairs Harrie Langman.[48] The report this commission produced was translated into a development program, called the "Compass for the North," for the three northern provinces. Most interestingly, the program copied the spatial-economic ideas that had already been implemented on a national scale. The report distinguished five core economic areas in the northern Netherlands, two of which were located in the province of Friesland, while the rest of the northern Netherlands was classified as rural territory (see figure 8.5). New industrial estates and infrastructural improvement would be prioritized in the core economic areas, with firms relocating from outside the northern Netherlands receiving financial incentives through the IPR to move to the core areas. The core areas identified in the "Compass for the North" closely resembled the urban zones identified by the Friesland provincial plan. The core areas were meant not only to boost agglomeration effects and lower transportation costs, but also to allocate space for agriculture, nature preservation, and recreation outside them. Policymakers hoped that this selective investment strategy in the "northern corridor" would entice the national government to support a megaproject in the northern Netherlands. This project, called the Zuiderzeelijn (Zuiderzee Line), would connect the north and the Randstad with a high-speed railway line.

The long-term policy transition discussed above created a new hierarchy of priorities that affected the region of northeast Friesland in a profound way. The national competitive interest depended on the accessibility and vitality of its main ports, while the competitiveness of the northern Netherlands depended on the core areas. Northeast Friesland was reconceptualized as a rural region that would have a future in tourism

Figure 8.5. Regional policy in the province of Friesland 1994 to the present

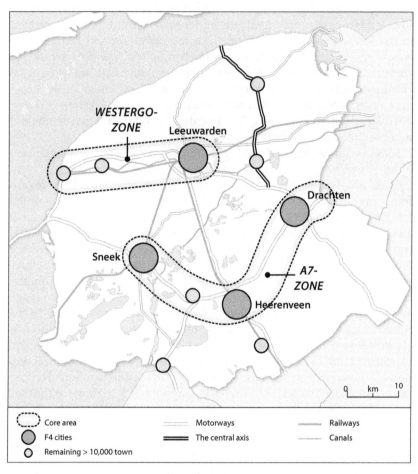

Source: Province of Friesland, drawn by UvA Kaartenmakers.

and multifunctional agriculture. In terms of investments in physical and knowledge infrastructure, northeast Friesland, which had previously occupied a special position as an area that was heavily affected by the "regional problem," dropped to the bottom of the priority list.

Opposition from Northeast Friesland

Provincial planners were aware that the Regional Plan Friesland of 1994 was a break with past policy. It abandoned the idea of harmonious development, which had been valued since the postwar industrial planning period and was reinforced during the public debate on the regional plan of 1982.[49] In the late 1970s, the province of Friesland asked its citizens to choose between two alternatives for the regional plan: one that would impose policies that would protect *Fryske eigene* and another that would stimulate growth.[50] Although it is questionable whether policies could steer development at will, Frisians overwhelmingly voted to retain their identity and support harmonious and small-scale development rather than rapid growth and urbanization.

The new direction in the regional plan of 1994 sparked considerable outrage. The loudest voice of dissent was the long-term mayor of Dongeradeel, Haije Sybesma, who occupied the office from 1976 until the end of 1999. As a politician, he promoted several projects in northeast Friesland, including the "Central Axis" motorway through the heart of the region (see figure 8.4). However, by 1994, the provincial government was no longer willing to prioritize projects for northeast Friesland. Sybesma's response to the first draft of the regional plan was that the province was "actively euthanizing" the countryside.[51] On another occasion, he criticized the limited financial appropriations made available for investment programs for rural development.

Meanwhile, the municipalities in northeast Friesland responded with their own program, the "Compass for Northeast Friesland." Accepting the new policy framework, the northeast Frisians targeted funds related to rural areas, to develop tourism and multifunctional agriculture. However, the regional program also emphasized the industrial nature of the region. The document identified "restrictive spatial policies" as one of the greatest threats to the development of the region, running the risk of becoming an "open-air museum" or a "nature-preservation area."[52] A few years later, the municipalities asked Jarig van Sinderen, then director of the Scientific Council of Government Policy (WRR), to write a rebuttal of the core-area strategy. The main argument of his rebuttal was that companies forced to relocate to the designated areas would look for even more favourable locations outside the province because they would have to incur the cost of relocation anyway. This would damage the Friesland economy rather than strengthening it.[53] This report was sent to the members of the provincial assembly, accompanied by a letter of petition, which reflects a similar ambivalence toward the spatial and regional policies in place: "Special attention needs to be paid to the important position of the manufacturing sector in our region and the opportunities that further development of recreation and tourism will offer."[54]

On first view of the consequences of the shift in policies, there do appear to be reasons for northeast Friesland to attack the new policy

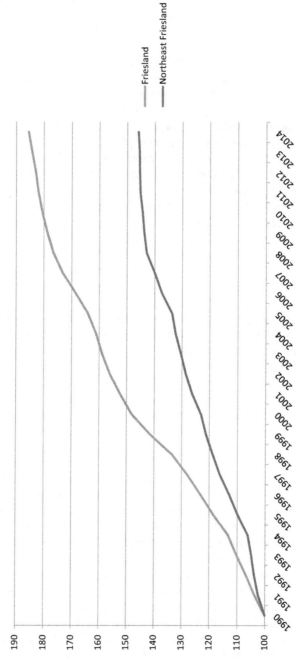

Figure 8.6. Growth in the surface area of industrial estates (index)

Friesland
Northeast Friesland

Source: Province of Friesland. Information not publicly accessible.

framework.[55] If we compare the growth of employment in business parks in northeast Friesland (+15%) to the growth in the five largest cities in the region (+27%) between 1994 and 2000, there is a clear divergence.[56] Whether this is due to policy interventions or to autonomous developments is difficult to ascertain. However, looking more closely at specific sectors, it is apparent that the transportation and service sectors account for most of the growth, while manufacturing and construction companies grew at similar rates in rural areas and towns compared to cities. The most notable migrations from northeast Friesland to the core areas were transportation companies. They include Broersma (2003) and Brant Visser (1999), both moving to Heerenveen from Anjum and Surhuisterveen, respectively. If we look at the expansion of industrial estates in terms of surface area, then we see a similar divergence (figure 8.6). This index shows the surface area of plots in industrial parks that had been sold. While the surface area almost doubled in the province as a whole in two decades, northeast Friesland experienced only about half that growth.

It is striking to note that the crown jewel of the core-area strategy in Friesland, the International Business Park in Heerenveen, was not particularly successful in attracting large multinationals. The only real success story quickly turned sour. American computer manufacturing firm SCI built a large plant in the industrial park in 1999, claiming that it would employ 1,500 workers, but the actual number of employees turned out to be significantly lower, and the firm relocated in 2002 when it found a better location in Eastern Europe.[57] A significant subsidy was paid to attract the firm, and the price for the plot was far below market value. The IBF would become a success only after 2004, when it started to reduce the plot sizes in order to attract smaller firms. However, many of the companies locating there moved from other parts of the province.[58] The share of total employment in Friesland located in Heerenveen increased from 9.1 per cent to 10.6 per cent between 2005 and 2015. The municipality absorbed more than 80 per cent of total provincial employment growth, with more than half of the growth in sectors frequently located on business parks, including transportation, business-related services, and manufacturing.[59]

Conclusion and Discussion

This chapter has focused on the geographical aspects of economic transformations from the late 1960s and 1970s and the way these changes influenced spatial-economic policies. By looking closely at the six municipalities that constitute the Dutch region of northeast Friesland, our case study has illustrated that a narrative of deindustrialization might blur our understanding of contemporary history and overlook the inherent political aspects that are entrenched in our view of the past decades. Our qualitative as well as quantitative analysis has shown that industrial sectors are still very important for the region's economy, a result of postwar development policies. Thus, we argue against the view that political intervention failed to develop the region. On many occasions, the disqualification of regional economic policies was part of a rhetorical strategy that backed the neoliberal shift in spatial-economic strategies. Economic transformations from the 1970s onwards destroyed the premises on which regional policies in Europe were built – namely, an even spread of economic prosperity throughout the country, driven by a uniform industrial development path. In search of new economic ideas, a paradigmatic shift occurred, in which economic opportunities were to be regionally specific, in the sense that each region had to identify and stimulate its own qualities. These ideas were popularized and translated into pragmatic policy measures with the help of the ideas of scholars such as Michael Porter. They also gave politicians and policymakers the instruments to present new policies that helped to respond to economic transformations.

Porter's ideas about the advantageous aspects of clustered activities, for example, stimulated national investment in Dutch infrastructure. Fundamental to these investments was the image of the Netherlands as an important link in the chain of global trade. As a result, attention to less central regions was overridden by an emphasis on national transport and other sectors, which were framed as being of major significance to the Dutch economy. Nevertheless, an emphasis on strong sectors and regional specifics was copied at the lower level of provincial government. Agglomeration and corridor strategies replaced an egalitarian approach, in which economic investments were spread evenly across the whole province. Despite its industrial nature, which was developed carefully with the help of the national and provincial governments, northeast Friesland was framed as a rural region, and some preliminary quantitative assessments indicate that its industrial structure has developed more slowly compared to the province as a whole. It is difficult to measure the extent to which this is driven by the shifts in spatial-economic policies. However, what is certain is that the new economic ideas are not favourable for maintaining and adapting the industrial nature of the region.

Our emphasis on the continuities between the period of the economic boom in the 1950s and 1960s and afterwards does not mean that we deny that, in absolute terms, there was a drop in the number of industrial jobs, which also took place in the Dutch economy generally. The industrial sector did change significantly from the 1980s onwards. We agree with the conclusion of Hartmut Berghoff in the following chapter, which notes the "parallel existence of continuities and changes" in the last decades of the twentieth century. However, we also agree with the argument in Wirsching's chapter, which makes a case for the way political and socio-cultural dimensions affect the way we make sense of our contemporary history. Northeast Friesland, which stands as a model for other regions that are peripheral to core economic areas, illustrates this approach. In the 1980s, national and provincial policymakers started to neglect the industrial successes of postwar development policies. From the 1980s onwards, political attention that had been paid to the development of vulnerable areas made way for neoliberal policies focused on national sectors of economic growth. The emphasis on industrial decline helped to legitimate new policy directions at the expense of vulnerable regions, but also at the expense of a balanced view of our contemporary history. Case studies such as these help to address overgeneralized accounts, unveiling the political and socio-cultural construction of the deindustrialization narrative, and illustrating that place matters.

NOTES

1 Derek H. Aldcroft, *The European Economy, 1914–2000* (London and New York: Routledge, 2002), 202.

2 Werner Abelshauser, *Deutsche Wirtschaftsgeschichte seit 1945* (Munich: C.H. Beck, 2004), 314.

3 Carl Koopmans and Carlijn Bijvoet, *De effectiviteit van regionaal beleid in wetenschappelijk onderzoek vanaf 1970* (Amsterdam: SEO Economisch Onderzoek, 2004).

4 Kevin R. Cox, *The Politics of Urban and Regional Development and the American Exception* (New York: Syracuse University Press, 2016), 315.

5 Douglas Yuill, Kevin Allen, and Chris Hull, eds., *Regional Policy in the European Community: The Role of Regional Incentives* (London: Croom Helm, 1980).

6 François Perroux, "Economic Space: Theory and Applications," *Quarterly Journal of Economics* 64, no 1 (February 1950): 89–104.

7 Quoted in P.W.M.A. Hoogstraten, *De ontwikkeling van het regionaal beleid in Nederland 1949–1977: Een verkenning van de mogelijkheden en grenzen van overheidsingrijpen in de ruimtelijke struktuur* (Nijmegen, NL: Stichting Politiek en Ruimte, 1983), 36.

8 J.L. van Zanden and R.T. Griffiths, *Economische geschiedenis van Nederland in de 20e eeuw. Van een veelzijdige volkshuishouding met een omvangrijk koloniaal bezit naar een "klein land" binnen Europa* (Utrecht: Het Spectrum, 1989), 245–6.

9 Ulrich Herbert, "Europe in High Modernity: Reflections on a Theory in the 20th Century," *Journal of Modern European History* 5, no. 2 (2007): 5–21; Anselm Doering-Manteuffel and Lutz Raphael, *Nach dem Boom: Perspektiven auf die Zeitgeschichte seit 1970* (Göttingen: Vandenhoeck & Ruprecht, 2008).

10 Ariane Leendertz, "Zeitbögen, Neoliberalismus und das Ende des Westens, oder: Wie kann man die deutsche Geschichte des 20. Jahrhunderts schreiben?" *Vierteljahreshefte für Zeitgeschichte* 65, no. 2 (2017): 191–217.

11 Roberta Cappelo, "Space, Growth and Development," in *Handbook of Regional Growth and Development Theories*, ed. Roberta Capello and Peter Nijkamp (Cheltenham, UK: Edward Elgar, 2009), 33–52.

12 Paul R. Krugman, "Increasing Returns and Economic Geography," *Journal of Political Economy* 99, no. 21 (1991): 483–99.

13 Michael E. Porter, *Competitive Advantage of Nations* (New York: Free Press, 1990).

14 Brief Ministerie Economische Zaken, "Vervolgrapportage economie met open grenzen," Vergaderjaar 1991–92, Kamerstuk 21670, ondernummer 6, 27 May 1992, 5.

15 In the coalition agreement of the Lubbers III Government, 1989–94, the concept of "the Netherlands as a distribution country" is mentioned twice alongside several passages on prioritizing infrastructural developments.

16 Handeling Tweede Kamer der Staten Generaal, Kamerstuk 20705, 5 May 1990.

17 Statistics Netherlands (CBS), Bedrijfstelling 1963; Landelijke informatie van Arbeidsplaatsen en Vestigingen (LISA), 2008.

18 Doering-Manteuffel and Raphael, *Nach dem Boom*, 34.

19 Handeling Tweede Kamer der Staten Generaal, Vergadernummer 18, 13 October 1997.

20 The six municipalities are Achtkarspelen, Dantumadiel, Dongeradeel, Ferwerderadiel, Kollumerland c.a., and Tytsjerksteradiel. In 2018 the municipalities of Dongeradeel, Ferwerderadiel, and Kollumerland c.a. merged and became Noardeast-Fryslân.

21 Marijn Molema and Bart Hoogeboom, *Omarm het verleden, heb zorg voor de toekomst. Vitaliteitsscan Noordoost-Fryslân 2016* (Leeuwarden, NL: Fryske Akademy & Provincie Fryslân, 2016), 11.

22 Stuurgroep Actieprogramma Noordoost-Friesland, *Actie programma Noord-Oost Friesland 1e fase* (1987).

23 Eastern Friesland's appropriation amounted to 21 million guilders out of a total of 50 million, see D. Vanhove, *De Doelmatigheid van het*

Regionaal-Economisch beleid in Nederland (Hilversum, NL: Paul Brand N.V., 1962), 11.

24 This subsidy was 25 guilders per square metre for the construction of new buildings up to 25 per cent of the total sum of investment. In order to apply for this subsidy, one unemployed worker had to be hired for every fifty square metres of built area. See: Staatscourant 30, July 1953, no. 145.

25 O.A.L.C. Atzema and E. Wever, *De Nederlandse Industrie. Ontwikkeling, spreiding en uitdaging* (Assen, NL: Van Gorcum, 1994), 115.

26 Approximately 40 per cent of the Netherlands and 20 per cent of its population were included in this second phase of regional development policies: P.W.M.A. Hoogstraten, *De ontwikkeling van het regionaal beleid in Nederland 1949–1977: Een verkenning van de mogelijkheden en grenzen van overheidsingrijpen in de ruimtelijke struktuur* (Nijmegen, NL: Stichting Politiek en Ruimte, 1983), 121.

27 J.H. Zoon, *Friesland Tussen Hoop en Vrees: Enige beschouwingen over de invloed van de industrialisatie gedurende de periode 1950–1964 op de Friese Welvaart* (Drachten, NL: Laverman, 1969), 53–61.

28 The town of Kootstertille had 999 inhabitants according to the 1960 population census.

29 The IPR subsidy from 1967 onwards targeted the same eleven "centres of industry" up to the 1986–90 policy cycle. See Atzema and Wever, *De Nederlandse Industrie*, 70–80.

30 Th. G. Heyke, "De na-oorlogse industriële ontwikkeling in het Noorden des Lands," *Economisch Statistische Berichten* 44, no. 2208/2209, special issue "Het Noorden" (1959): 914.

31 ETIF Rapport 842, *De industriële bedrijfsmigratie in Friesland in de periode 1960–1976* (Leeuwarden, NL, 1978).

32 Statistics Netherlands (CBS), Bedrijfstelling 1963.

33 G.J. Reinink, *Industriële bedrijfsmigratie in Nederland in de jaren 1950–1962: Een onderzoek naar verplaatsingsfactoren* (Amsterdam: SISWO, 1970), 25.

34 All of these companies had more than a hundred employees in 1976; see ETIF, *Adresboek Friese Industrie* (Leeuwarden, NL: ETIF, 1976).

35 Molema and Hoogeboom, *Omarm het verleden*, 34–5.

36 A.M. Molema, B. Hoogeboom, R. Plantinga, and B. Riemersma, *Economische vitaliteitsscan Noordoost-Fryslân* (Leeuwarden, NL: Fryske Akademy & Provincie Fryslân, 2017).

37 CBS bedrijfstelling 1950.

38 These policies were initiated in the *Selective Investment Report* (1976), *Sector Report* (1979), and the *Technological Innovation Report* (1979). For a discussion of these policies, see E-J. Velzing, *Innovatiepolitiek: Een reconstructie van het innovatiebeleid van het ministerie van Economische Zaken van 1976 tot en met 2010* (Delft: Eburon, 2013), 41–72.

39 Adviescommissie inzake het industriebeleid, *Een nieuw industrieel elan* (The Hague, 1981), 37–8.

40 The authors of the study were able to obtain a copy of the manuscript of Porter's magnum opus about one year prior to publication and could therefore publish a report that applied his theory to the Dutch economy only three months after his book appeared. D. Jacobs, P. Boekholt, and W. Zegveld, *De economische kracht van Nederland: Een toepassing van Porters benadering van de concurrentiekracht van landen* (The Hague: SMO, 1990), 9.

41 Ministerie van Economische Zaken, *Economie met open grenzen* (The Hague, 1990).

42 Jacobs, Boekholt, and Zegveld, *De economische kracht van Nederland*, 195.

43 Northeast Friesland would, together with parts of the neighbouring province of Groningen, be a test case for a special rural development program initiated in VINEX.

44 Algemene Rekenkamer, *Aardgasbaten: Feiten en cijfers* (The Hague, 2014), 5.

45 WRR, *Ruimtelijke ontwikkelingspolitiek* (The Hague: SDU, 1998); Maarten Hajer and Wil Zonneveld, "Spatial Planning in the Network Society: Rethinking the Principles of Planning in the Netherlands," *European Planning Studies* 8, no. 3 (2000): 337–55.

46 Authors' interview with Peter Danz, 25 February 2016.

47 Authors' interview with Anne Dijkstra and Bert Scheper, 23 June 2016.

48 Commissie Langman, *Ruimtelijk-economisch perspectief Noord-Nederland* (The Hague, 1997).

49 Although this plan had been updated in 1989, only minor changes were implemented, while the conceptual framework remained more or less the same.

50 "Friesland staat voor keuze: Groene provincie of 'stedelijke gemeenschap,'" *Leeuwarder Courant*, 30 August 1978.

51 "Provincie pleegt euthanasie op het platteland," *Leeuwarder Courant*, 9 November 1993.

52 KPMG, *Kompas voor Noordoost-Fryslân* (Zwolle, NL: KPMG, 2000), 2–3.

53 Jarig van Sinderen, *Noordoost-Fryslân wel duurzaam, niet langzaam* (n.p., 2002), 323.

54 Actieprogramma Noordoost-Friesland, "Brief aan de fractievoorzitters in de staten van Fryslân," 19 April 2003.

55 F.J. Sijtsema et al., *Uitgifte van bedrijventerreinen op het Friese platteland* (Groningen: Universiteitsdrukkerij Rijksuniversiteit Groningen, 2002).

56 These cities are the urban zones in the regional plan: Leeuwarden, Harlingen, Sneek, Heerenveen, and Drachten.

57 Annemarie Kok, "Droomfabriek blijkt grote Zeepbel," *Trouw*, 7 August 2002.

58 "Ommezwaai megapark groot succes," *Leeuwarder Courant*, 9 July 2008.

59 Provincial employment data, Province of Friesland.

9 The End of Long-Established Certainties: The Transformation of Germany Inc. since the Late 1980s

HARTMUT BERGHOFF

The 1990s mark a historical caesura on a global scale. Some decisive events like the end of the Cold War and the completion of the European Single Market happened in a certain year, but mostly there were flowing transitions and long-running trends. Many developments that had been visible since the 1970s culminated in, or accelerated after, 1990. The global economy underwent far-reaching transformations, which affected Germany in profound ways. There were five dramatic changes that interacted with each other. First, the end of the Cold War opened up Eastern Europe and transformed centrally planned economies into capitalistic markets. The ensuing reduction of spending on arms increased investments in non-military projects and facilitated a "peace dividend."

The second change was the breakthrough of the digital revolution. The Internet for everyone went live in 1993 and spread like wildfire. For more and more users, it became possible to transmit data in real time. Time and space compression reached an unprecedented level. As the speed of processors increased exponentially, hardware prices eroded fast. Dramatically reduced information costs made it easier to exchange information and coordinate processes across long distances. At the same time, the automation and digitization of industrial production made substantial progress.

Third, the disintegration of the world economy of the first half of the twentieth century was finally overcome by the 1970s and 1980s, when pre-1914 levels of market integration were reached again. Neoliberalism was in its prime: protective regulations were torn down on a grand scale, and the mobility of capital, goods, and services reached record dimensions.[1] The Uruguay Round of the General Agreement on Tariffs and Trade (GATT) was concluded in 1994. It embraced 123 counties, created the World Trade Organization, and extended the GATT trade rules to areas previously excluded. Generally, it reduced tariffs and lowered other trade barriers significantly. China and India, but also many smaller emerging market economies, opened up. At the same time, transportation costs tumbled. The diffusion of the intermodal container had begun in the 1970s and 1980s. In the 1990s, it became the standard mode of transporting finished goods. Airfreight had been used since the 1970s for the transportation of perishable and expensive goods, but in the 1990s it reached unprecedented market shares. Measured by its value, airfreight accounted for 13.9 per cent of all global imports in 1980, but 36 per cent in 2000, when freight rates had almost been halved.[2]

The forth factor was the introduction of the Single European Market in 1993, the most important step toward European integration since the Treaty of Rome in 1957. The territory of this market expanded significantly when thirteen new member states joined in 2004. The euro was introduced in 1999–2002. Exchange-rate manipulations in order to protect one's national market were no longer possible among the twelve participating countries. Transactions across their borders became easier, and markets much more transparent. European integration went hand in hand with deregulation. Public enterprises were privatized, markets opened up to international competitors, and monopoly privileges (rail services, post office, utilities) abandoned.[3]

Finally, the capital market became increasingly important for industrial finance. Cross-border capital flows multiplied in the 1990s by a factor of three, measured as percentage of GDP.[4] Trading in US equity (stock) markets grew from $1.671 trillion (or 28.8 per cent of US GDP) in 1990 to $14.222 trillion (144.9 per cent of GDP) in 2000. The financial sector grew much faster than the economy as a whole, and "profit making occurred increasingly through financial channels rather than through trade and commodity production."[5] Progressing financialization also triggered profound changes in the way corporations were run: conglomerates were split up and a booming market for corporate control emerged.[6]

How did all these changes affect Germany? This chapter explores the relationship between continuities and discontinuities in the 1990s. Does this decade represent a caesura in German business and social history? How did politicians, regulators, and corporations react to these external challenges, which increased the pressure on Germany Inc.? Did the level of protection and security that the traditional Germany Inc. was able to provide evaporate, or did it survive in a modified version?

This chapter was stimulated by two academic debates, one in the field of contemporary history and the other in political economics. Lutz Raphael and Anselm Doering-Manteuffel claimed in their widely read book, *After the Boom*, that a paradigm change and structural rupture took place in the last third of the twentieth century. Fordism and "Rhenish capitalism" as well as the traditional industrial world "became history," while post-industrial "digital financial market capitalism" took over.[7] Neoliberal market euphoria replaced the belief in the regulatory power of the state. Flexibility and individualization, the dominance of mass consumption, as well as the end of industrialism and, with it, of proletarian culture are assumed to have become key features of the epoch that began to emerge from the 1970s but took shape only in the 1980s and 1990s.

The second vantage point of this article is the debate in the varieties-of-capitalism literature on the alleged morbidity of Germany Inc. This system, which is also referred to as "coordinated," "cooperative," or "Rhenish" capitalism,[8] was characterized by a strong containment of market forces through trade associations, unions, and government supervision. Germany Inc. produced a large variety of technologically advanced products. Its foundations were a solid school system, thorough vocational training, and a vibrant research landscape. For several years, scholars have discussed whether this model lost its vigour or even faded away around 2000. Wolfgang Streeck claims that the decline of Germany Inc. has reached an advanced stage.[9] For him, its dissolution began in the 1980s and accelerated in the 1990s, as German capitalism moved toward the Anglo-Saxon model of liberal market economies. This chapter inquires into whether the interpretation of Streeck, Raphael, and Doering-Manteuffel can be confirmed or whether it has to be refuted or modified. The following sections deal with reform of capital markets, the internationalization and financialization of German corporations, with their increasing plasticity, as well as changes in management and labour relations.

The Partial Unleashing of the Capital Market

In Germany, corporations had traditionally kept their distance from capital markets and had relied on banks or their own assets. Political regulators went to considerable lengths to change this trend, especially from the late 1990s onwards. They wanted to make Germany more attractive for foreign investors, and, in this spirit, carried out several important reforms. The Christian-liberal coalition under Helmut Kohl strengthened the traditionally weak protections for investors. In 1998, the Law on Control and Transparency in Businesses Act (KonTraG) set new standards for corporate governance, extending the liability of boards and the duties of chartered accountants. Multiple voting rights were abolished, which, since the days of the Weimar Republic, had acted as protective shields against unfriendly takeovers. In 1988, the official justification read: "To have influence without property rights does not conform to the expectations of the capital market." [10] The KonTraG strengthened supervisory boards, shareholder rights, and shareholder equality and thus took Germany a step further toward conforming to international standards.

It marked only the beginning of a series of far-reaching laws that were passed after 1998 by the coalition of Social Democrats and Greens under Chancellor Gerhard Schröder. To them and many observers, Kohl's last term had left behind political gridlock. His government had been unable to find adequate responses to the double challenge of the 1990s, German reunification and mounting globalization.[11] Even the conservative president Roman Herzog called for a departure into a new era to overcome complacency and the "loss of economic dynamism." Unlike many Asian countries, "where venturous visions are ... realized that motivate people again and again, ... we lack the drive for innovation, the readiness to take on risk, and to leave the trodden paths."[12] Indeed, Germany suffered from slow growth and high unemployment.

Complaints about excessive wages and structural incrustation on all levels were the central issues in the debates about the *Standort Deutschland* – that is, the economic viability of Germany. The debate gained in poignancy due to high unemployment and modest growth compared to the Anglo-Saxon countries. Therefore it was not entirely counterintuitive that several pro-business, almost neoliberal, reforms were implemented by a government under Social Democrat leadership. The top bracket of income tax was reduced from 53 to 42 per cent between 1998 and 2005, while corporate tax shrank even further, from 45 to 25 per cent. Unincorporated firms were de facto freed from the business tax (*Gewerbesteuer*) while corporations enjoyed significant concessions. By international standards, social contributions and taxes had put a heavy burden on businesses in Germany. Now these businesses benefited from substantial cuts. In 2003 – under the label "Agenda 2010" – Chancellor Schröder announced the flexibilization of the labour market and a radical overhaul of the welfare state.

In 2002, capital gains taxes for corporations divesting equity stakes in other companies were repealed. This remarkable measure accelerated the disentanglement of Germany's densely knit business networks, a process that had already started in the 1990s. Firms now reduced cross-holdings, and banks divested themselves of equity stakes in industrial corporations. The agenda behind this reform was to dissolve or weaken powerful and inward-looking networks and to promote the market for corporate control. As a consequence, foreign and institutional investors increased their stakes in German corporations. In 1997, foreign investors held only 10 per cent of the shares in DAX 30 companies. Following the tax reform, which triggered a massive sale of equity, the proportion of foreign investors reached 52.6 per cent by 2008.

In 2002, the Securities Acquisition and Takeover Law (WpÜG) weakened defence mechanisms against takeovers and strengthened small shareholders.[13] In 2004, hedge funds were allowed to operate in Germany for the first time. The entry of foreign players into the asset-management business was eased, and a level playing field between domestic and foreign actors established.[14] As a consequence, the market capitalization of German stock exchanges rose steeply. While it had been 7.6 per cent of GNP in 1979 and 20 per cent in 1990, it skyrocketed to 65 per cent of GNP in 1999. Despite this explosive growth, German figures trailed those of the United Kingdom and the United States (179 per cent and 153 per cent, respectively, in 1999) by a huge margin.[15] The number of joint-stock corporations had been between 2,100 and 2,600 in the period 1960–89. In 2000, this figured reached 10,582; in 2004, it was 16,002.[16] New stock markets, especially for smaller companies, opened up. The stock exchange tax was abolished in 1991. Still, compared with the United Kingdom and the United States, a profound scepticism with respect to stock exchanges remained in place. The number of listed companies increased from an extremely low base – 413 in 1990 to only 744 in 2000.[17] In other words, most German joint-stock corporations still kept their distance from the stock exchange. For them, preserving control remained key. In 2000, 55 per cent of all German corporations listed on stock exchanges were dominated by individual families.[18] Germany did not switch to a dispersed-ownership system. Despite a clear trend toward the principles of liberal market economies, the country preserved many features of the traditional Germany Inc.[19]

Towards Transnationalism: The Internationalization of Germany Inc.

More radical changes affected the ownership structure of large German corporations. Shares of the DAX 30 corporations were increasingly bought by foreign and institutional investors after capital market reforms had opened the door for these new players. By 2001, foreign investment had already reached 35.5 per cent, rising to 56 per cent in 2011.[20] In 2001, only three firms – Adidas, Continental, and Deutsche Bank – were dominated by foreign capital; by 2008, this number had reached thirteen.

As foreign capital poured in, jobs were increasingly transferred abroad. In 2005, the DAX 30 corporations employed only 45 per cent of their staff in Germany. Nineteen of these companies had more than half of their workforces abroad. The highest proportions were reached by Fresenius Medical Care, with 93.5 per cent of its workforce outside Germany; Adidas with 82 per cent; and Henkel with 78.9 per cent.[21] While the workforce in Germany shrank dramatically, it increased elsewhere. Between 1991 and 2002, the total number of industrial jobs in Germany declined from 12.1 to 9.8 million in West Germany, and, in all of Germany, from 15.4 to 11.7 million. In total, 3.7 million jobs were lost in all of Germany in this period due to offshoring, the closure of facilities, and gains in productivity.[22] All in all, the 1990s were characterized by the rapid internationalization of capital and labour.

Siemens AG, an archetypal representative of Germany Inc., reflects these developments in an exemplary way (see table 9.1).[23] In 1980, its equity was overwhelmingly in German hands; by 2001, foreigners held 49 per cent of the company's shares; ten years later, that figure had grown to 71 per cent. Between 1990 and 2000, the number of the company's employees in Germany decreased by 50,000, while the proportion of jobs outside Germany soared to almost 60 per cent of the total workforce. At the same time, the share of foreign sales jumped from 55 to 76 per cent. What once had been a German export company was becoming a transnational corporation with factories and equity owners all over the world.

Production sites were increasingly evaluated by their cost efficiency. The trend to replace exports by products manufactured abroad was reinforced by demands of foreign customers for "local content" – that is, production in their own countries. The entire value chain was supposed to be split around the globe. Most large German corporations did not yet reach this level of transnational structure, but they had found a new orientation and, with it, the direction of their future development.

The highest increase in German foreign direct investments (FDI) in manufacturing facilities was recorded in Eastern Europe and Asia, although the old European Union members (EU 15) and the United States still attracted the majority of investments. In 1993, the Asia-Pacific Committee of German Business was founded. China, which had opened up to foreign investors only after 1979, experienced unprecedented flows of incoming foreign capital in the 1990s.[24] In 1994, the Delegation of German Industry and Commerce opened an office in Shanghai, and other regional branches followed. In 1987, the stock of German FDI in China was a mere 101 million euros; by 2002, that figure had skyrocketed to 6.6 billion.[25]

Table 9.1. Internationalization at Siemens AG, 1970–2010

Indicator	1970–1	1979–80	1989–90	1999–2000	2009–10
Staff (1,000s)	306	344	373	447	405
Percentage of staff outside Germany	23	31.6	38.3	59.7	68.4
Percentage of foreign sales	42	54	55	76	85
Percentage of foreign investment	22.3	32.1	45.1	57.6	Not available
Percentage of shares held by foreign investors	23 (1970)	29 (1979)	43 (1990)	48 (2001)	71

Source: Annual reports of Siemens AG; Ladislaus Erdödy, *Ausgewählte Kapitel zur Eigenfinanzierung des Hauses Siemens* (Munich: Siemens AG, 2004), 15–16.

The annual value of German outward FDI flows was $24 billion in 1990, $109 billion in 1999, and $169 billion in 2007. The FDI stock more than tripled between 1990 and 2000.[26] These enormous investments profoundly affected the organizational matrix of most corporations. The move toward transnationality was driven by cost-benefit analyses, political imperatives (market access in exchange for local production), and the example of international competitors. Another factor was the influence of management studies and the consultancy industry.

Within academia, Michael Porter (Harvard Business School) was the most important source of inspiration. He divided the value chain into its components and recommended placing them exactly where the locational advantages were largest.[27] Each component should be judged by itself in comparison to the best competitor. Benchmarking became a very strong argument for reconfiguring organically grown spatial structures. The classic form, which was a highly integrated and hierarchical organization, was increasingly complemented or replaced by more flexible network structures. The boundaries of the firm became more fluid and adaptable at short notice. Relocating, outsourcing, divesting, and joint ventures became permanent strategic options. In the 1990s, more and more companies cooperated with their suppliers and formed global manufacturing networks. Foreign top managers, however, remained rare for the time being. After 2000, their numbers increased significantly. In that year, only 13 per cent of all executive directors of the DAX 30 companies were foreigners, but ten years later this proportion had risen to 28 per cent.[28]

Most large German corporations did not follow their American peers' example and engage in systematic tax avoidance. DAX-30 companies paid taxes amounting to 26 per cent of their profits in 2011, whereas the 280 largest American concerns only paid 18.5 per cent in 2009–11.[29] As far as taxation is concerned, German firms did not fully use their room to manoeuvre but kept strong bonds to their home country.

Financialization

The term "financialization" denotes not only the growing importance of financial institutions but also a megatrend in the non-financial economy. In manufacturing, it means reorientation from the logic of production to the logic of finance. Corporations increasingly perceive themselves as malleable portfolios rather than integrated technical and social entities, and the interests of shareholders increasingly become more important than those of other stakeholders.[30]

Prior to this change, which began in the 1980s, shareholders had been neglected by complacent and incompetent managers. The cartel of management and unions had the same effect. General protests against the disregard for shareholders' interests were frequent in the early 1990s, yet by the end of the decade they were gone or extremely rare.[31] The mantra of shareholder value deeply affected the DNA of German corporations, which were increasingly scrutinized by outside forces. The new opinion-leaders were critical journalists as well as analysts from investment banks and consultancy firms. As they pinpointed weaknesses and demanded remedial action, their judgment gained more and more weight. It influenced stock quotations, which became the central parameter for the future of corporations as well as the careers and bonuses of managers.

Consultants moved centre stage in the 1990s and increased the pressure on managers and staff, as they demanded changes in ever-shorter intervals.[32] In Germany, they had long encountered pronounced reservations. Nevertheless, the American management consultant firm McKinsey established an early bridgehead, opening a Düsseldorf office in 1964 with four consultants. Expansion was slow – new offices were set up in Hamburg and Stuttgart in 1970 and 1986, respectively. In 1990, McKinsey came to Berlin, where it prospered through large mandates from *Treuhandanstalt*, the gigantic privatization agency for East Germany.

In the 1990s, change management became a perennial task for all major corporations and required the routine hiring of consultants. Their deployment became necessary because core industries such as electrical engineering, car manufacturing, and machine tools production had forfeited their competitive edge in "the lost 80s."[33] Their productivity had fallen behind international, especially Japanese, competitors. In addition, advances in the fields of automation as well as information and communication technologies triggered many disruptive changes and made traditional structures obsolete. Furthermore, globalization and deregulation intensified competition. As a result, prices and margins eroded in many sectors with frightening speed.

As a consequence, productivity drives were implemented. They aimed at speeding up innovation processes (time to market) and cutting throughput times, reducing costs, and remaking corporate cultures. Buzzwords were "re-engineering" as well as "lean" and "total quality" management. All employees were to develop an entrepreneurial mindset and to focus on the customer. The primacy of efficiency was intended to overcome the hierarchical way of thinking, which is deeply rooted in German culture.

Analysts and consultants abundantly used the concept of "global best practice" from which they deduced criteria for benchmarking, regardless of national variations. In 1990, the influential book *The Machine That Changed the World* was published by MIT-based researchers.[34] It recommended lean production as an all-encompassing paradigm. This model, like that of shareholder value and benchmarking, contradicted the traditional culture of German corporations. Nevertheless, these impulses made deep inroads into Germany Inc., although they often met with scepticism.

At Siemens, employee attitude surveys demonstrated that, by the mid-1990s, not even one-third of all staff considered shareholder value as very important.[35] This stance was in retreat by the second half of the 1990s, when the assumptions of external observers became all persuasive. Older employees and directors found it hard to accept this shift. External pressures on them were intensified by an increasingly aggressive climate in the media. In 1992, a book titled *Losers in Pinstripe Suits* became a bestseller.[36] Full of malice, it delved into the mistakes of Germany's corporate elite. Its bottom line was that German top managers had a lot to learn from their American and Japanese counterparts. Newspapers and the business press did not go easy on corporations and their directors either. When BMW experienced a serious crisis, Eberhard von Kuenheim, CEO from 1970 to 1993 and a representative of the older generation of managers, was inundated with criticism. *Manager Magazin* called him "aloof" and "unteachable," governing like a "Prussian general" and argued that the 1990s "require different talents and managers."[37] His successor, Bernd Peter Pischetsrieder, had to leave BMW in 1999, after his acquisition of the Rover group turned out to be a debacle.

Analysts did not show any mercy either and bashed iconic companies of Germany Inc. McKinsey and Goldman Sachs criticized that the unit costs of some Siemens products were 25 to 50 per cent above those of their competitors.[38] For analysts, the firm was "an ailing corporate monster: no competitive culture, too slow, extremely low profitability and, as a result, generating no shareholder value."[39] Indeed, the operational profitability was alarmingly low, which provoked severe criticism from the media, from shareholders, and even from the Siemens family, who had become minority shareholders. Peter von Siemens, a member of the supervisory board, complained publicly in 1996 that, "for such a meagre yield, the milkman around the corner would not open his shop."[40]

The company had adopted a productivity program called "Top" in 1992 and had realized with it savings of 36 billion DM by 1997; yet, the situation did not substantially improve. The combined effects of price erosion, currency appreciations through the strengthening DM, and restructuring costs exceeded those impressive savings. In 1996–7, the crunch escalated, in part because of the Asian crisis. At the same time, the semiconductor market nosedived, and prices for memory chips collapsed. The company's mobile phone and transportation divisions operated at a loss, and its gas turbines experienced serious technological problems.[41]

It had become obvious that the conservative modernization of the early 1990s was insufficient. In July 1998, Siemens presented its "Ten-Point Program," a radical change of policy. The company announced that, from now on, it would play by the rules of financial markets. For the first time in its long history since 1847, the sale of entire divisions was announced. Part of this new departure was the adaptation of American accounting principles. In 1999–2000, Siemens switched to Generally Accepted Accounting Principles (GAAP), which increased the transparency of the firm's financial statements. Since 1998, German law had allowed companies to abandon the German Commercial Code in favour of international standards. By 2000, almost all of the DAX 30 corporations prepared their balance sheets according to either GAAP or International Accounting Standards.[42] The Americanization of accounting methods paved the way for listing on the New York Stock Exchange, which more and more German companies aspired to. Daimler (1993) was the pioneer in being listed there; by 2002, sixteen other German firms had followed suit.[43]

Corporate reforms in the spirit of financialization required detailed data and quantitative business indicators. To this time, many companies had been rather opaque, and it was hard for both inside and outside actors to get a clear picture. At Siemens, only a very few people knew the financial status of the divisions. After two years of controversy, their results were published for the first time in 1995–6 in order to pass the pressure on the corporation on to the divisions and to discourage the traditional practice of concealed cross-subsidies. Solidarity among divisions was renounced, and long-established security networks began to crumble. Transparency and management by figures were the new guiding principles. In 2000, the executive board defined target returns for all divisions. Pressure mounted, as the figures were accessible by everyone inside and outside the corporation.

The traditional tolerance for underperforming units was officially abandoned with the Ten-Point Program. In 1997, Siemens had already introduced economic value added (EVA) as its key performance indicator. It measures a company's or a unit's financial results based on the residual wealth calculated after deducting its cost of capital. If EVA is negative, no value is generated from the funds invested. This measure allowed management to discover in the blink of an eye which unit created – or failed to create – value. At Daimler, the passing of the reins from Edzard Reuter to Jürgen Schrempp in 1995 resulted in the introduction of a management system based on financial indicators. All divisions and subdivisions became profit centres. By 2000, 39 per cent of all DAX 100 companies had introduced EVA, and 86 per cent of them worked with indicators that were geared toward shareholder value.[44]

EVA was the epitome of financialization. The concept had been developed 1991 by the US consultancy firm Stern, Steward & Co and had spread throughout the 1990s.[45] EVA represented a completely new approach that identified "dead capital" within the corporation. This capital had to be revived or shed. This approach spelled out the end of solidarity within corporate groups. Hectic reorganizations spread, along with existential fear among units that did not meet their EVA targets.

This climate also encouraged corporate malfeasance. Indeed, Siemens was responsible for one of the largest corruption scandals in history. The amounts of dubious payments reached their pinnacle in the 1990s. It was no coincidence that the company's communications division, which had lost its technological edge and whose future at Siemens was under discussion, accounted for the lion share of the dark money flows. Ultimately, the company was penalized by record financial sanctions amounting to $1.6 billion in 2008.[46] For its part, to boost sales, Daimler offered bribes in at least twenty-two countries between 1998 and 2002. For this purpose, the company had created an non-transparent network of middlemen, offshore accounts, and more than two hundred "internal third-party accounts." This carefully designed infrastructure facilitated the covert transfer of funds to corrupt clients who were the official owners of these accounts, which were managed and restocked by Daimler.[47]

Economic pressure alone does not explain the extent of corruption. The "tone from the top" was rather lackadaisical, and efficient controls were missing. Furthermore, managers acted in an environment in which foreign corruption had been traditionally treated as a kind of export promotion. Until 1999, bribes were tax deductible in Germany under the rubric of "useful expenditures" when the recipients were foreign officials. Until 2002, bribes paid to other businesspeople enjoyed the same privilege. The sudden criminalization of a widespread and officially recognized practice was part of a "compliance revolution" that changed the rules of economic life in Germany and elsewhere in an abrupt way.[48] This rupture is another reason for classifying the 1990s as a threshold to a new era.

The Plasticity of the Firm

In the 1990s, a fundamental new perception of corporations proliferated. They were no longer seen as organically grown, long-standing entities but as investment portfolios that could be reshuffled at short notice. The belief in the superiority of conglomerates had been waning in the United States since the 1970s. These doubts reached Germany in 1980s and unfolded fully in the 1990s. The new mantra was to concentrate on core competencies and to divest units without strong synergies.

The German market in corporate control expanded significantly in the 1990s. It became much easier to buy and sell firms or parts thereof. In 1997, the Neue Markt, a stock market for small and medium-sized enterprises, opened its gates, twenty-six years after the American model of the NASDAQ. The investment banks benefited from a highly profitable, fast-growing line of business. A hectic reshuffling of the German business landscape got underway. Spin-offs, mergers, and acquisitions took place with rapid speed. Many traditional companies were fragmented or wound up. Bremer Vulkan, one of the largest shipyard combines in Europe, first bought a large number of ailing shipyards in the 1980s before it collapsed in 1996.[49] In 1985, Daimler took over the loss-making electrical engineering giant AEG and divided it up into its parts, which were integrated into Daimler, sold, or closed.[50]

Daimler turned itself upside down twice in the 1990s. First, Edzard Reuter, CEO from 1987 onwards, pursued the strategy of morphing the dyed-in-the-wool motor vehicle manufacturer into an integrated technology group that would build trains and aircraft and also be active in electronics and aerospace. This vision triggered a wave of acquisitions of firms from different branches of industry, which in the end turned out to be a huge waste of capital. Reuter's successor, Jürgen Schrempp, refocused on car manufacturing and began to sell the recently acquired companies. In the automotive business, he wanted to form a "Welt AG" (global corporation). In 1998, Daimler merged with Chrysler. Two years later, it acquired interests in Mitsubishi and Hyundai. These investments also turned out to be disasters and were rescinded in 2007.

The new plasticity of corporations could result in their complete dismantling. Hoechst AG is probably the most extreme example. In 1994, Jürgen Dormann, the new CEO, started a radical restructuring. Various divisions were sold or inserted into joint ventures. Within ten years, a once unified firm disintegrated into a vast multitude of components.[51] In 1993, Crédit Lyonnais acquired Bank für Gemeinwirtschaft (BfG), which had its roots in the labour movement. Then, in 2000, BfG was bought by the Swedish bank SEB, which later sold the BfG retail banking division to the Spanish Banco Santander.

The 1990s began with the first hostile takeover of a large German corporation – the acquisition of Hoesch by Krupp in 1991. The decade ended with the hostile takeover in 2000 of Mannesmann by the British mobile phone company Vodafone. Prior to this, hostile takeovers, not to mention international ones, had been almost unknown in Germany. Mannesmann experienced the dismantling and sale of its entire manufacturing capacity.[52]

These spectacular cases should not tempt us to overestimate the extent of mergers and acquisitions activities. Although the numbers were rising in the 1990s, overall figures remained quite modest. A study of acquisitions by German corporations from outside the financial sector found 23 cases in the 1980s, 136 in the 1990s, and 179 in the 2000s.[53] This was a significant increase but not a torrent. Moreover, consensual deals still prevailed. The authors of the acquisitions study could identify only 5 hostile takeovers out of 338 cases.

Corporate crises overshadowed the 1990s and became warning signs for the surviving firms. Siemens carefully analysed the demise of its once most important domestic rival AEG and was well aware that far-reaching reforms were necessary in order to survive in the long run. The new CEO, Heinrich von Pierer, was told in 1992 to re-establish a satisfactory level of profitability but to keep the company together at the same time. By 1997, it had become obvious that these two targets were incompatible, and Siemens was redefined as a flexible structure with interchangeable parts. The firm had long been referred to as the "Siemens family," but this metaphor, which signalled continuity and security, was now dropped. Von Pierer's successor called Siemens a "living organism." Every position of the "portfolio" was held for disposal.[54] The security that the classic industrial society had been able to provide eroded fast. What Giddens described as the dissolution of predictability became a tangible reality, especially for the workforce.[55]

As part of its Ten-Point Program, Siemens announced its intention, in 1998, "to remove about 60,000 people from its group."[56] Ten years earlier, such a dispassionate notification would have been unthinkable. In 2001, Siemens managers received the following instruction: "The term 'core business' has largely disappeared from our internal language." Everybody knows that "there are no inalienable units. There is no protection to hide behind." In the past, Siemens had acted very cautiously when it came to divestments and acquisitions, but "our traditional way of thinking has been replaced by striving for global leadership. This implies totally different aspirations when it comes to our performance. Above all, Siemens has internalized the high demands of the capital market." Today, "there is only one dogma left: the business has to be successful."[57]

By 2005, seven of the fifteen divisions that had existed in 1996 were sold or phased out, among them communication technologies, the historic heart of Siemens; the entire semiconductor business; and the recently (1990) acquired computer manufacturing division Siemens Nixdorf. These divestments were accompanied by a mind-boggling number of acquisitions. Between 1991 and 2001, Siemens bought more than a thousand companies – many of them small start-ups – and spent 17 billion euros on all of its mergers and acquisitions.[58] Such fluidity was unprecedented: the structure of Germany Inc. had become more flexible and increasingly consisted of modules that could be shuffled around at short notice.

Management and Corporate Governance

Financialization created new types of managers who were young, ambitious, and media savvy. They had often worked outside Germany and were shaped by American corporate cultures. To this group belonged Ron Sommer, previously CEO of Sony USA, who became CEO of Deutsche Telekom, which had emerged from the privatized post office. A similar figure was Thomas Middelhoff, CEO of Bertelsmann, Europe's largest media corporation, from 1998 to 2002. He steered the conservative family firm in the direction of the internet economy until he lost the confidence of the Mohn family.[59] Klaus Esser, a lawyer with an MBA from MIT, who had practised law in New York, joined the Mannesmann board in 1994 and became CEO in 1998. Initially, he fought against Vodafone's takeover bid; when he suddenly began to support it, allegations were made that financial motives accounted for the change. The subsequent dismantling of a 110-year-old company was, according to the *Economist*, "for many Germans an affront to the traditional way of doing business in their country, where consensus is valued and executives are paid modest amounts compared with those in America and Britain. Indeed, in a country where hostile takeovers are a rarity, and hostile takeovers by foreigners virtually unknown, almost everything about Vodafone's tilt at Mannesmann was deeply unpopular."[60]

Sommer, Middelhoff, and Esser were harbingers of changes to come but, in the 1990s, they were not yet typical of the German business elite, which overwhelmingly still conformed to more traditional patterns. The tenure of CEOs of the fifty largest German corporations dropped between 1990 and 2000 only from 9.9 to 8.4 years. The career pattern with very long, mainly in-house trial periods remained predominant. [61] For decades, candidates had to climb the career ladder one step at a time. CEOs were appointed in their early fifties, and in most cases they remained in this position until they retired. They were extremely well connected, inside and outside the firms, and had intimate knowledge of their companies. Experiences with other, especially foreign, corporate cultures were rarely found in this generation.[62]

Now, consultancy firms were becoming an important springboard into top management positions. On boards, the number of technicians without degrees or academically trained engineers decreased. Production lost in importance vis-à-vis finance. More and more graduates of economics and business administration moved to the top. With them, a stronger focus on returns advanced. Loyalties toward individual locations and units waned as corporations were increasingly seen as malleable organizations. With the generational shift, biographical profiles changed. The new board members were strongly influenced by Anglo-Saxon management styles, which they had often experienced firsthand during periods abroad. In the 1990s, most young managers held the conviction that Germany, with its high unemployment and low growth rates, lagged behind the United States, which was perceived as a model.

Heinrich von Pierer, Siemens CEO from 1992 to 2005, represented very much the old type of manager. He started at the company at the age of twenty-eight and joined the management board twenty years later. Whereas his predecessors had been engineers, he had studied law. A more radical change occurred on the level immediately below the CEO. In 1997, Heinz-Joachim Neubürger, a graduate from INSEAD and an investment banker with J.P. Morgan from 1981 to 1989, became, after a relatively short in-house career, chief financial officer. The industrial divisions were restructured by Edward G. Krubasik, another INSEAD graduate, who had worked for McKinsey. In 1997, he was directly appointed to the board without any prior in-house experience, a hitherto unimaginable event.

Switching between employers became more frequent and more accepted. It was even increasingly seen as an advantage. The in-house pedigree and decades of internal networking declined somewhat in importance but still remained highly relevant in the 1990s. At the same time, the job security of top managers began to crumble. Until the 1980s, they could be pretty much certain to stay in their position until retirement age. In most cases, this was still realistic, but the number of early dismissals rose. In contrast to long-standing practices, nobody could feel entirely safe anymore, and the pressure on middle and top management increased considerably.

The share of variable salary components grew in the 1990s and continued to grow after 2000. This trend coincided with a steep rise in overall compensation. Table 9.2 shows the composition of executive directors' incomes in various DAX 30 companies. For the majority, more than 70 per cent of their total compensation was variable in 2008. The generational change in management went hand in hand with skyrocketing salaries. In 1990, the average compensation of the executive directors of DAX 30 companies was 14 times the average labour cost per employee (figure 9.1). This ratio jumped to 24:1 in 1999, reaching 54:1 in 2007. From an American perspective, this might still look moderate; for the German context, it is fair to speak of a radical – and controversial – change.

Improved balance sheets translated into higher bonuses and thus into immense rises in overall compensation. Another factor was the increasing disclosure of individual salaries, which set off a spiral of envy. Outside hires were often better paid than internal directors, who then required similar incomes. The new transparency disrupted the traditional culture of secrecy. Making salaries public was meant to have a moderating effect, but the opposite was true. One other factor was the advance of compensation consultants, who used the new transparency to propel salaries to unprecedented levels.

Table 9.2. Share of fixed and variable compensation of executive board members of various DAX 30 companies in 2008

Corporation	Share of fixed compensation (%)	Share of variable compensation (%)
Allianz	29	71
BASF	27	73
Bayer	33	67
BMW	27	73
Daimler	29	71
Deutsche Post	59	41
Deutsche Telekom	39	61
Linde	25	75
Münchner Rück	24	76
Siemens	23	77
ThyssenKrupp	25	75
Volkswagen	12	88

Source: Peter Wilke et al., *Kriterien für die Vorstandsvergütung in deutschen Unternehmen nach Einführung des Gesetztes zur Angemessenheit der Vorstandsvergütung* (Düsseldorf: Hans-Böckler-Stiftung, 2011), 22.

Figure 9.1. Average compensation of board members per capita as a multiple of labour costs per head in all DAX 30 companies, 1987–2008

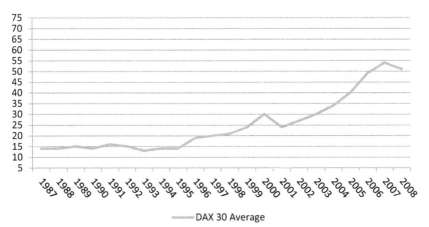

DAX 30 Average

Source: Joachim Schwalbach, Vorstandsvergütung, Pay-for-Performance und Fair Pay. Dax30-Unternehmen, 1987–2010 (Berlin 2011), http://www.wiwi.hu-berlin.de/professuren /bwl/management/managerverguetung/Verguetungsstudie_2011%20Schwalbach %20Humboldt-Uni.pdf/ (accessed 14 April 2015).

Labour Relations: Transformations and Continuities
of the Social Contract

Bankruptcies, offshoring, and rationalization reduced employment in industry by almost four million people between 1991 and 2002. Flexibility instruments like temporary or part-time work, and (pseudo-) self-employment created more and more jobs that were precarious. The depth of production was reduced as input materials were internationally procured (global sourcing) and internal processes were relocated to external suppliers or former internal units were spun off (outsourcing). After 1995, employment subject to compulsory social security contributions declined while the number of self-employed rose slightly and temporary employment increased strongly. Temporary agency work more than tripled between 1995 and 2006. The government extended the maximum duration of this type of work between 1985 and 2002 from three to twenty-four months. The number of temporary work agencies rose to 7,700 in 2007, at which time they employed 670,000 people. Thirty-five per cent of all businesses with five hundred or more employees used temporary workers in 2007. These workers helped to cope with peaks in demand but very often replaced permanent workers. The share of temporary agency staff among unqualified workers was 21 per cent in 1998 but rose to 41 per cent in 2006. This type of work also spread through the higher levels of the labour market. Skilled workers and even highly qualified specialists could be hired through agencies. They took over very demanding temporary tasks in research and development or software updates. Thus a growing minority of graduates from engineering and management schools as well as information technology specialist were sent on temporary assignments.[63]

This development was discussed with great sorrow and ambivalence. Chancellor Schröder, who had facilitated the internationalization of the German economy through capital markets reforms, massively criticized the offshoring of jobs. The media, the public, and politicians scolded managers as "unpatriotic."[64] Some union functionaries demanded to exclude such firms from public contracts. These reactions did not stop any of the trends. Management replied that stiff competition forced them to reduce their German staff and that these measures protected the remaining jobs.

As a consequence, conditions deteriorated for those who became unemployed or were not protected by strong collective agreements. Core employment was shrinking while marginal employment rose significantly. People with different contracts often worked side by side, receiving different salaries for identical work. Under these conditions, ties between employers and staff loosened. The average duration of employment within one firm decreased. The consequences were interrupted work histories, the de-standardization of employment biographies, and the loss of calculability and security.[65] In 1980, about four-fifths of the German workforce were in permanent positions. By 2004, this proportion had fallen to three-fifths. A growing minority of people were stuck in the low-wage segment of the labour market. Precarious employment created working poor who survived only by social transfers or undeclared work. The parallel increase in one-person households and childlessness was, in part, a direct result of the shifting of labour market risks onto the individual. For more and more people, salaries were too low to support a family. In 2005, 20 per cent of the German labour force aged twenty-five to forty – the classic phase of starting a family – lived in one-person households. In 1991, this proportion had been only 13 per cent.[66]

The number of unemployed in Germany rose from 2.1 to 4.9 million between 1991 and 2006. This had a dampening effect on wage growth and weakened collective bargaining. More and more companies turned away from employers' associations or opted for membership without bargaining coverage. In 2004, only 43 per cent of all companies in West Germany were bound by collective agreements. In what had been the GDR, this proportion was even lower, at 22 per cent.[67] Collective agreements increasingly had flexibility clauses, which allowed local exceptions. Large companies outsourced entire factories or converted them into new legal entities in order to get rid of expensive agreements (for example, with the strong metalworkers union IG-Metall). In doing so, German industry gained a "cost flexibility ... that had been unthinkable two decades ago."[68] From the mid-1990s, the traditionally high unit labour costs rose only moderately: between 1996 and 2007, the annual increase was always below 1 per cent. In other words, productivity grew faster than real wages.[69]

Under these circumstances, unions found themselves on the defensive. The German Trade Union Confederation (DGB) had 11 million members in 1990, but only 6.7 million in 2005.[70] In industrial disputes, the unions acted cautiously. Essentially they supported a relative smooth transition from the old to the new labour market. Downsizing and plant closures provoked short token strikes but no prolonged and bitter disputes. Of course, there were frequent protests, but they generally stayed relatively calm. Factory occupations like that in 1993 in the Bischofferode Kali works remained rare exceptions.

In 1996, however, the metalworkers union succeeded in warding off attempts of Daimler to cut wages paid on sick leave. They basically brought car production to a complete standstill through a resolute token strike. Other companies also failed in similar attacks on long-standing social entitlements. The other car manufacturers and most businesses did not touch earlier agreements on the payment of full wages on sick leave, much to the ire of the employers' association Gesamtmetall.[71]

The social partnership persisted, at least for the majority of workers in permanent jobs. Management and workers' representatives remained loyal to the rules of Germany Inc. The generally accepted practice of co-determination gave both sides influence and responsibility and thus prevented aggravated confrontations. On supervisory boards, they not only cooperated in making decisions but they often did so unanimously. Relations between management and workers representatives continued to honour a culture of co-management.

Another reason for relatively smooth labour relations was the various privileges bestowed on members of works councils like company cars or exceptionally high wages. This kind of favouritism is sometimes hard to distinguish from downright corruption. In 2005, it became known that Volkswagen had manipulated members of the works council through illegal payments, luxurious trips, and the services of prostitutes.[72] Nonetheless, employee representatives supported managements' proposals for productivity drives and work intensification, job cuts, and FDI largely because they were aware of the need for reform. Although these fundamental changes threatened the workforce, they were implemented without serious conflicts, which again underlines the strength of the co-determination model. Management and unions concentrated on bargaining over attractive severance packages that made redundancies socially acceptable. Negotiations were sometimes tough, but there were no unbridgeable gaps. In order to secure jobs, union representatives sometimes accepted wage cuts, the loss of voluntary allowances, or longer and more flexible hours.

Siemens illustrates the relocation of labour market risks from employer to individual worker. Since 1975, employees who had served more than twenty-five years at the company had enjoyed protection from redundancies for operational reasons. But senior management came to see in this generous rule an obstacle to restructuring. In 1995, this concession was abandoned with a grace period for older staff. This again demonstrates that pressure increased on all levels. Optimization initiatives became a permanent feature of working life. All units and all processes were constantly put on trial. Permanent benchmarking became standard practice, which meant that one did not rely on one's own experiences anymore but on the parameters of one's best competitor.

Employees and unions had no choice but to tag along. The pressure from the market could not be denied, and without fundamental changes the companies would have lost their future sustainability. The unions took a defensive stance but fought hard and in most cases successfully to help those who lost their jobs. Redundancy plans were generally rather generous. This is one reason – apart from high unemployment – why the number of working days lost through strikes declined significantly. In the period 1995 to 2000, the number had fallen to 1.6 per 1,000 workers, the lowest level since 1960.[73] All in all, the culture of consensus remained intact. Given the degree of change, the prevention of destructive conflicts was an enormous achievement.

Company housing was deeply rooted in long traditions of paternalism. Its demise is another symbol of transformed labour relations. Thyssen-Krupp sold 48,000 apartments to a consortium of Morgan Stanley and others in 2004–5. Most of them had been built by Krupp for their workers around 1900. In the cold rhetoric of the capital market, Thyssen-Krupp announced in 2004 that "the corporation wants to divest themselves from investments which no longer belong to their core business."[74] The revenue from the sale amounted to 2.1 billion euros. Prior to the transaction, the heavily indebted corporation had been downgraded by rating agencies below investment grade. Analysts applauded the sale. The share value rose immediately, and bonds regained investment grade.[75] To sell the family silver and to succumb to the rules of the capital market amounted to a radical breach with tradition and hit local communities hard.

Siemens sold 2,300 apartments in 2002 and 4,000 in 2009. Tenants and IG Metall were up in arms. Many families had lived in their apartments for two or three generations. One slogan was "Siemens flogs its 'family'."[76] IG Metall argued that company housing had been part of the corporate culture for ninety years and that the sale was short-sighted and corresponded to a stock market–oriented, Anglo-Saxon way of thinking."[77]

Again the company cushioned the immediate social effects. The new owners could increase rents only moderately and had to keep the apartments for ten years. Tenants were protected from the termination of their contracts. Here the same mechanism as with layoffs applied. Those who were directly concerned benefited from considerable compensations while the next generations had to cope with the new uncertainty by themselves.

The traditional social contract was further eroded by the transition of company pensions from a system of defined benefits to one of defined contributions. Originally the companies stipulated certain amounts to be paid to retired employees in addition to statutory pensions. Now they promised only fixed contributions to capital funds. The final pay-off depended on the performance of these funds. The reasons for the shift were rising life expectancy and volatile capital markets. The system of defined contribution reduced the corporations' risk and accrued liabilities. From now on, the pensioners directly participated in the risks and the opportunities of the market. In worst-case scenarios like stock market crashes, however, the system of defined contribution offers no protection at all.

As a kind of compensation and very much in line with the principles of shareholder capitalism, more and more companies started or expanded employee share programs. Lufthansa introduced a new scheme in 1996 that allocated a certain number of shares to employees and helped them buy more shares through interest-free credit. The value of such programs depended on the fate of the firm. EM.TV & Merchandising AG went public in 1997 and offered each employee convertible bonds that entitled them to buy shares later on. The value of these debentures increased by a factor of 80 within two years before it nosedived due to acquisitions of firms and movie rights at inflated prices. Books were cooked, and the founders secretly sold shares prior to the release of negative news. The employees not only lost their jobs but were left with a pile of rubble instead of secure old-age benefits.[78]

Capital markets offer nobody any guarantees. The logic behind these changes is the transfer of risks from corporations to the employees or retirees. The traditional certainties that had been an integral part of the Bonn Republic were replaced by the shimmering promise to participate in the opportunities and risks of the market.[79] The bursting of the dot-com bubble in 2000 and the financial crisis in 2007–8 dampened the euphoria that had temporarily prevailed. As a result, share ownership of Germans plummeted and is still very low by international standards.

Conclusion

Germany Inc. used to provide calculable careers and lifetime employment. This was possible against the backdrop of high-growth and low-competition markets during the postwar "boom." These prerequisites disappeared in the 1980s. Globalization, deregulation, and digitization weakened the foundations of the old arrangements. Monopolistic markets like telecommunications, energy generation, and utilities were opened up for real competition, which made prices and margins collapse. The steel, mining, and shipbuilding industries had already slipped into long structural crises in the 1960s and 70s.

Increased market pressure coincided with rising profit expectations. Together these factors forced corporations to improve their performance and undergo massive reforms. Firms became malleable as spinning off units, outsourcing processes, and acquiring new units could be done with increased speed and ease. At the same time, transnational and hybrid elements made corporations more flexible and blurred their boundaries. German big businesses opened up to the logic of capital markets for the first time and therefore became suddenly driven by external expectations. It is not easy to judge whether this was beneficial or detrimental. Many corporations underwent long-overdue modernization processes. All in all, however, only "moderate steps rather than decisive leaps" towards a liberal market model took place.[80]

Germany Inc. did not dissolve in the 1990s and did not "become history." Instead it gained in flexibility and opened up to some elements of the Anglo-Saxon model, which resulted in a partial hybridization of German capitalism. And yet, many important pillars of the old model remained in place, like specialization in high-quality products, the dual vocational training system, close relations to politicians and bureaucrats, a high share of in-house careers among top managers, and the smooth coordination through associations. Co-determination continued to minimize conflicts. At least for the majority of workers with permanent jobs, a significant part of the social partnership persisted.[81] The unavoidable drive for flexibilization and cost cutting progressed incrementally and without the destructive conflicts that would have endangered the consensual culture of Germany Inc.

Germany did not enter a post-industrial era either. Industrial production remained the hallmark of its economy. Industry coexisted with the fast-growing service sector, which was mostly intertwined with industry.[82] Multigenerational family firms continued to play an important role even if they were increasingly run by non-family managers. These companies had technologically advanced products and increasingly conquered markets around the world. At the same time, they remained loyal to their original locations and maintained traditional forms of paternalism. Financial markets played only a minor role for them as they were interested in the long-term preservation of their assets and cultivated close relationships to their house banks and employees. Professional modernization, global focus, and generally admired success were compatible with cultural conservatism. Conversely, the preservation of many traditional elements might explain the vitality of this sector that, to this day, is so characteristic of Germany.[83]

The parallel existence of continuities and changes created a peculiar ambivalence. Public discourse on these fundamental transformations oscillated between scandalization and demonization on the one hand and demands for more radical reforms on the other. The transition to the new Germany Inc. was accompanied by tension and angst. Contradicting political signals further added to the confusion.

Under outside pressure, coordinated capitalism displayed a remarkable adaptability. Many companies made up for some long-overdue reforms. Despite public avowal to follow Anglo-Saxon methods and to play by the rules of capital markets, German companies became no clones of their British and American competitors. In 2002, the Neue Markt was dissolved. Germany Inc. was not liquidated but reformed, rebuilt, and, above all, made more flexible. While at the beginning of the 1990s Germany was still considered "the sick man of Europe,"[84] it displayed a remarkable growth dynamic after 1995. Rising productivity combined with moderate wage growth improved export prospects.[85] The willingness to undergo far-reaching reforms coupled with the conservation of some part of the country's traditional strengths might be the key reason why the Federal Republic regained its international competitiveness. The price, however, was permanent pressure to improve one's performance as well as a deepening social inequality and a general erosion of long-established certainties.

NOTES

1 Karl Gunnar Persson and Paul Sharp, *An Economic History of Europe: Knowledge, Institutions and Growth, 600 to the Present* (Cambridge: Cambridge University Press, 2015), 256–77; Andreas Wirsching, *Der Preis der Freiheit: Geschichte Europas in Unserer Zeit.* (Munich: Beck, 2012), 226–41.

2 David Hummels, "Transportation Costs and International Trade in the Second Era of Globalization," *Journal of Economic Perspectives* 21, no. 3 (2007): 131–54.

3 Gerd Hardach, "Wettbewerbspolitik in der Sozialen Marktwirtschaft," in *Das Bundeswirtschaftsministerium in der Ära der Sozialen Marktwirtschaft: Der deutsche Weg der Wirtschaftspolitik*, ed. Werner Abelshauser (Berlin: de Gruyter Oldenbourg, 2016), 254–61.

4 IMF, "The Fund's Role Regarding Cross-Border Capital Flows," Washington 2010, accessed 7 July 2018, http://www.imf.org/en/Publications/Policy-Papers/Issues/2016/12/31/The-Fund-s-Role-Regarding-Cross-Border-Capital-Flows-PP4516.

5 Gretna R. Krippner, "The Financialization of the American Economy," *Socio-Economic Review* 3, no. 2 (2005): 174 and 179.

6 Gerald A. Epstein, ed., *Financialization and the World Economy* (Cheltenham, UK: Edward Elgar, 2005); Hartmut Berghoff and Julia Laura Rischbieter, "Debt

and Credit: From Post-War Reconstruction to the Age of Financialization," *Journal of Modern European History* 15, no. 4 (2017): 489–502; Hartmut Berghoff, "Varieties of Financialization? Evidence from German Industry in the 1990s," *Business History Review* 90, no. 1 (2016): 81–108.

7 Lutz Raphael and Anselm Doering-Manteuffel, *Nach dem Boom: Perspektiven auf die Zeitgeschichte seit 1970*, 3rd ed. (Göttingen: Vandenhoeck & Ruprecht, 2012), 27 and 98.

8 Peter A. Hall and David Soskice, eds., *Varieties of Capitalism: The Institutional Foundations of Comparative Advantage* (Oxford: Oxford University Press, 2001); Werner Abelshauser, *The Dynamics of German Industry: Germany's Path toward the New Economy and the American Challenge* (New York: Berghahn, 2005).

9 Wolfgang Streeck, *Re-Forming Capitalism: Institutional Change in the German Political Economy* (Oxford: Oxford University Press, 2009). See also Saskia Freye, *Führungswechsel: Die Wirtschaftselite und das Ende der Deutschland AG* (Frankfurt am Main: Campus, 2009), 13–30.

10 Gesetz zur Kontrolle und Transparenz im Unternehmensbereich (KonTraG), 29, accessed 7 July 2018, http://www.wildensee.de/kontrag.pdf.

11 Karl Heinz Paqué, "Hat die Deutsche Einheit die Soziale Marktwirtschaft Verändert? Eine Zwischenbilanz 1990–2010," in *Der Staat und die Ordnung der Wirtschaft: Vom Kaiserreich bis zur Bundesrepublik*, ed. Werner Plumpe and André Steiner (Stuttgart: Steiner, 2016), 179–203.

12 For the complete speech, see Spiegel Online, 10 January 2017, accessed 7 July 2018, http://www.spiegel.de/politik/deutschland/roman-herzog -die-ruck-rede-im-wortlaut-a-1129316.html.

13 John W. Cioffi and Martin Höpner, "The Political Paradox of Finance Capitalism: Interests, Preferences, and Center-Left Party Politics in Corporate Governance Reform," *Politics and Society* 34, no. 4 (2006): 477–80.

14 David Furch, *Marktwirtschaften unter dem Druck globalisierter Finanzmärkte: Finanzsysteme und Corporate-Governance-Strukturen in Deutschland und Italien* (Wiesbaden: Springer VS, 2012), 153–69.

15 "Market Capitalization of Listed Domestic Companies (% of GDP)," World Bank, accessed 7 July 2018, https://data.worldbank.org/indicator /CM.MKT.LCAP.GD.ZS?locations=DE-GB-US.

16 Deutsches Aktieninstitut, *Factbook* (2013).

17 "Deutschland: Börsennotierte Unternehmen," Global Economy.com, accessed 7 July 2018, http://de.theglobaleconomy.com/Germany/Listed _companies/.

18 Markus Ampenberger, *Unternehmenspolitik in börsennotierten Familienunternehmen* (Wiesbaden: Springer VS, 2010), 237.

19 Hartmut Berghoff and Ingo Köhler, *Familienunternehmen in Deutschland und den USA seit der Industrialisierung: Eine historische Langzeitstudie* (Munich: Stiftung Familienunternehmen, 2019), 67–109.

20 These are unweighted arithmetic means. "Übersicht: Anteil der Ausländer am Grundkapital der Dax-Unternehmen," *Handelsblatt*, 28 December 2008; Ulf Sommer, "Ausländische Investoren profitieren vom Dax-Boom," in *Handelsblatt*, 1 January 2011; "Ausländische Investoren dominieren im Dax," *Frankfurter Rundschau*, 10 May 2013.

21 Christof Römer, "Offshoring: Wie viele Jobs gehen in die Neuen Mitgliedsstaaten der EU?" in *EU-Osterweiterung: Erste Zwischenbilanz für das Handwerk*, ed. Klaus Müller (Duderstadt: Mecke, 2008), 103; Werner Voss and Norbert in der Weide, *Beschäftigungsentwicklung in den Dax-30-Unternehmen in den Jahren 2000 und 2006* (Düsseldorf: Hans Böckler Stiftung, 2009), 21.

22 Statistisches Bundesamt, ed., *Datenreport 2004* (Bonn: Bundeszentrale für politische Bildung, 2004), 102.

23 All information on Siemens stems from publicly available sources. In-house documents have been available for research on the company's recent history. The resulting book manuscript, Hartmut Berghoff and Cornelia Rauh, *Die Große Transformation: Die Geschichte der Siemens AG im Zeitalter der Globalisierung, 1966–2011* (2015), has been barred from publication by Siemens AG. This 816-page study is stored in the Siemens Corporate Archives.

24 Caroline Wang, *Deutsche Direktinvestitionen in der Volksrepublik China: Gestaltungsfaktoren und Internationales Management* (Wiesbaden: Gabler, 2014).

25 Statistisches Jahrbuch 1994, 725; 1997, 706u.; 2005, 660.

26 "OECD Germany – Foreign Direct Investment (FDI)," Knoema, World Data Atlas, accessed 17 July 2018, https://knoema.com/OECDFDIS2014/oecd-foreign-direct-investment-fdi-statistics?tsId=1001700 and http://www.bundesfinanzministerium.de/Content/DE/Monatsberichte/2014/09/Inhalte/Kapitel-3-Analysen/3-2-deutsche-direktinvestitionen-im-ausland.html, accessed 9 July 2018.

27 Michael E. Porter, *Competitive Advantage: Creating and Sustaining Superior Performance* (New York: Free Press, 1985).

28 Kathrin Justen, "Deutschlands Vorstände werden internationaler," 18 July 2013, accessed 7 July 2017, https://www.humanresourcesmanager.de/ressorts/artikel/deutschlands-vorstaende-werden-internationaler.

29 Ernst & Young, *Entwicklung der Dax-30-Unternehmen im Geschäftsjahr 2012*, 19, accessed 14 May 2014, http://www.ey.com/Publication/vwLUAssets/Dax-30-Unternehmen_2012/$FILE/Dax30_Praesentation_2012.pdf.

30 Krippner, "Financialization"; Berghoff, "Varieties of Financialization."

31 "Manager unter Druck," *Manager Magazin*, 1 May 1991.

32 Alfred Kieser and Berit Ernst, "In Search of Explanations for the Consulting Explosion," in *The Expansion of Management Knowledge: Carriers, Ideas, and Sources*, ed. Kerstin Sahlin-Andersson and Lars Engwall (Stanford, CA: Stanford University Press, 2002), 47–73; Michael Faust,

"Consultancies as Actors in Knowledge Arenas: Evidence from Germany," in *Management Consulting: Emergence and Dynamics of a Knowledge Industry*, ed. Matthias Kipping and Lars Engwall (Oxford: Oxford University Press, 2003), 146–63.

33 Soziologisches Forschungsinstitut Göttingen, *Im Zeichen des Umbruchs: Beiträge zu einer anderen Standortdebatte* (Opladen: Leske + Budrich, 1995), 142.

34 James P. Womack, Daniel T. Jones, and Daniel Roos, *The Machine That Changed the World* (New York: Rawson Associates, 1990).

35 Christian Stadler, *Unternehmenskultur bei Royal Dutch/Shell, Siemens und DaimlerChrysler* (Stuttgart: Steiner, 2004), 195.

36 Günter Ogger, *Nieten in Nadelstreifen: Deutschlands Manager im Zwielicht* (Munich: Droemer Knaur, 1992).

37 F.A. Linden and W. Wilhelm, "Ein Konzern rotiert," *Manager Magazin*, 1 March 1992.

38 McKinsey & Co., Jürgen Kluge, u.a., *Wachstum durch Verzicht. Schneller Wandel zur Weltklasse: Vorbild Elektroindustrie* (Stuttgart: Schäffer-Poeschel, 1994), 63–5; "Eine Revolution von oben," *Der Spiegel*, 7 November 1994.

39 ABN AMRO, *Siemens: Scanning for Returns* (London: AMRO, 2003), 2 and 28. See also Stadler, *Unternehmenskultur*, 294.

40 Peter von Siemens interview, *trend* 11 (1996).

41 Geschäftsbericht der Siemens AG, 1997/98, 45 and 54; 1998/99, 52.

42 See Anke Hassel, Martin Höpner, Antje Kurdelbusch, Britta Rehder, and Rainer Zugehör, "Zwei Dimensionen der Internationalisierung: Eine Empirische Analyse Deutscher Grossunternehmen," *Kölner Zeitschrift für Soziologie und Sozialpsychologie* 52, no. 3 (2000): 500–19.

43 Simon Hage, "Deutsche Konzerne: Flucht von der Wall Street," *Manager Magazin*, 6 September 2007.

44 KPMG, ed., *Shareholder Value-Konzepte: Eine Untersuchung der Dax-100 Unternehmen* (Frankfurt am Main: KPMG, 2002).

45 VA has a short-term bias and gives incentives to keep research and investments low. Peter C. Brewer, Gyan Chandra, and Clayton A. Hock. "Economic Value Added (Eva): Its Uses and Limitations," *SAM Advanced Management Journal* 64, no. 2 (1999): 4–10.

46 Hartmut Berghoff, "Organised Irresponsibility? The Siemens Corruption Scandal of the 1990s and 2000s," *Business History* 60, nos 2–3 (2018): 423–45.

47 Department of Justice, *US v. Daimler AG*, court docket number 10-CR-063 -RJL, accessed 1 June 2017, https://www.justice.gov/criminal-fraud/case /united-states-v-daimler-ag-court-docket-number-10-cr-063-rjl.

48 Hartmut Berghoff, "From the Watergate Scandal to the Compliance Revolution: The Fight against Corporate Corruption in the United States and Germany, 1972–2012," *Bulletin of the German Historical Institute* 49, no. 2 (2013): 7–30.

49　Reinhold Thiel, *Die Geschichte des Bremer Vulkan 1805–1997*, vol. 3, *1946–1997* (Bremen: Hauschild, 2008).

50　Peter Strunk, *Die AEG: Aufstieg und Niedergang einer Industrielegende* (Berlin: Nicolaische Verlags-Buchhandlung, 1999).

51　Christoph Wehnelt, *Hoechst: Untergang des Deutschen Weltkonzerns* (Lindenberg: Fink, 2009).

52　Geschäftsbericht Mannesmann 1999, 21.

53　Ferdinand Mager and Martin Meyer-Fackler, "Mergers and Acquisitions in Germany, 1981–2010," *Global Finance Journal*, online publication, 2017, 2, accessed 7 July 2018, http://www.sciencedirect.com/science/article/pii /S1044028316300941.

54　Klaus Kleinfeld, in Siemens AG Geschäftsbericht 2005, 9.

55　Anthony Giddens, *The Consequences of Modernity* (Stanford, CA: Stanford University Press, 1990), 14.

56　Geschäftsbericht Siemens AG, 1997/98, 7 and 60.

57　*Dialog intern*, 2 June 2001, 7–9.

58　Ibid., 15.

59　Hartmut Berghoff, "Blending Personal and Managerial Capitalism: Bertelsmann's Rise from a Medium-Sized Publisher to a Global Media Corporation, 1950–2002," *Business History* 45, no. 1 (2013): 855–74.

60　"Corporate Germany on Trial," *Economist*, 23 January 2004.

61　In 1980 it had been 12.3 years. Freye, *Führungswechsel*, 58–65.

62　Michael Hartmann, "Soziale Homogenität und Generationelle Muster der Deutschen Wirtschaftselite seit 1945," in *Die Deutsche Wirtschaftselite im 20. Jahrhundert*, ed. Volker R. Berghahn, Stefan Unger, and Dieter Ziegler (Essen: Verlag, 2003), 31–50; Hartmut Berghoff and Ingo Köhler, "Redesigning a Class of Its Own: Social and Human Capital Formation in the German Banking Elite, 1870–1990," *Financial History Review* (2007): 63–87.

63　Meinhard Miegel, Stefanie Wahl, and Martin Schulte, *Die Rolle der Zeitarbeit in einem sich Ändernden Arbeitsmarkt* (Bonn: IWG, 2007), 7–43.

64　Quoted in Dietmar Hawranek, Frank Hornig, and Alexander Jung, "Bye-bye 'Made in Germany,'" *Spiegel*, 25 October 2004. See also "Unanständig? Wirtschaft wehrt sich," *Welt*, 14 April 2004, and Christian Ramthun and Julia Leendertse, "Deutsche Firmen: Verantwortungslos, unsozial, unpatriotisch?" *Wirtschaftswoche*, 18 March 2005.

65　Andreas Wirsching, "Erwerbsbiographien und Privatheitsformen: Die Entstandardisierung von Lebensläufen," in *Auf dem Weg in eine Neue Moderne? Die Bundesrepublik Deutschland in den Siebziger und Achtziger Jahren*, ed. Thomas Raithel, Andreas Rödder, and Andreas Wirsching (Munich: Oldenbourg, 2009), 83–97.

66　Miegel, Wahl, and Schulte, *Rolle*, 40–3.

67　Rheinhard Bispinck and Thorsten Schulten, "Deutschland vor dem Tarifpolitischen Systemwechsel?" *WSI Mitteilungen* 8 (2005): 467.

68 Paqué, "Deutsche Einheit," 195.

69 Georg Erber and Harald Hagemann, *Zur Produktivitätsentwicklung Deutschlands im Internationalen Vergleich: Expertise im Auftrag der Abteilung Wirtschafts- und Sozialpolitik der Friedrich-Ebert-Stiftung* (Bonn: Friedrich-Ebert-Stiftung, 2012), 18–21.

70 "DGB Bundesvorstand, Mitgliederstatistik," Mitgliederstatistik, accessed 7 July 2018, http://www.dgb.de/uber-uns/dgb-heute/mitgliederzahlen/.

71 Stefan Zimmer, *Jenseits von Arbeit und Kapital? Unternehmerverbände und Gewerkschaften im Zeitalter der Globalisierung* (Opladen: Leske + Budrich, 2002), 130–3.

72 Rainer Dombois, "Die VW-Affäre: Lehrstück zu den Risiken Deutschen Co-Managements?" *Industrielle Beziehungen* 16, no. 3 (2009): 207–31.

73 Heiner Dribbusch, "Arbeitskampf im Wandel: Zur Streikentwicklung seit 1990," *WSI Mitteilungen*, no. 7 (2006): 382–8.

74 Quoted in Ulla Jasper, "Thyssen sucht Käufer für 50.000 Wohnungen," *Die Tageszeitung*, 20 August 2004.

75 "Thyssen-Krupp hebt den Stahlpreis an," *Handelsblatt*, 10 February 2005.

76 "Siemens verscherbelt seine 'Familie,'" *Erlanger Rot* 4 (2008).

77 Quoted in "Mitarbeiter protestieren gegen Wohnungsverkäufe. Siemens," *Fränkischer Tag, Regionalausgabe Bamberg*, 12 September 2008.

78 Mathias Stuhr, *Mythos New Economy: Die Arbeit an der Geschichte der Informationsgesellschaft* (Bielefeld: Transcript, 2010), 136–9.

79 Eckart Conze, *Die Suche nach Sicherheit: Eine Geschichte der Bundesrepublik Deutschland von 1949 bis in die Gegenwart* (Munich: Siedler, 2009), 16–18.

80 Daniel Detzer et al., *The German Financial System and the Financial and Economic Crisis* (Cham: Verlag 2017), 185.

81 Stephen J. Silvia, *Holding the Shop Together. German Industrial Relations in the Postwar Era* (Ithaca, NY: Cornell University Press, 2013), 220–6.

82 André Steiner, "Abschied von der Industrie? Wirtschaftlicher Strukturwandel in West- und Ostdeutschland seit den 1960er Jahren," in *Der Mythos von der Postindustriellen Welt: Wirtschaftlicher Strukturwandel in Deutschland 1960 bis 1990*, ed. Werner Plumpe and André Steiner (Göttingen: Wallstein, 2016), 47–54.

83 Hartmut Berghoff, "The End of Family Business? The Mittelstand and German Capitalism in Transition, 1949–2000," *Business History Review* 80, no. 2 (2006): 263–95; Jeffrey R. Fear, "Straight Outta Oberberg: Transforming Mid-Sized Family Firms into Global Champions 1970–2010," *Jahrbuch für Wirtschaftsgeschichte* 53, no. 1 (2012): 125–69.

84 L. Siegele, "Germany on the Mend," *Economist*, 17 November 2004.

85 Christian Dustmann, Bernd Fitzenberger, Uta Schoenberg, and Alexandra Spitz-Oener, "From 'Sick Man of Europe' to the 'Economic Superstar': Germany's Resurging Economy," *Journal of Economic Perspectives* 28, no. 1 (2014): 167–88.

Contributors

Hartmut Berghoff, Director of the Institute of Economic and Social History at the Georg-August-University Göttingen; former director of the German Historical Institute in Washington, DC, 2008–15

Eileen Boris, Hull Professor and Distinguished Professor of feminist studies and Distinguished Professor of history, black studies, and global studies, University of California Santa Barbara

Jessica Burch, Assistant Professor of global commerce, Denison University, Ohio

Sina Fabian, Assistant Professor of history at Humboldt University of Berlin

Bart Hoogeboom, Researcher at the Dutch Centre of Expertise in Family Business at the Windesheim University of Applied Sciences

Michael Kozakowski, Lecturer at Central European University

Marijn Molema, Professor at the University of Groningen, the Netherlands

Franziska Rehlinghaus, Assistant Professor at the Georg-August-University Göttingen

Karsten Uhl, Director of the Mitelbau-Dora Concentration Camp Memorial, Nordhausen, Germany

Sebastian Voigt, Postdoctoral researcher at the Leibniz Institute for Contemporary History Munich – Berlin; Fellow at the Institute for Social Movements, Bochum, Germany

Andreas Wirsching, Director of the Leibniz Institute for Contemporary History Munich – Berlin; Professor of history at Ludwig Maximilians University, Munich

Index

Abzug, Bella, 82, 91
Algeria, 103, 106–8, 110–12
Amway Corporation, 36f, 40
Ash, Mary Kay, 37, 39, 49
Asia, 9, 16, 79, 85, 120, 240, 242, 246
Automation, 104, 129–35, 139, 141, 145–7, 222, 237, 245
Avon Corporation/California Perfume Company, 17, 37f, 40, 47

Barksdale-Sloan, Edith, 84, 90, 92f, 97
Bayer AG, 22, 156, 159–64, 167, 170, 176, 253
Bell, Daniel, 5, 13, 15
Bertelsmann AG, 159f, 162f, 167f, 173, 251
Blair, Tony (British PM), 8, 57
blue-collar work, 13, 36, 39, 43, 45, 115, 118, 13f, 135, 167
Bretton Woods system, 7, 16, 46

capitalism, 6f, 10, 12, 14–16, 18, 22, 25f, 30, 35, 38, 49, 154, 200, 237, 239, 258. *See also* digital financial capitalism; neoliberalism; Rhenish capitalism
care work, 19, 39, 50, 79, 82, 85, 88, 94
Carter, Jimmy (US president), 4, 35, 37f, 45, 49
China, 9, 29, 190, 238, 242

civil rights, 80, 85, 90, 93
class, 3, 10f, 18f, 43, 45, 64, 71, 79–81, 83f, 87, 94, 118f, 145, 200. *See also* working class
coal mining industry, 3f, 16, 58, 60f, 64, 70, 117, 170, 192, 258. *See also* miner
collective bargaining agreement, 94, 117, 121, 255
computerization/computer manufacturing, 15, 21, 129–32, 135, 137, 139–46, 231, 250
consumer society/consumption, 7, 12, 14, 17–20, 35, 42, 56–9, 61–5, 67, 70f, 110, 153, 239
contingent work, 18, 44–6, 50
continuing education, 153–8, 160, 164–8, 173–6

Daimler-Benz AG, 246–9, 253, 255
decline, 4, 6, 8, 10, 13f, 16–18, 23–6, 35–8, 45 f, 58, 61, 63, 65, 67, 69–72, 84, 113, 121, 158, 161, 189–92, 199, 201, 203, 212, 214, 222, 233, 239, 242, 252, 254, 257. *See also* economic crisis; Great Depression/financial crisis of 1929
deindustrialization, 18–20, 23–7, 37, 45f, 50f, 69, 78, 80, 83, 103, 106, 189–91, 193–9, 201f, 209f, 214, 216, 222, 232f
DeVos, Rich, 37f, 40, 49

Diebold, John, 129f, 132f, 145
digital financial capitalism, 6–9, 26, 239
direct sales/selling, 17f, 20, 26, 36–40, 43f, 45–50, 58
Doering-Manteuffel, Anselm, 6–9, 13, 15, 238f
domestic work(er), 9, 17, 19, 45, 48, 50, 58, 78–81, 83–6, 88–93, 115

Eastern Europe, 25, 85, 231, 237, 242
economic crisis, 12, 15, 18, 20, 27, 58–61, 63, 65, 67, 70f, 80, 106, 108, 110, 130, 154f, 158, 160, 165, 167, 192, 194. *See also* decline; Great Depression/financial crisis of 1929
Edding Commission, 158–60
Eribon, Didier, 11, 13
European Union (EU), 25, 118, 202, 213, 242

Fair Labor Standards Act (FLSA), 39, 84, 88–90, 92
Federal Republic of Germany, 8, 107, 109, 111, 113. *See also* West Germany
financialization, 78, 238f, 244, 247, 250
Fordism, 104, 117, 120–2, 153, 163, 196, 198, 239
France, 4, 10f, 20f, 23f, 26, 56, 67, 79, 103–11, 113–16, 118f, 189–94, 197–202
Friedrich Krupp AG/ThyssenKrupp AG, 162, 168, 170, 172, 249, 253, 257
Friesland, 24f, 212, 214–33

Global South, 9, 132
globalization, 16, 19, 23–6, **77**, 129, 139, 146, 189f, 193, 199, 201f, 240, 245, 258
Great Britain/United Kingdom (UK), 10, 13, 17f, 36, 42, 56, 58, 62, 65, 69–71, 132–4, 193, 203, 211, 241, 260

Great Depression/financial crisis of 1929, 12, 38, 116

housework/household labour, 78–83, 85, 89, 91f
human capital, 160f, 163, 170, 172, 174

immigration/immigrants, 10, 19–21, 48, 79f, 85–9, 91, 93, 107, 116, 118, 139, 193, 196f, 199, 202, 206
India, 9, 190
individualism/individualization, 6, 14, 24, 58, 153, 163, 167, 175, 197, 199, 203, 239
Industriegewerkschaft Druck und Papier (IG Drupa), 132, 145
Industriegewerkschaft Metall (IG Metall), 165, 255, 257
inequality, 3, 7, 12f, 18, 22, 60, 71, 79, 154, 156, 175, 194, 260
inflation, 35, 40–2, 44, 57–60, 62, 64, 70, 81, 104f
International Business Machines Corporation (IBM), 129, 160
International Graphical Federation (IGF), 129f, 133–5, 137–40, 147
International Monetary Fund (IMF), 59, 70

Keynes, John Maynard/Keynesianism, 5, 7, 9, 14, 72, 194, 213
Kohl, Helmut, 13, 239f
Krugman, Paul, 12, 213f

labour relations, 26, 170, 239, 254, 256f
Latin America, 19, 85

Mannesmann AG, 249, 251
manufacturing industry, 3, 191
marketing, 37f, 41–3, 69

McKinsey, 244, 246, 252

Mitterrand, François (French president), 104, 112, 194f, 200f

multinational corporations/multinationals, 121, 135f, 139, 191, 200, 227, 231

National Committee on Household Employment (NCHE), 84, 89f, 93

neoliberalism, 6f, 13f, 19, 25, 58, 93, 153, 175, 199, 212, 232, 237, 239f

Netherlands, the, 10, 24, 26, 137, 210–19, 221, 223–5, 227, 232

New Deal, 4, 39, 89

new economy, 18, 50, 110, 212f, 224, 226, 232

New York Times, the, 12, 83, 85, 87, 136–40

Nixon, Richard (US president), 4, 82, 86, 90

oil (price) crisis, 7, 14, 17, 20f, 46, 59f, 62–4, 67, 104f, 107, 113, 118–20, 153, 157, 161, 171, 194

Organization for Economic Co-operation and Development (OECD), 3, 156

periphery, 21, 214f, 224, 227, 233

populism, 10f, 24, 189, 202

post-Fordism, 122, 153

post-industrial society, 5, 13, 26, 50

postwar boom, 6, 10, 16, 20, 104, 121

Raphael, Lutz, 6–9, 13, 15, 238f

Reagan, Ronald (US president), 4f, 13

regional industrialization policies, 24, 209–11, 216, 219f, 222

Rhine/Rhenish capitalism, 8, 25f, 239

Ruhr area, 4, 16

Rust Belt (US), 4, 16, 80, 83

Schröder, Gerhard, 8, 240, 254

Second World War, 3, 10, 12, 14, 45, 69, 79, 86, 103, 116, 121, 141, 155, 170, 220

self-employment, 44, 48f, 115f, 121, 254

service economy/service sector, 3, 5, 8, 13, 17, 20f, 25, 36–8, 46, 50, 65, 71, 79–81, 86, 92f, 105, 113–16, 120f, 153f, 158, 197, 209, 216, 222, 231, 259

Siemens AG, 156, 160–3, 242f, 245–7, 249f, 252f, 256f

South Korea, 9, 190

Spain, 42, 67, 69, 88, 103, 109f, 112, 116, 119, 249

Stanley Home Products (Fuller Brush), 37f, 49

steel industry, 4, 10, 191f, 197

Streeck, Wolfgang, 15, 23

strike, 21, 46f, 56f, 59f, **77**, 118f, 130f, 135–41, 143, 193, 196, 255–7

structural change, 13, 15, 25, 155, 196–8, 203, 209, 215. *See also* transformation

Taiwan, 9, 190

Thatcher, Margaret (British PM), 13, 57f, 64, 71, 140

tourism, 36, 65, 67, 69–71, 177, 227, 229

transformation, 6–11, 13–23, 25f, 35, 37, 50f, 65, 69f, 78, 81f, 103f, 129f, 133–5, 138f, 142, 145f, 153, 174, 189f, 202, 210, 212, 214, 226, 231f, 237, 254, 257, 259. *See also* structural change

Trente Glorieuses (thirty glorious years), 13, 103, 120, 189, 200, 203

Tupperware, Inc., 17, 37, 39, 47, 49

unemployment, 7, 16–18, 20, 22, 35, 37, 40, 42f, 46–8, 50, 57–9, 61, 64f, 68, 70f, 85, 89, 91, 103, 105–15, 117, 120, 158, 165, 174, 189, 195–7, 199f, 202, 211f, 215, 218, 222, 240, 251,

254f, 257. *See also* decline; economic crisis; Great Depression/financial crisis of 1929

United States of America (USA), 3–6, 9–15, 17, 19, 26f, 35f, 42, 44–7, 49–51, 78–81, 85f, 89f, 94, 114f, 132, 134, 139, 141, 168, 170, 173, 189f, 193, 198, 203f, 211f, 238, 241f, 247f, 250f

Van Andel, Jay, 37f, 40, 49

vocational training, 25, 112f, 135, 155, 158f, 222, 239, 259

Vodafone, 249, 251

wages, 3f, 11f, 14, 18, 36, 38–40, 42, 50, 59f, 80–2, 84–6, 88–92, 94f, 104, 108, 115, 117f, 120f, 145, 156, 160, 167, 192, 194, 197, 240, 255f, 260

welfare, 45, 59, 78, 81–4, 90, 92, 111, 153, 156, 240

West Germany, 6, 13f, 16, 22f, 25f, 56, 70, 130, 132, 138, 153–6, 159, 174, 193, 195, 242, 255. *See also* Federal Republic of Germany

Western Europe, 3, 6, 8f, 12, 14, 21, 26, 67, 103, 137, 190, 192

white-collar work, 17, 43f., 50, 115, 131, 135, 165, 167

"winter of discontent," 36, 56f, 70

working class, 11, 18, 64, 66, 68, 70–2, 88, 193

work council, 21, 131, 145f

GERMAN AND EUROPEAN STUDIES
General Editor: Jennifer L. Jenkins

1 Emanuel Adler, Beverly Crawford, Federica Bicchi, and Rafaella Del Sarto, *The Convergence of Civilizations: Constructing a Mediterranean Region*

2 James Retallack, *The German Right, 1860–1920: Political Limits of the Authoritarian Imagination*

3 Silvija Jestrovic, *Theatre of Estrangement: Theory, Practice, Ideology*

4 Susan Gross Solomon, ed., *Doing Medicine Together: Germany and Russia between the Wars*

5 Laurence McFalls, ed., *Max Weber's "Objectivity" Revisited*

6 Robin Ostow, ed., *(Re)Visualizing National History: Museums and National Identities in Europe in the New Millennium*

7 David Blackbourn and James Retallack, eds., *Localism, Landscape, and the Ambiguities of Place: German-Speaking Central Europe, 1860–1930*

8 John Zilcosky, ed., *Writing Travel: The Poetics and Politics of the Modern Journey*

9 Angelica Fenner, *Race under Reconstruction in German Cinema: Robert Stemmle's Toxi*

10 Martina Kessel and Patrick Merziger, eds., *The Politics of Humour: Laughter, Inclusion, and Exclusion in the Twentieth Century*

11 Jeffrey K. Wilson, *The German Forest: Nature, Identity, and the Contestation of a National Symbol, 1871–1914*

12 David G. John, *Bennewitz, Goethe,* Faust: *German and Intercultural Stagings*

13 Jennifer Ruth Hosek, *Sun, Sex, and Socialism: Cuba in the German Imaginary*

14 Steven M. Schroeder, *To Forget It All and Begin Again: Reconciliation in Occupied Germany, 1944–1954*

15 Kenneth S. Calhoon, *Affecting Grace: Theatre, Subject, and the Shakespearean Paradox in German Literature from Lessing to Kleist*

16 Martina Kolb, *Nietzsche, Freud, Benn, and the Azure Spell of Liguria*

17 Hoi-eun Kim, *Doctors of Empire: Medical and Cultural Encounters between Imperial Germany and Meiji Japan*

18 J. Laurence Hare, *Excavating Nations: Archeology, Museums, and the German-Danish Borderlands*

19 Jacques Kornberg, *The Pope's Dilemma: Pius XII Faces Atrocities and Genocide in the Second World War*

20 Patrick O'Neill, *Transforming Kafka: Translation Effects*

21 John K. Noyes, *Herder: Aesthetics against Imperialism*

22 James Retallack, *Germany's Second Reich: Portraits and Pathways*

23 Laurie Marhoefer, *Sex and the Weimar Republic: German Homosexual Emancipation and the Rise of the Nazis*

24 Bettina Brandt and Daniel L. Purdy, eds., *China in the German Enlightenment*

25 Michael Hau, *Performance Anxiety: Sport and Work in Germany from the Empire to Nazism*

26 Celia Applegate, *The Necessity of Music: Variations on a German Theme*

27 Richard J. Golsan and Sarah M. Misemer, eds., *The Trial That Never Ends: Hannah Arendt's* Eichmann in Jerusalem *in Retrospect*

28 Lynne Taylor, *In the Children's Best Interests: Unaccompanied Children in American-Occupied Germany, 1945–1952*

29 Jennifer A. Miller, *Turkish Guest Workers in Germany: Hidden Lives and Contested Borders, 1960s to 1980s*

30 Amy Carney, *Marriage and Fatherhood in the Nazi SS*

31 Michael E. O'Sullivan, *Disruptive Power: Catholic Women, Miracles, and Politics in Modern Germany, 1918–1965*

32 Gabriel N. Finder and Alexander V. Prusin, *Justice behind the Iron Curtain: Nazis on Trial in Communist Poland*

33 Parker Daly Everett, *Urban Transformations: From Liberalism to Corporatism in Greater Berlin, 1871–1933*

34 Melissa Kravetz, *Women Doctors in Weimar and Nazi Germany: Maternalism, Eugenics, and Professional Identity*

35 Javier Samper Vendrell, *Seduction of Youth: Print Culture and Homosexual Rights in the Weimar Republic*

36 Sebastian Voigt, ed., *Since the Boom: Continuity and Change in the Western Industrialized World after 1970*

Ingram Content Group UK Ltd.
Milton Keynes UK
UKHW040752080323
418181UK00053B/169/J